The Meeting of the Tracks

Rock Art in Ancient Wales

John Sharkey

ISBN: 0-86381-853-6

Design of illustrated pages & photography: Maura Hazelden

Photography: Mick Sharp

Cover design: Sian Parri

First published in 2004 by
Gwasg Carreg Gwalch, 12 Iard yr Orsaf, Llanrwst,
Wales LL26 0EH
01492 642031 01492 641502
books@carreg-gwalch.co.uk website: www.carreg-gwalch.co.uk

For Jack Arnell of Castell Gorfod.
A reminder of our many conversations
of stones, landscape and sacred places.

Acknowledgements

A special thanks to Maura Hazelden for designing the full-page illustrations, for the inclusion of her photographs and for her invaluable help throughout.

To Mick Sharp for photographs and to James Warburton for those of the Blaenawen stone.

To Mark Lodwick of the Welsh National Museum, Cardiff; to Ron Cowell of the National Museums and Galleries on Merseyside; to Stuart Ó Seanóir, Assistant Librarian of Trinity College, Dublin; to the staff of The National Library of Wales, Aberystwyth, Cardigan Library and the Haverfordwest County Library.

To 'The Board of the Trinity College Dublin' for permission to reproduce the plan of New Grange by Edward Lhuyd. To *Archaeologia Cambrensis* for the reproductions from Barclodiad y Gawres, Bryn Celli Ddu and detail of the crosses from Tŷ Illtud. To Ron Cowell for detail of the Calderstones; to Heinemann London for the cupmarks from Le Ferrassie; to the Metropolitan Museum of Art for the drawing of the Turoe stone; to the Blandford Press, Poole for details of the Newgrange stones; to Batsford Press for the Kendrick's Cave mandible; to Oxford University Press for detail of the Scara Brae markings; to the Irish Academic Press for detail of Design Alphabet; to The Other Clare No. 19 for the Mount Callan ogham; to Sutton Publications, Stroud for the Rhuddlan pebble; to Flammarion SA, Paris for detail of Camonica Valley rock art; to the Anglesey Antiquarian Society for the Llwydiarth Esgob cupmarks; to John Guilbert for the Cerrig Bank slates and Peter Crew for the Maentwrog 'head', both first published in *Archaeology in Wales*. The Roman glass dish is, 'reproduced by the permission of The Stationary Office'.

To Gomer Press, Llandysul for permission to use the quotation from George Borrow's *Wild Wales*. To the Blandford Press for brief quotations by G. Coffey and R. Morris; by G. Melville Richards to The University of Liverpool Press; by G.T. Meaden to the Souvenir Press; and by Terry Breverton to Glyndwr Publishing.

In the search for current information on early rock carvings and in compiling the 'Site List of Welsh Cupmarks', I gratefully acknowledge the help of the officers of the Regional Sites and Monuments Records (SMR), Cambria Archaeology, The Dyfed Archaeological Trust Ltd., The Clwyd-Powys Archaeological Trust, The Glamorgan Gwent Archaeological Trust Ltd., The Gwynedd Archaeological Trust.

To Myrddin ap Dafydd and his team at Gwasg Carreg Gwalch for their patience with the many rewritings of the text.

Contents

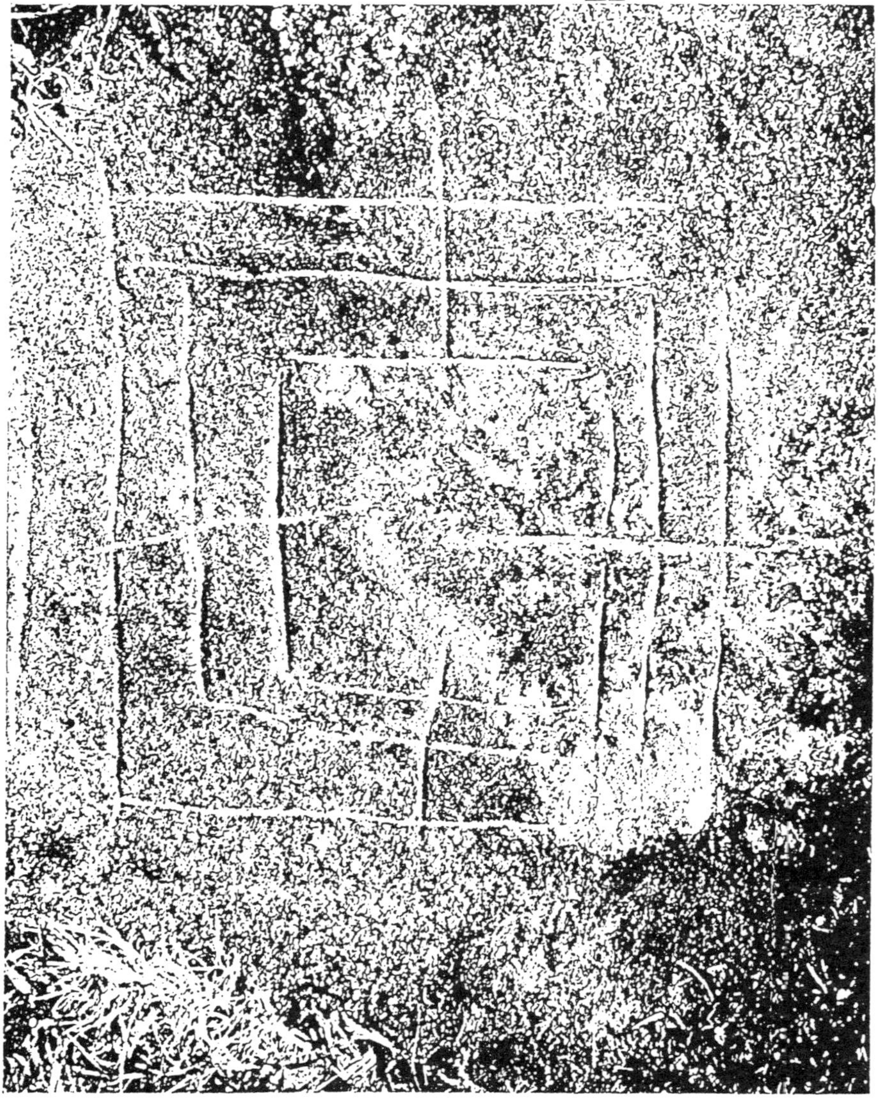

Stone at the meeting of the tracks, near Llanfairfechan, Conwy (Edna Knowles)

At the meeting of the tracks

> I passed on; the country was neither grand nor pretty – it exhibited a kind of wildness, however, which did not fail to interest me – here were stones, rocks and furze in abundance.
>
> George Borrow (1865)

The fun in writing this book has been following up the observations, hints, asides and suggestions of earlier writers. Antiquarians, prehistorians, travellers and archaeologists have unknowingly contributed to the making of the work, although any conclusions drawn are mine. As the number of original carvings in Wales are quite small or concentrated at a site like Barclodiad y Gawres, it seemed necessary to opt for an individual approach to each. This is different to the more usual treatment of rock art in describing works as representative of a particular class or genre. Nor did I presume the reader would be overfamiliar with the cultural and artistic influences from elsewhere, so I sought to give as much general information as necessary. This was done with the archaeological background and the initial excavations or findings of the early Welsh stone carvings.

Such work is often perfunctory included in the general studies published during past decades, and particularly sketchy in a more recent book on British prehistoric art by Stan Beckensall. So each chapter here evolved into a rather intensive exploration of a particular carving or group of carved stones, while including some personal, philosophical or social interpretations. It even includes the often very tiresome physical exploration of hills and moors whilst looking at single boulders for recorded sites of minute hollowed-out cupmarks. In retrospect my method has been to follow the tracks others uncovered. I researched from the present to the earliest findings and reports, then move forwards in time to conclude with any recent investigations. Two examples are the acoustic properties recorded inside the passage grave of Bryn Celli Ddu, and the magnetic variations associated with the uprights for the extensively cupmarked capstone of the Bachwen dolmen in Gwynedd.

The small number of megalithic carvings found in Wales, in comparison with the numbers to be seen in Ireland and Brittany, should not restrict the need for an elucidation in terms of their context, style or meaning. Nor does it necessarily invalidate what was then a basic or common artistic relationship with the many hundreds of individually carved stones known in the passage grave art of the western seaways, from Portugal to the northern isles of Scotland.

One of the ideas that I have put forward in relation to the art of the passage tombs on Ynys Môn (Anglesey) (and by implication in Ireland where nearly a thousand carved stones are known) is that of a key work by which the other carvings may have been meaningfully invoked, and that motifs like the small spirals could also function as a form of ritual protection for the carvings, the monument or its people. The overall effect, I would suggest, helped to create a visual bond and strong reinforcement between the inner sacred space and their religious concerns. So the finished carvings – as seen by light of torches and enhanced perhaps by the carbonised shale pebbles found in the excavations of Barclodiad y Gawres – could be read in an universal sense. This is different to what archaeologists seem to imply when referring to the ancient carved rock as if they were yet another illustrated form of modern design. Earlier prehistorians were very much concerned about comparisons between the many different kinds of decoration, where they may have originated from and how they fused into eventual use here. The resulting tendency to categorise and quantify the carvings is still marked among many researchers. This may be useful as a notational tool but it strengthens the presumption that such abstract workings are not meaningful in the objective sense of the term. Such work appears to be more acceptable within current cultural aesthetics. So whatever meanings the art may had held for the carvers and their contemporaries, published observations and commentary tend to shy away from the further question as to why some megalithic structures were so decorated, unlike the majority of rough stone edifices that were left unadorned. Was it artistic creativity that impelled certain groups in ancient Britain to carve such particularly abstract forms in the interiors, as well as on the kerbstones of the major tumuli? Or was this emergence of megalithic art part of a social response to the religious culture of particular groups, who felt that a visible manifestation was a necessary adjunct to the ancestral rites? In relation to what remains of the ruins of the earliest large-stone burial architecture that proliferated throughout all these islands from the third millennium BC, it is now impossible to know – collectively or individually – what the completed structures may have looked like within their immediate environment or how society appropriated such monumental creations, then or later.

We are also unlikely to appreciate the subtle differences in the geometric forms of spirals and chevrons, that may have illuminated a world view for the preliterate peoples of the Neolithic and Early Bronze

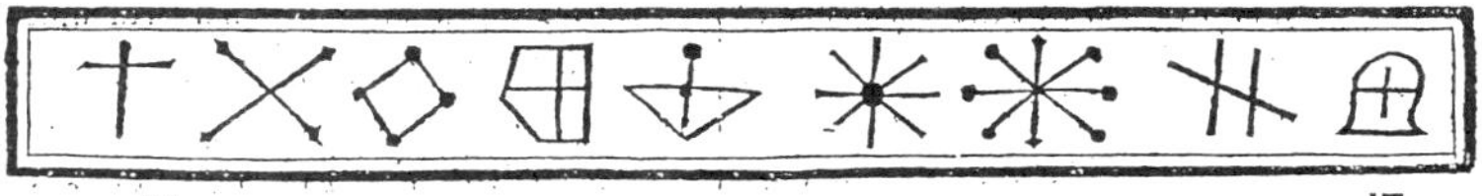

Carvings from inside Tŷ Illtud, near Brecon, Edward Lhuyd 'Brittania', 1694

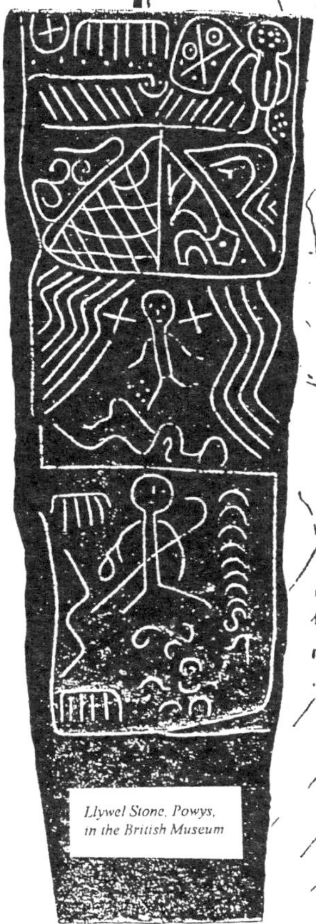

Llywel Stone, Powys, in the British Museum

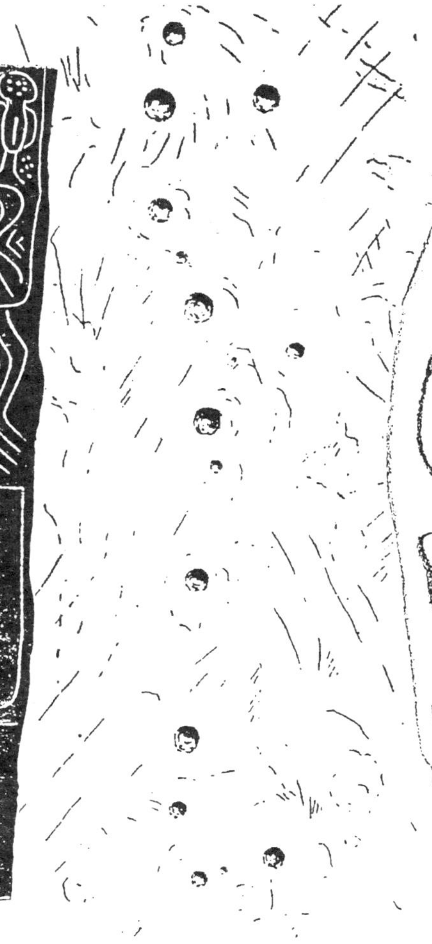

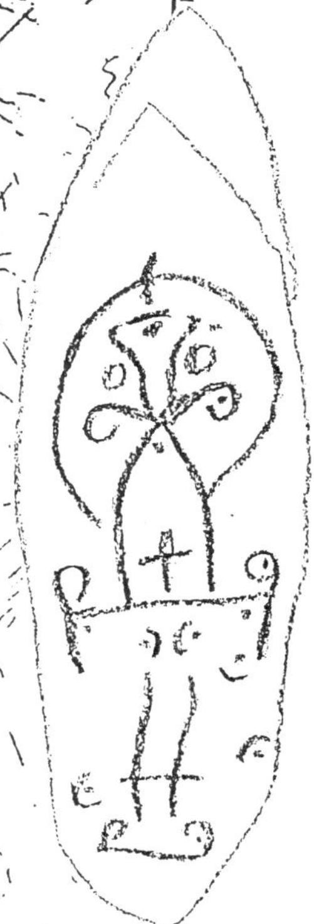

Blaenawen Stone, Pembrokeshire

Cupmarks on stone by Cist Cerrig burial chamber, Gwynedd

Ages. Yet the stone carvings force us to recognise the context and the placement of their art. The tomb shrines were private sanctuaries for a limited number of peoples to have access into the sacred realms of their ancestors. The carved stone walls inside would have held a comprehensive meaning for those groups who could recognise the markings as confirmation of their common reality. Such recognition would have been an acquired mental process, as our own assimilation of an abstract logo in modern advertising occurs without seemingly conscious effort. They would have had no need to break down the constituent signs on a carved stone for meanings – hidden or otherwise – as we are forced to.

The marks on the stones could be all that is left of the linguistic principles underlying the creative process of such sacred architecture. They may, as has often been suggested, be messages carved in stone for the tutelary deities or even for us – as visitors in an uncertain future – to decipher! Whatever suppositions we may come up with, there is no denying the power extruding from the high smoothly dressed stones when moving through the 19m long passageway at Newgrange. This is one of the largest and best known visitor friendly passage tombs in Ireland. The overwhelming effects on people at the dawn of its creation when confronted with such magical creativity, has long ago been leached from modern consciousness yet, like children in a metaphysical corner of a time machine, we can still feel a cultural link here with the dreams of those who ritually indented the hard outer surfaces. Their primal markings have somehow survived the tangle of time and time's reduction of form and substance. The art of the Boyne Valley tumuli and other enclosed passage tombs exists because of the hardness of the medium on which the carvings were initially created. We are fortunate within such decorated sacred places to be able to encounter a singular engagement of prehistoric time and space. It is an interior liminal arena that still takes the breath away. Complete with the carved mysteries of a possibly even older mythic period. We have turned their hermetic vision into an expressive aspect of our own linear history, part of a numerical chronology that trips off the tongue, without a thought that it is as far back in time again as the beginning of our Christian-Judaic era. Yet it is possible to relocate ourselves there, if only through the touch of a finger following the curving outline of the massive triple spiral at the entrance to Newgrange. In the feeling that may permeate our senses tracing the finger along the grooves of the stones, our mind's eye informs us of the message of the makers, if that delicate physical interaction of soft skin on hard stone is sufficient to open us to the inner worlds of nature they explored over five thousand years ago.

Unfortunately we have become so attuned to the literal exterior values of things, to the outer realms of meaning even of the natural landscapes we see before us, that it has become difficult to imagine a different country of the mind. One that may have blossomed in a world without the noisy detritus and insidious pollutants that continually assail us now, whether we are consciously informed or otherwise aware of the state of the world we live in.

* * *

It is only since the nineteenth century that stone carvings have been given some recognition and artistic appreciation as an important body of ancient ethnic art. This is quite unlike the barbaric sculpture seen by Edward Lhuyd when he ventured down the long stone passageway in 1696, soon after the initial opening of the Newgrange tumulus. Yet he was the first person to actually describe and record such carvings. The Welsh scholar and natural historian's detailed explorations from Oxford, where he was Keeper of the Ashmolean Museum, across England into Wales and then through Ireland, Scotland, Cornwall and Brittany revealed the rich natural and man-made landscapes that still retained remnants of the distant past. This was prior to the antiquarian craze, and decades before the wild romantic and druidic splendour of Wales had become a fashionable back-drop for artists and their patrons. It is regrettable that Lhuyd did not live long enough to complete the projected five volumes of his *Archaeologia Brittanica* that would have included the languages, monuments, natural history, fossils and plants of his native Wales. The first book *Glossography* dealt with Celtic etymology and philology and was published in 1707, two years before his sudden death from pleurisy. To some extent, we would have been able to read his words and perhaps fill out the natural landscaped forms of the artifactual structures he described. Unfortunately, without the notes of his field work from the two explorations of Wales in 1694 and 1699 recording the antiquities and monuments, we have no such details before general industrialisation began, apart from the few descriptive and scientific cameos by Lhuyd that were published in his lifetime. It is unfortunate that his notes, manuscripts and letters were burned in two devastating fires during the late eighteenth century at Hafod the house of Sir William Williams-Wynn, and at the London bookbinders where the bulk of Lhuyd's manuscripts and other works had been sent to be bound. It could be said that it was on a par with the burning of the old library at

Alexandria, as it resulted in a devastating loss for modern scholarship, even if accidental, that destroyed much of the then available ancient manuscript literature of Wales.

It was Lhuyd who first mentioned the inscribed stone at Pentre Poeth farm that was later called the Trecastell stone when bought by the British Museum in 1878. It has Latin and ogham inscriptions as well as a series of enigmatic carvings on the other face. He also made the first notation of the miniature carvings inside the chambered tomb known as Tŷ Illtud. The saintly attribution in the name of the monument is not as unusual as the sixty-odd surviving diamonds, sunbursts and small crosses that have been variously suggested to have been done as far back as the prehistoric era, to the mediaeval period or even more recently as masons marks. Along with the graffiti dates on the outside stones, the combination of all three elements are a rarity, and unique to Wales. These two very different kinds of stone carving have been subject to some scholarly debate. However, no similar carvings have been found that would help elucidate or create a stylistic and aesthetic context in which to place such work. Another problematic figure carved on the Blaenawen stone near Aberteifi (Cardigan), that was rediscovered by the author in 1984, seems equally to be without precedence within a Welsh medieval context. In a sense the final chapters on these carvings are an attempt to fill that void. By using a compilation, or more accurately a frottage of reference and paraphrase from the explanations that have been recorded I have tried to indicate the rich veins of symbolism and associated meanings that underscore the carvings.

The rationale for writing the book is that, apart from carvings to be seen inside the megalithic structures of Barclodiad y Gawres in Ynys Môn and Tŷ Illtud near Aberhonddu (Brecon), little attention has been paid to the extensive Early Bronze Age cupmarks associated with capstones of dolmens. This is particularly true on what seems to have been a selected number of monuments in two particular areas of western Wales, north and south of Bae Ceredigion (Cardigan Bay). As with the artificially made hollows found on isolated boulders and on a small number of standing stones throughout Wales, they are usually singular or irregular cups without obvious patterns and without the embellishment of carved grooves, runners or concentric rings that are prominent elsewhere along the western Atlantic coastal routes. Yet even these most simple carvings tend to generate the wildest explanations. For example, the purpose of the small rounded hollows – made in rocks usually about 5cm in diameter by 3cm deep and generically called cupmarks – has been variously suggested as ritual, magical and astronomical marks symbolic of the sun and stars. Some have even suggested that they are site markings – especially those with grooves – by copper-smiths as they appear to have been close to ancient mine workings. The latter may be more applicable to the many groups of petroglyphs found in Galicia, south-west Ireland and western Scotland.

The carvings are often visibly difficult to locate. Yet they are available to any interested individual who cares to look for them. And unlike other prehistoric artifacts hidden in the ground or in museums, they are open to personal conjecture. In that sense every explanation, no matter how crazy, is valid if it reflects the empathy of the observer to the miniature art of the unknown carvers. They do not go out of date, unlike many archaeological explanations of the past. Cupmarks may appear empty, but in the way of such hollowed containers they shelter unseen life, tiny debris and naturally distilled water. They are generally considered to be indicative of ritual usage during the Bronze Age, and even much later when reused at some Early Christian sites. However, remember that cupmarks associated with burial ritual have been discovered as early as the Neanderthal period. At Newgrange examples have been found on nearly one out of every two decorated kerbstones as well as on many of the outer stones of the Knowth tumulus. It is thought they may have represented aspects of the renewal of life in death.

A representative collection of prehistoric carvings can be appreciated in the silence of the reconstructed stone passage tomb of Barclodiad y Gawres on Ynys Môn. This is possible notwithstanding the manner in which the heritage industry strives to represent the actual surroundings, so that they are providing the visitor with the experience of being inside a genuine prehistoric burial chamber. Like its near neighbour on Ynys Môn that was a heap of old stones in the 1920's, the totally reconstructed inner stone and grass covered dome of Bryn Celli Ddu is also listed and protected under state guardianship. Many of the larger ancient sites, such as dolmens and hill forts are now isolated from the once surrounding ritual landscape, seemingly preserved solely as individual monuments. Even the Norman castles have also been rebuilt in such a manner so that they confuse all but the professional eye, especially foreign visitors who assume they are photographing original structures. Much of what visibly survives in Wales has been repackaged with the collusion of archaeologists who during the past fifty years have elevated their stock as concerned guardians of the land, while being the sly handmaidens of the tourist industry.

Fortunately, rock art does not fit into such easily defined contexts. There are probably thousands of unrecognised examples of doodlings, scratchings and scribblings on boulders, gate-posts and stone slabs throughout rural Wales. Many of these may originally have been pictographic. However, it is easy to get carried away by curious stone markings that may well have been due to natural causation. It is equally true with some oddly iconic additions that were symbolically carved on many of the stone slabs and Christian high crosses. Two examples are the decorative spirals from Llangeinwen in Ynys Môn, or the snakes and animals on the side panels of the 3.4m high free-standing cross at Chwitffordd (Whitford) near Prestatyn. There are also the fascinating human and animal outlines in massive rock formations that we have all come across at some time or other. This is a study which is now known as Simulacra. However, in general the book confines itself to the more prominent carvings discovered by antiquarians, prehistorians and amateurs like myself, dedicated to what is still essentially a genre artform.

* * *

This introduction, like the title of the book, is named after the site of a carving high above Llanfairfechan in Conwy. The incision of three roughly expanded squares intersected by four centre lines may have been a ritual protective device. It is also suggestive of the game known as Merels or Nine Men's Morris, played by two people using nine counters or small stones and placed on the intersections in order to get three in a row. A slate with a similar figure of a 20cm x 20cm carving, was found at Bryn Glas near Machynlleth in a small area of an old enclosure with the remains of a stone structure. When excavated it was among other small finds. The game was called Triothi in ancient Greece and was probably introduced into areas of western Europe by the Romans. A few similar slate examples are in the Beja museum in southern Portugal – formally a Roman colony – and were called Ric-Rac. In the hills of the Isle of Man, at least three such carvings are known and probably, as in northern Wales, the game was played by shepherds whilst following their flocks. The Trios carvings are similar in form to some of the square mazes on old Cretan coins, and the name itself may be a corruption of the Welsh troia (from 'troi' meaning to 'turn') or from the Greek Troie or Caerdroia (the Troy Town) which was a common term for mazes in many parts of Britain. There are two such Troy Towns on the Isles of Scilly that are composed of large stones (now painted white) and are said to date from the seventeenth century. On a number of equally small islands off Scandinavia, much earlier stone mazes have been recorded, some formed of massive boulders. Unlike the mazes that often have many turns, blind alleys and repetitive loops, the spiral labyrinths are unicursal with a short pathway to the centre, and an equally short loop from the centre to the periphery. They can invoke magical protection by representing the power of nature or the tutelary guardians.

It is important to recognise that different levels of knowledge and initiation could relate to the same ancestral figure, or as in the case of known signs have many symbolic meanings. Each could be inclusive from one group to another and even from one explanation to another. A creative approach to this ancient art is not to view the images in a literal manner, as if they were predetermined letters of an unknown alphabet. The lines on stone were etched by physical endeavour. Matter was displaced, which brought about a transfer of energy. The symbols and motifs as experienced in the mind of the beholder could equally be related to the origins of their people. The frequent inclusion of quartz – perhaps to heighten sound qualities – and the use of differently coloured stones as a ritual enhancement, is a reminder that the stone passage and the round central chamber involved a ritual movement into the realms of the ancestor. Memory, emotion and desire could be re-experienced in the carved stone, as with the triple squared device at the Meeting of the Tracks, coded so that multiple meanings be applied without denying any one of them as less meaningful than the others. What it comes down to is a cachet of lateral readings, rather than grasping at a single interpretation. This is different to how ancient stone carvings in Wales and Ireland are currently explained. A concentric circle means a circle. A cupmark remains a cupmark!

Edward Lhuyd at Newgrange in 1699

> Edward Lhuyd and his three companions, with knapsacks on their shoulders, travelled on foot for the better searching of samples, viewing, and taking draughts of everything remarkable, and for that reason prying out every hole and cranny.
>
> William Price (eighteenth century)

Edward Lhuyd, the naturalist and antiquarian, was a many-sided genius who has been described as the founding figure of modern philology, field archaeology, British palaeontology and even of Welsh field naturalists. He had intelligence, physical stamina and will-power with an acute grasp of the world he grew up in. The restoration of Charles II took place in the year of Lhuyd's birth, 1660. The nobles and gentry regained their hereditary rights as leaders of local and national life, alongside the bishops and clergy of the Anglican church. The Royal Society was also founded. Experimental and applied science became popular, appealing as it did to the practical mind, a period in which Isaac Newton and Christopher Wren produced their notable work.

From his initial passionate interest in the flora of his native northern Wales, to collecting fossils and geology, and then to archaeology and the Celtic languages, Lhuyd has been described as lacking the concentration or patience to devote himself to a particular field of study. However, in an age when the natural sciences were in the ascendant, he unfortunately did not have the private means to pursue such a course even had he wanted to, but had to make do on a low paid post as the Keeper of the Ashmolean Museum in Oxford, and what he could earn from collecting fossils or leading small field expeditions. He was therefore dependant on the results of the research in his varied fields of interest and on the publication of such work. He was a prodigious letter writer and it is from this surviving material that we now know anything about his intellectual fascinations, his field travels around Britain, and that he had to ingratiate himself with the wealthy, the well-known, and with scores of would-be subscribers to fund his publications. The lack of response from the Welsh gentry in this regard often made him despondent. At his sudden death from pleurisy at the age of 49, his papers and books were seized because he had been in debt. Oxford University and the Bodleian Library refused to purchase them which meant that the notebooks of his unfinished work and the extraordinary range of manuscripts he collected throughout his adult life became dispersed. In fact most were eventually destroyed in the fire at Wynnstay, the house of Sir Watkin Williams-Wynn and in an earlier 1810 fire at a bookbinders in London where the manuscripts had been sent when acquired at auction. Eleven volumes of his papers are thought to have been burnt. His few published works, generally badly edited, and the remaining letters give a rather inadequate account of his undertakings. Yet they are a record of his ambitions and achievements, his feelings and frustrations. And in relation to Newgrange in Ireland, which he visited in 1699 soon after the tumulus had been opened, his first-hand account of the monument – with its long passage, inner chambers and the stone carvings – is unique. In fact Edward Lhuyd was the first person to describe and illustrate what we now know as one of the most important repositories of the earliest manifestations of such art, carved in Ireland more than five thousand years ago.

His father Edward Lloyd, of Llanforda near Croesoswallt (Oswestry) was reputed to have been a rogue and squandered his estates. Lloyd who was an ardent Royalist had stayed hidden with Sir Thomas Price of Gogerddan during the Civil War. In the year that it ended his daughter Bridget Price, of Glanffraid near Llandre in Ceredigion gave birth to Edward. Since Lloyd never married her, Edward Lhuyd who did not use the older form of his father's name, was illegitimate. He had a warm and close relationship with his mother's family at Gogerddan, where he spent his holidays from Croesoswallt Grammar School. It was said that he acquired the love of plants from his father, but it was an active interest that was nurtured by his mother's sister Elizabeth Price at a formative period of his life, that led him into botany. Edward had acquired such knowledge, not only of the local flora, but also of the Eryri (Snowdonia) region of northern Wales. As a young man he was drawn to the mountains, and there is a 1682 list of the plants he collected there. His name is commemorated in the discovery of *Lloydia serotina*, Lili'r Wyddfa (the Snowdon Lilly) that is accorded pride of place in the Welsh flora. The small alpine, which is quite rare today with a few habitats in the most inaccessible areas of the mountains, has several local names – y Bryfedog (the Spiderwort) and Brwynddail y Mynydd. or the rush-leaved mountain plant. (Rhind & Evans, 2001)

He probably taught at the Croesoswallt school, before he went up to Oxford when he was twenty-one. After matriculating, due to his lack of means, he became assistant to his tutor Dr. Plot, Professor of Chemistry, who was first Keeper of the Ashmolean Museum. The list of plants collected by Lhuyd had been sent to the eminent botanist, John Ray, who included it in the second edition of his *History of Plants*. It began a correspondence between them and it was when Lhuyd had become less fascinated by growing nature and more interested in ancient fossils that he asked Ray about his 'formed stones'. Lhuyd was of the opinion that they were formed from the seeds of sea vapours but Ray concluded that fossils embedded in rocks were once alive. In 1691 Lhuyd became Keeper at the Museum, and this allowed him to travel and explore the Oxfordshire quarries in search of rocks and fossils, which he collected and sold to supplement his meagre income. A quantity of fossil ferns in the Bristol coal measures were exhibited there to the public for the first time along with his other fossil collections. Lhuyd was equally innovative in considering the drawings of them to be worth publishing. However the University of Oxford had refused to publish his catalogue, but in 1699 Sir Hans Sloane and Samuel Pepys paid for the printing of a limited edition of 120 copies. It was the first publication of its kind on fossil plants in England, but Lhuyd was absent on his tour and so was unable to correct its many misprints and errors.

It was some years previously that the field study of ancient monuments and philology had begun to displace his earlier interests in natural history and geology. Bishop Edmund Gibson in 1693 was asked to edit an English version of William Camden's *Brittania* and Lhuyd agreed to supply notes for three counties of northern Wales, and eventually for the whole of Wales. These he offered to the publisher for £10 and 20 copies of the completed edition. The publisher considered his offer absurd that he should want to travel abroad when all the information needed was at the Bodleian or other Oxford Libraries, and so he offered him £5 and 10 free copies. Lhuyd was determined to consult the sites first-hand by actually visiting the monuments in each county. They finely agreed and Edward Lhuyd left the city of Oxford for Sir Fynwy (Monmouthshire) and southern Wales in the middle of August. The last of his notes were sent off to Gibson a year later in 1694, who replied to him, 'that your countries came safe to hand and without flattery, are done like a gentleman and a scholar'. He was sent two maps of Wales – southern and northern – from the first edition for correction and alteration. As each English county had a separate map he was upset and refused to have anything to do with them. 'They care not how little is done for that country,' he wrote later. They were published as they were, without reference to Lhuyd's finished text. It covered 140 folio sized pages that are quite imaginatively set, with indexes in a smaller font on the left margins of the long pages to direct the reader to the particular places under review. The 1695 *Brittania* covering the whole of England and Wales was well received and went through many editions. Perhaps it was the kind of editing that Lhuyd needed for his other publications, none of which were ever quite up to the author's expectations. The first section of his *Archaeologia Brittanica* dealing with etymology, philology and grammar was ready by 1703 and published four years later. *Glossography* disappointed many of his Welsh subscribers because of its erudite material and the learned in Paris were dissatisfied as it had not been written in Latin. He had also prepared the second volume which was to deal with the antiquities and the monuments of Wales but it never appeared. Other projected volumes of this monumental work included a section on natural history in five parts, another to deal with fossils, a fourth on plants that grow spontaneously and the fifth devoted to animals. None were ever published. In 1909 after being elected to a post worth £100 a year, Lhuyd caught a chill that developed into pleurisy and a few days later died. (Carter, 1962)

A Tedious Ramble of Four Years

In May 1696 Edward Lhuyd began his journey from Oxford crossing southern England into southern Wales. In Sir Benfro (Pembrokeshire) he was molested and he and his party accused of being Jacobit (sic) spies and conjurors. It seems that these allegations originated from the amount of letters he wrote and received. In northern Wales he was robbed by bandits. By July 1699 he had crossed over to Dublin and on his way north to see the Giants Causeway, he explored Newgrange. He left Scotland early in the following year and sailed back to Ireland. On his way south through the western regions he visited Sligo, collecting fossils and rare plants around Ben Bulben, Longford and Galway from where he took a boat to the Aran islands. After his return journey to Doolin in Co. Clare he explored the shale cliffs at Fisherstreet for fossil stones and sea shells. He reached the Killarney lakes in the extreme south-west by July 1700. Lhuyd had hoped to find some rare plants in Kerry, 'but the Tories frustrated our curiosity here, tho' no where else in the Kingdom'. He was forced to leave and travelled by sea to Penzance from some unknown port. Prior to this at Trabeg a few miles from Dingle he recorded an ogham carved stone which may be the earliest of such accounts. In fact Lhuyd complained in his letters that modern scholars he met could not read the ancient Irish manuscripts he had purchased. On 28th August, he wrote to Dr Tancred Robinson about his observations of Ireland, so it is possible that he may have just then arrived in Cornwall. However at

Helston he was taken for a thief, arrested and brought before a Justice of the Peace. He had then decided to leave by the end of November but had trouble getting a boat to Brittany. When Lhuyd and Parry eventually arrived in the second week of January 1701 they were accused of being spies and imprisoned for eighteen days. He was released and his papers returned when they were found to have nothing of treason in them. They sailed to Poole and then to Oxford, after Lhuyd himself described his journey as, 'a tedious ramble of four years return'd to the place from whence I set out'. Oxford University conferred an honorary degree of MA on Edward Lhuyd after his return. (Ellis, 1906/07)

His chest, or what has been described as a moving library, contained magnifying glasses and other instruments, books of reference and the ancient manuscripts he purchased so that they could be collated together. Along with his assistants – such as David Parry and William Jones – Lhuyd with appropriate letters of introduction, appeared to have travelled from one country house to another where they stayed often for weeks on end. This enabled him and his assistants to explore on foot the surrounding countryside with its monuments while collecting geological and botanical items of interest, ancient manuscripts and local lore pertaining to his wide and varied interests before moving on to their next destination.

Lhuyd would have preferred to begin his travels in Cornwall early in May 1696 as stated in one of his letters, 'but having promised the gentry of Glamorganshire and Carmarthenshire where I have the greatest number of subscribers to survey their countries with all conversant sped, I found myself obliged to make that my first business'. In August he was detained at y Bont-Faen (Cowbridge) for two months – prior to which he had visited the Forest of Dean, Casnewydd (Newport), Caerdydd (Cardiff), Abergafenni, Pont-y-pŵl and Llanelli near Crucywel (Crickhowell)

Early October he was in Abertawe (Swansea) and by December he wrote from Aberteifi (Cardigan) that he had surveyed the counties of Mynwy (Monmouthshire), Morgannwg (Glamorganshire), Caerfyrddin (Carmarthenshire) and hoped to finish Sir Benfro by the following spring. It was at the Grammar School in Aberteifi that he recruited his most able assistant, David Parry. On their return to southern Wales they visited Thomas Watkins of Morgannwg where Parry recorded a medical treatise written by the hereditary physicians of Myddfai in Sir Gaerfyrddin. This was later transcribed by the Welsh scholar Iago ab Dewi (James Davies), and in 1766 was copied by William Bona of Llanpumsaint to eventually become incorporated into the English translation of *Meddygon Myddfai.* (Williams, 1861)

Lhuyd remained in Dinbych y Pysgod (Tenby) until May, then to Hwlffordd (Haverfordwest) and on to Narberth. By the sixth of July he was based in Aberteifi and arrived in Llanbedr Pont Steffan (Lampeter) towards the end of that month. Hereford by the first of August, Gelli Gandryll (Hay on Wye) in September, Drenewydd (Newtown) by October and he spent Christmas at Dolgellau. He remained in northern Wales for well over a year until he crossed to Ireland in July 1699. In Dublin Lhuyd was welcomed by the Irish Philosophical Society. He visited Trinity College and remained in the city for three days. On his north-east journey to see the Giants Causeway in Antrim, he visited Swords where he saw a round tower. Then he visited Tara Hill and Newgrange in Co. Meath which, 'impressed him greatly', so much so that he had his assistant William Jones sketch the first ever plan of the interior. At Dundalk he wrote down some common native expressions and greetings, a first step in Irish. In Armagh he listed the old manuscripts in the library of the Archbishop and at Ballymore near Carrigfergus he was shown a prehistoric bronze trumpet. At Larne, 'he made an easy purchase of a dozen ancient manuscripts on parchment', from a farmer called Eoin Agniw whose lands had been taken away from his father, the last of the hereditary poets to the U'Neills. At the Giants Causeway he noted that the basalts were the same as at Cadair Idris. From a haven in Cushenden Bay he took a sail boat to Kintyre and remained in Scotland for three months until January 1700.

He travelled through Kintyre, Knapdale and Lorne, then by sea to Mull and Iona. He recorded many of the ancient monuments of Argyll and stone crosses on Iona were sketched. When he came back to the mainland he visited Glasgow, Edinburgh, the lowlands and returned to Campbeltown in December but was stormbound there for five weeks. He used this period to explore the countryside and write letters to his many correspondents. The information on fossils, plants, shells and monuments such as Newgrange was clearly copied from his notebooks for often the same expressions are repeated in different letters. He was equally interested in popular beliefs of the people, the talismans and healing amulets they carried. In one letter he described the Cockskneestone that prevents a house burning; the Toadstone against the sinking of a boat, the Molestone, quartz pebbles and Elf-arrows. (Gunther, 1945)

From what has survived of his manuscripts and notes in Trinity

College Dublin, Lhuyd seemed mainly concerned with Scottish Gaelic and the different dialects in current use. He recorded Gaelic phrases, Highland place-names, river-names and places in the Lowlands, words lists from different regions, a translation of the John Ray's dictionary into three Gaelic dialects, and the names of people who owned manuscripts. He transcribed phonetically the Rev. John Beaton's Gaelic rendition of the first books of the Bible, that had been translated by Robert Kirk during the previous century. Beaton was the last member of the renowned hereditary medical family and an ardent collector of manuscripts. One of Lhuyd's notebooks contains a list of the Irish and Scottish Gaelic manuscripts owned by him but he clearly was not interested in selling any to the Welshman when they met (in Ireland) during February 1700. (Campbell, 1962)

There are over forty individual Lhuyd manuscripts among the Selbright material catalogued at Trinity College. Many had been bound by him, often with his seal, in a most diverse manner. He placed items of different sizes and content together, mixing those on paper with vellum and often using different numbering systems. He had collected the bulk of his ancient Irish manuscripts in the year he travelled through that country. Many that he valued most were the legal manuscripts whereas for the literary texts, he could not find anyone to translate a page from them. Yet the list of the works he collected is impressive, including a fragment of the *Yellow Book of Lecan* containing many of the famous Irish wonder tales (immrama), folk sagas such as the *Cattle Raid of Cooley*, and the sole surviving copy of the prose and metrical *Dindshenchas*. The Welsh material included an Irish version of Nennius' *Historia Brittonum*, Gerallt Gymro's *Topography of Ireland* (Giraldus Cambrensis), and the Expulsion of the Deisi (from Ireland into south-west Wales). His purpose in collecting was mainly philological so the Lhuyd material also contains glossaries, dictionaries and treatises on the Irish language, drafts for his *Archaeologia*, some notebooks with his rudimentary grasp of Irish and Scottish Gaelic, and a preface by him written in Irish for an Irish-English dictionary. (O'Sullivans, 1962)

The Cave of New Grange

Edward Lhuyd wrote three separate letters that included almost similar accounts of his 1699 entry into the tumulus. A cave was the term he used and anyone who has ever walked down that long narrow passage between its smooth massive stones will know how apt his expression was. It is likely that he copied these accounts from his own original notes, written down probably during the time he spent there exploring it and the immediate area around Newgrange, as there are drawings of other monuments by Lhuyd and his assistant. (B.M. Stowe, MS. 1024)

The first letter was from Scotland on 15th December to Dr. Tancred Robinson of the Royal Society. This account was published in the *Philosophical Translations.* The second was written to Dr. Thomas Molyneux of the Dublin Philosophical Society from Ballymoney after his return to Ireland on the 29th January. The third, written in March from Sligo was to the Rev. Henry Rowlands, an antiquarian living in Ynys Môn who published it in his *Mona Antiqua Restuarata* (1723). A further letter in May to Dr. Molyneux, from Sligo, included the William Jones drawing. Lhuyd states that, 'Will Jones gives you his humble Respects and sends you a Draught of the Cave at New Grange'. The one generally reproduced is the better of the two tracings from the original. Lhuyd's notes on the plan were apparently copied down in Molyneux's handwriting who subsequently visited Newgrange sometime afterwards and his account was published in 1726. (Herity, 1967)

The letters and the drawing together form a most valuable document in relation to the history of the Newgrange monument. The published accounts over the following two hundred years appear to lack the extraordinary creative insight, quality of exact description or intellectual coherence of Lhuyd's. Even Coffey's 1912 book on it – one of the last detailed accounts of the monument prior to its total excavation and reconstruction by O'Kelly from 1962 – appears to be somewhat confusing in comparison. It must be remembered that with the constant quarrying of stones and changes in vegetation, the entrance stone had been covered over until it was rediscovered during the 1840's along with the decorated lintel stone. So it is not surprising that few later commentators made any mention of the carvings there. Antiquarians of the druidic school tended to look upon the Welshman's unbiased account as lacking in substance or used it to show up their own inimical observations and viewpoint. It is worth looking at the plan and comments in some detail as these show the tenor of Lhuyd's mind as being thoroughly modern in approach and far in advance of his period. The outline of the stones uses quite a different approach from what became a convention based on an idealized projection from above, as drawn by General Vallancey (1775) and George Coffey in 1912, which is muddling as he has the same set of incomplete numbering for the stones in both chamber and passage. Lhuyd's plan portray the orthostats as lying outwards from their base as if drawn in situ from inside the cave. On a detailed examination, according to the

Irish prehistorian Michael Herity, it is a careful survey with its measurements agreeing quite closely with those of modern surveys.

The accounts in the letters are generally succinct, graphically detailed and written in a direct, almost scientific manner, without romantic embellishment. His reference to the basin in the right-hand chamber for 'Blood in Sacrifice', is discarded in the later letters. They are interesting also in the slight changes of emphasis that occurs when discussing the animal bones found when the cave was first opened. The labourers differed in their accounts, whereas later Dr. Molyneux said they were human bones. For Lhuyd, the Roman coins found on top of the mound showed it to have been built before the Danes arrived but that the carvings and 'rude sculpture, barbarous', proved it was much earlier. That he quoted Ole Worm's 1643 influential work on the Danish monuments showed he plainly disagreed with the popularly accepted idea that all British megaliths were built by them. He also mentions the stones in the circle at Newgrange in connection with those at Avebury and Stonehenge and was probably aware of the work of his older contemporary John Aubrey who had died two years earlier in 1697.

> The most remarkable curiousity we saw was a stately mount at a place called New Grange near Drogheda; having a number of huge stones pitched on end around it, and a single one on top.
>
> > The Entry is sixty-five foot long. The Cave 22 foot one way and about 18 the other.
> >
> > This Cave is in a large Artificial Mount surrounded at bottom (i) with huge stones pitched on End.
>
> The great pillars round this cave, supporting the mount, were not at all hewn or wrought; but were such rude stones at those of Abury in Wiltshire, and rather more rude than those of Stonehenge. The entry in to this cave is at the bottom, and before it we found a great flat stone, like a large tomb-stone, placed edgewise, having on the outside certain barbarous carvings, like snakes encircled, but without heads.
>
> > (a.a.a) The Entry and floor of the Cave is nothing but loose Stones confusedly Dispersed.
>
> At Bottom within it is a cave, the entry thereof is guarded on each side with large rude stones standing on end, having sometimes barbarous sculpture on them not unlike the ruined monuments in Wormius's

'Monumenta Danica' and on top of these are other stones laid across, but no letters at all.

(b) The large rude Pillars supporting ye Entry in number 42, ye heights of these at ye first Entrance is about 5 foot & afterwards they are gradually higher till nearly ye midst, whereas ye Entry is about 8 & thence to ye Cave ten foot high.

At the first entry these supporters are so pressed with ye weight of the hill and the overhead stones are so, that they that go in must creep, but by degrees 'tis still higher till you go into the cave which may be about 6 or 7 yards in height

(c) The pillars about ye Area or Walls of ye Cave some of these are still higher ye those in ye Entry & ye height of ye Cave may be about 20 foot.

(d) Rude carving on some of ye Pillars

Many of the pillars about the right-hand basons were carved as the stones above-mentioned; but underfoot there was nothing but loose stones of any size in confusion and amongst them a great many bones of beasts and some pieces of deer horn. In this cave on each hand of us was a cell or apartment. In those on each hand was a very broad shallow bason of stone, situated at the edge. The bason in the right-hand apartment stood in another; that on the left-hand was single; and in the apartment straight forward there was none at all. We observed that water dropt into the right-hand bason, tho' it had rained but little in many days; and suspected that the lower bason was intended to preserve the superfluous liquor of the upper that none might come to the ground.

(e.e.e) Three Cisterns which are placed in ye 3 several apartments of ye Cave.

(f) A kind of Font or Bason standing in ye right hand Cistern.

Within this bason was some very clear water which drop'd from the cave above, which made me imagine the use of this bason was for receiving such water, and that the use of the lower was to receive the water of the upper when full, for some sacred use, and therefore not to be spill'd.

(g) A Carved stone placed edgewise (not erect like ye other Pillars) behind ye left-hand Cistern.

(h) Carved Stones above ye right-hand Cistern.

Those about the basons, and some elsewhere, had such barbarous sculpture (viz. spiral like a snake, but without distinction of head and tail) as the fore-mentioned stone at the entry of the cave.

(i) Part of ye Roof of ye Cave which is Vaulted like an Oven.

(k) The Carved Stone above ye right-hand Cistern more fully

(l) A Stone wrought in the form of a Cone, half a yard long & about 20 inches in the Girth having a small hole at ye big End. This I found within ye right-hand Cistern under ye bason above mentioned.

Near the top of the mount they found a gold coin, which Mr Campbell, the proprietor of this village, shew'd me, and 'tis a coin of the Emperor Valentinian.

A gold coin of the Emperor Valentinian, being found near the top of this mount, might bespeak it Roman; but the rude carving at the entry and in the cave seems to denote it a barbarous monument. So, the coin proving it ancienter than any invasion of the Danes; and the carving and rude sculpture, barbarous; it should follow, that it was some place of sacrifice or burial of the ancient Irish.

Enlarging the minute drawings of the carvings from the sketch of Newgrange and by comparing them with the appropriate illustrations from Coffey's work, it is possible to appreciate the earliest illustrated accounts of Irish megalithic art. The clear thinking and foresight of Edward Lhuyd in providing a visual record to his own notes and written accounts can also be seen in his notations of the Latin inscriptions on early Welsh crosses and from the carvings on the inside stones of Tŷ Illtud, a megalithic chambered tomb in Powys (page 9).

A backward glance

> In the early years of the Museum the registers appear to have been carelessly kept, and the 'finds' distributed according to a hard-and-fast 'three-ages' classification by material – stone, bronze, and iron – so that at present much confusion exists in portions of the collection of the Royal Irish Academy.
>
> George Coffey (1912)

Like many seemingly simple discoveries or explanations, the three-age technical model published in a 1836 paper by Thomsen the Danish writer, not only seemed an obvious answer to the dating conundrum of that time, but has gradually been accepted by prehistorians and the general public alike, as the basis or framework by which the past can best be understood. It has also become the corner-stone of prehistoric archaeology. Initially the Ages of Stone, Bronze and Iron, as applied to existing artifacts and their technology, made it possible to situate a prehistory or protohistory before known history was said to have begun. In essence time began to be expanded backwards into ever-earlier eras. This was made possible by typology or classification of tools and monuments into a new time-scale of early to late, and of superior to inferior categories. For any particular class of objects it was possible to apply historical analysis. It not only freed such categorization from mere static description, but gave individual objects a technical context and a new dynamic conceptual mould. Focus on the technology meant objects could be seen primarily in terms of function. Pioneered by General Pitt-Rivers, stratification then gave yet another dimension to the archaeological tenet of digging into the earth in search of the past. Any found object could be related to a depositional event that was time-scaled within its local setting. It was universal in so far as it was also linked to the natural history of the ground around it. So it was the reciprocal relationships between type, technology and stratification that laid the foundations of scientific archaeology. (Schnapp, 1994)

The archaeology of ancient Britain was determined during the last century by diffusionist notions and the spread of the Bronze-Age people to every area of the islands. In turn it was modified by other theories based on exchange in border trade and gift-giving as the essential medium of change. The ideas were wrapped in socio-scientific jargon, discussed in symposia and journals, then published as the latest prehistory. Their conceptual basis was nevertheless the three-tiered scenario of Stone, Bronze and Iron Ages. The key textbooks in relation to the early archaeology of Wales, by doyens such as Wheeler (1925), Daniel (1950) and Lynch (2000) clearly show how the initial date-lines were being constantly qualified by the introduction of late and early prefixes for each era. But perhaps more important is how the inclusion of new scientific data – such as in relation to the exact radio-carbon dating when artifacts were interred in burials – muddled the former chronological foundations on which earlier books were based. This can best be illustrated in relation to the New Stone Age with the arrival of the first farmers and the megalithic structures they erected to honour the dead. For many writers following in the footsteps of the influential Gordon Childe, Professor of Archaeology at Edinburgh, diffusion from a second millenium classical Mediterranean world explained the very existence of the stone monuments here. Of course an exodus from the cradle of civilisation is an endemic notion that underpinned early Welsh history from the work of Sieffre o Fynwy (Geoffrey of Monmouth) onwards.

The archaeological establishment throughout the twentieth century had created for itself a mandate of authority on prehistory and how it should be defined and presented as an exact science. It occasionally rubbished some of the marginal and so-called antiquarian studies as unscientific in their books and journals. It was a new breed of professionals that were to determine the heritage of Britain and the way forward. The dip in public confidence during the 1960's over the squabble of carbon 14 dating in relation to accepted archaeological data was quickly forgotten. This was especially true when the later tree-ring dating and the pollen analyses of findings from excavations provided a firm scientific backbone to the beleaguered profession. The bristle-cone pine *(Pinus longaeva)* is a gnarled tree in the semi-desert region of Arizona, and it's rhythmic patterns of yearly growth provide a direct reflection of environmental changes from six to four thousand years ago. It was variations in climate that created broad bands, due to wet years and narrower ones in years of drought. In archaeological terms this new development in chronology provided an absolute date as a check on previous radio-carbon dating, recalibrating it. Equally important, since the tree-rings were controlled by climate their patterns could be used as a record of the past, one that could be matched with the pollen analyses. Pollen grains have a remarkable resistance to decay, and proliferation of trees and plants at different periods can now be ascertained to build a picture of local and regional changes within the environmental flora of the past. (Dimbleby, 1978)

One result is that the corner-stone of prehistory, based on the so-called first farmers in Britain, has been seriously questioned. As with the previous conceptual shifts of prehistoric time, it is as if the removal of a stereotype allows fresh thought to flower. Within the former idea of the Neolithic era, the early scavengers living on berries and shellfish were the real Stone Age primitives, who not only decimated the ancient animal kingdom by hunting them to extinction, but whose knowledge of the surrounding world was so limited, that they lived like children in a garden of Eden. We now have a broader picture of how such peoples used the natural plant world around them for nourishment, shelter, healing and magic. A credible first step in understanding the intimate relationship with the land was to reconsider the actual environment in which they lived rather than the stone axe, that wonderfully shaped icon so idealised by earlier generations of writers. The data now available to prehistorians are botanical studies of pollen analyses, tree-ring dating, and the science of fossiliferous plants. By the use of advanced techniques, the sequences of growth from the grasses of a post-glacial tundra era to the deciduous mixed forest of about ten thousand years ago can now be untangled from many overlapping geophysical strata. Possession of fire and the domestication of grazing animals like sheep, pigs, goats and red deer had a prolonged intrusive effect on the woodlands. As people became more sedentary and began to depend on such animals for food, clothing and other commodities they probably changed some wild habitats in order to attract or retain certain species of game. They may have even induced wild animals in for hunting purposes. The former notion of the early people in Britain running the elk, reindeer and wild horse to extinction has been modified. It was in fact climatic disruption that affected the vegetation over periodic time and hastened their decline.

To early twentieth century archaeologists, the Neolithic farmers represented a solid recognizable breed of workers who tilled the land and built massive stone funerary monuments. Yet time-scales were gradually being extended so that by the end of the century the Mesolithic period was no longer recognizable as a protracted outdoor life with vast shell middens built around the coastal regions. Their provenance from many inland excavations during the past decades show the possible interaction of such people with primitive agriculture and herding. It was in a sense the old and new cultures learning from the knowledge and technology of each other. Even the building of large-stone tombs seems to have precursors in low-lying boulder burials, and that some Bronze Age cairns were found to have been erected over plain internments from the Late Neolithic era. However confusing this is, what is emerging is an evolutionary continuum in which the sacred recognition of the world around them was a paramount factor in the lives and the monuments of early peoples in these islands.

To begin with the triad of prehistoric chronology by way of an introduction may seem elaborately pedantic, but it is not fortuitous in relation to the subject of the book. Good examples of rock art in Wales are not that numerous. The meanings or explanations of the most important carvings, like the monuments they decorated, hinged on the prism of archaeological interpretation. Situated in the landscape, they are subject to environmental and physical changes. Even in the protective atmosphere provided by the reconstructions of monuments like Barclodiad y Gawres and Bryn Celli Ddu on Ynys Môn, the once clear incisions on stone slabs fuzz over and become hard to distinguish. Many of the small diamond shape and cross motifs on the inside stones of the megalithic chamber known as Tŷ Illtud near Aberhonddu are now indecipherable. Nearly a decade after the discovery of the Blaenawen stone, its clear incised figure had gradually faded and has all but now disappeared. In most instances it is from the early published accounts of the findings that we can really appreciate the work and creativity of the unknown carvers who decorated the stones.

An interesting foray into their world-view is tracking down the large number of cupmarks that are to be found on tombs, standing stones and movable boulders from all parts of the country. This is a subject that is often relegated to a reference or footnote in the important archaeological surveys of Wales published during the last century. The art is often quite wrongly compared to the more numerous and prominent cup and ring petroglyphs to be found in Ireland, Scotland and Northern England. The minute artificially made depressions on the capstones of dolmens in western Wales around the Preseli Hills and Pen Llŷn (Llŷn peninsula) were often dismissed as natural hollows. Yet they offer a hidden ritual configuration in relation to the larger physical monuments and landscape. The sense of the sacred these carvings embody is as important as their material aspect. The carvers – artisans and ordinary folk – created a synonymous world of symbols which we can hardly decipher. The outward forms may provide explanations. Yet in terms of inner meaning they retain that enigmatic quality which is expressive of much of the wild countryside of Wales.

Writing on the Late Bronze Age culture in Britain, a prominent archaeologist stated that the people on this side of the English Channel had little interest in the decorative arts. Lacking any trace of figurine art, he finds their techniques were of the simplest and that decoration – if present – was basic and repetitive. He does concede that perhaps rock carving may have some aesthetic sense beyond the functional. However, the passage grave art (of the Neolithic) and the cup and rings (of the Bronze Age) were equally abstract and repetitive, and were created for purely ritual or religious purposes. Whilst highlighting the value of their functional motifs, his inference that abstract repeats of decorative motifs in clay, stone, bone or other materials that have survived can be other than repetitive, is as silly as the compounding of ritual with religion without attempting to define the former in relation to a function, or the latter within a specific social identification of the sacred. It is when seeking clarification of the author's meaning in relation to the actual carvings that it becomes a bit of a smokescreen. Colin Burges states that for him 'the meaning of cup and ring art is a mystery', but that their use was part of the total religious fabric of the period. Whatever significance that can be attributed to the art may be safely expressed as a function, rather than as any kind of spiritual embellishment. (Burges, 1980)

Archaeological ideas altered radically during the last century, especially in relation to the expansion of prehistoric time. The changes brought about in the Neolithic era by primitive farming, animal husbandry and stone tomb building are now seen as part of a cultural fusion with the earlier Mesolithic society. However rock carvings, by their association with the earliest of the established three-age technologies, were considered as a form of primitive expressionism. Fossil-like, they tended to be regarded as anomalous within megalithic artifacts, and served as visual comment to be plucked from source books as illustrations. Unlike the study of pottery, with its mass of evidence from burial rituals as the basis for rigorous classification of shards and as evidence of the many types of beaker used at different times and in different regions, the distinct lack of megalithic stone carving to be found in Britain has been marginalized.

Passage Grave Art

Barclodiad y Gawres in Ynys Môn, with its five decorated stones in situ is a singular example. The six carved Calderstones in a greenhouse near Liverpool were retrieved from a destroyed site by Birkenhead and a few lintels from Orkney tombs are now in the Royal Museum of Scotland. The meandering spiral incised on both sides and top of a 2m high stone from Bryn Celli Ddu is problematic as archaeological opinion now tends towards a two-phase structure. The stone may have originally been a central part of an old henge monument, or later carved to be ritually interred along with the long smooth undecorated pillar during the creation of the circular cairn. It is now in the National Museum of Wales and a cement cast stands behind the reconstructed tumulus. The main decorative motifs that are found on the above stones are geometric and curvilinear, and seem part of the common decoration prevailing in the Irish passage grave art of the Boyne Valley tumuli, and from passage graves over to the west and north of Ireland. Therefore the carvings in Britain are most often described as Irish intrusion into Wales and Orkney. Yet a different hypothesis is that the art of Ynys Môn owes more to Brittany than Ireland. Some of the double carved footmarks on three of the Calderstones are similar to the motif on a stone at Petit Mont, and may be an artistic example of such influence. (O'Sullivan, 1993)

To put the few examples of megalithic rock carvings in Wales into a proper context, the general reader may be surprised at the scale of such work to be found in Ireland, where it has been estimated that there are over a thousand individually carved stones in nearly three hundred passage-type round structures. Not all contain carvings, and some tumuli remain unopened and therefore unexplored. Many in the Boyne Valley had carved kerbstones outside the tumulus as well as those in the inner passages and chambers. During the twenty year extensive excavations of Newgrange and Knowth, some were found to be carved on both sides and sited so that the symbols on the hidden surface faced into the very fabric of the mound building. It brings up some stark differences in interpretation. For instance, the back of kerbstone K13 at Newgrange has what appears to be a mass of undifferentiated doddles all over the stone. They include spirals, concentric rings, dots in rings, curved lines and a series of cupmarks. These are all seemingly carved by many different hands. This is especially noticeable when compared with the outer visible surface and its fully realised design. In Brittany there is a similar kind of outward display. On the bottom hidden part of a reused stone of La Table Des Marchands at Locmariaquer are the remains of earlier less professional forms that also include cups. For incorporating in its new setting, the stone was stripped back for a well designed composition of multiple hooks, surrounding what Marija Gimbutas describes as a symbolic vulva. This might suggest that such finished carvings – as are also obvious from the complete mural-like layout and designs on the passage and inner chamber stones at Gavrinis – were worked by individual artists. Perhaps the earlier marks were the result of communal ritual participation. If as it is often claimed, that symbolically the architecture of the passage tomb generally represented the body of the Earth or Mother Goddess, then why should such a small number in Ireland, Brittany and Britain in relation to the overall total found in each region, be chosen to be so decorated? And within their curvilinear abstract art, certain carvings – especially those with cupmarks previously executed – were placed inward as at Newgrange or into the ground as in Brittany.

The main focus of megalithic archaeology has been directed at the architecture of tomb building, and considerations of rock carvings are minimal. Prehistorians, if trying to make sense of the enormous quantity of stone carving in Ireland, naturally tended to view it from that perspective, or were overtly influenced by associations with diffusion. So traditionally the art of the Boyne Valley – at Newgrange, Knowth and Dowth – was seen as the more complex and primary source of inspiration. And the areas westwards in Ireland and eastwards in Britain – from centre to periphery – were equated in terms of more simpler and cruder styles, and from later periods. A few mid-third millenium carbon 14 dates for Newgrange was a confirmation for many researchers, but for others the dates from a millenium before for passage tombs at Carrowmore on the western coast indicated much earlier building. At present there seems to be a tacit Irish compromise in that within each of the four large scale cemeteries across Ireland, where the overwhelming number of tombs are located, there is sufficient evidence to trace an evolution from the simpler to more complex finished styles. Those at Carrowkeel and Carrowmore in Sligo are devoid of carvings, but the art of Loughcrew and the Boyne Valley contains an evolutionary shift in motifs and final forms. It mirrors the differences in each area, from the purely undifferentiated collections of carvings to the more complex designed stones. (Bergh, 1995)

The latter half of the nineteenth century was a period when research and subsequent publication of discovery revealed the rich decorative heritage that lay within many of the ruinous Irish monuments. W.F. Wakeman in 1858 seems to have been the first to mention the carvings at Loughcrew. Accounts by Eugene Conwell of his excavations there, alongside the plans and artwork of du Noyer were published in the following decades. Wakeman had described many of the hilltop siting of such tumuli but drew a contrast between single tombs like Knockmany in the north, and the large-scale megalithic cemeteries of Co. Meath and

Carrowmore near Sligo. The latter were first recorded by Wood-Martin. Sir James Fergussan wrote about these Irish sites in his large compilation of *Rude Stone Monuments* of 1872, and towards the end of the century the Cornish antiquary W. Borlase published a remarkable collection of the dolmens of Ireland, culled from the manuscripts and above printed sources. He included Bryn Celli Ddu in Ynys Môn, as well as illustrating plans of little known monuments in Portugal and Brittany. G. Coffey's *New Grange & Incised Tumuli* of 1912 also brought in the corrective view of outside influences, especially in relation to the art of Newgrange and Loughcrew. In the 1920's it was R.A.S. Macalister who carried on with this kind of synthesis. He excavated the many tombs at Carrowkeel and attempted to correlate the aesthetic outlooks of Dechelette and L'Abbe Breuil in relation to the parallels found in the passage grave art of Ireland and Brittany, and in particular to the oracular idols and stone plaques found along the coasts of western Europe. (Herity, 1974)

O.G.S. Crawford, the influential editor of the archaeological journal *Antiquity* from 1927 to his death in 1957, was a firm advocate of the Mother Goddess. He traced her images in the passage graves of classic form from Crete around western Iberia to Brittany and Ireland. In studying the circular designs that represented her human face he was identifying Breuil's evolutionary process, by which the recognizable carvings of a pair of eyes, eyelashes, eyebrows, a nose and mouth, a fringe of hair and side-tresses, with perhaps a necklace and breasts below had 'disintegrated into a jumble of spirals, circles, multiple arcs, and zigzag and wavy lines'. We now accept of course that it may well have been the other way around, as the latter rock scribblings predate the former by as much as a millenium. Crawford had the grace to admit he was not successful in getting 'a really good face' to photograph in Ireland, but the few examples he quotes as anthropomorphs were some single stone compositions from Newgrange and Knowth in the Boyne Valley, and elsewhere at Knockmany, Fournocks, Loughcrew and at Barclodiad y Gawres. (Crawford, 1957)

Whatever individual meanings had been attributed to the Irish passage grave art, multiple levels of interpretation were slowly leached from the carved stones, with the lead from Britain in discussing them in two-dimensional terms of modern design. In analysing the ornamentation solely in terms of tables of motifs or styles, and by cherry-picking such identifiable elements from the background of rock doodles and scribbles, the ritualistic aesthetic and pains-taking time-consuming practice of the unknown artists was ignored. The work was clinically

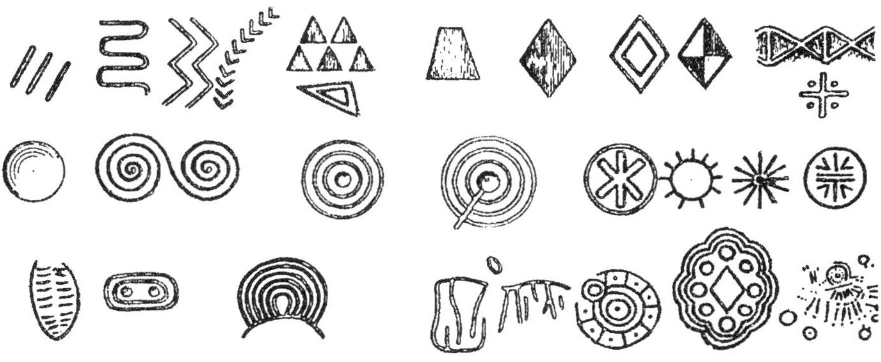

Alphabet of symbols (after Macalister)

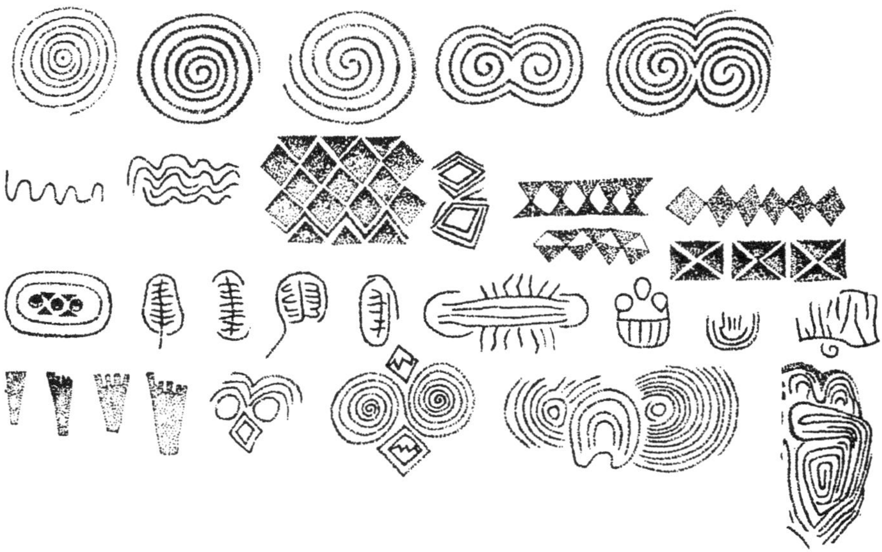

Detail of Alphabet of passage grave designs and motifs (after Herity)

Note the *feet* at the Calderstones; ocular symbol combined with lozenges from Barclodiad y Gawres; double spiral from Newgrange; the *face* designs at Loughcrew and Knowth.

discussed in terms of shapes or their amalgamation to create the basic abstract forms. Like journeymen working too close to their material, the spiritual and religious power underpinning the total creation of the larger tomb shrines, the technology of the buildings as well as their ritual decoration, could safely be ignored. Instead they opted for designs based on what came to be known as a standard insular style of ornament. Earlier scholars had argued about its origins in Iberia, Brittany or even Scandinavia but since the bulk of the Boyne Valley carvings have now been photographed and published, it has been suggested that each of the major tumuli of Knowth, Newgrange, Dowth and at Loughcrew had in their own stylistic manner drawn inspiration from a common font of ancient European art. (O'Kelly, 1982 and Eogan, 1986)

However, to map out any transition in terms of influences from abroad, or to hypothesise on crucial incursions from here southwards, is as difficult as it always has been. Devoid of figurative elements, the geometric passage grave art appears to have evolved locally, fully realised within its stylistic parameters. None of the more realistic motifs that are evident in late Palaeolithic or western megalithic art have been recognised as being within the body of Irish or British indigenous carving. The exception may be in terms of anthropomorphic concerns, in which there has been a revival of interest. This is partly in reaction to the clinical archaeological approach to the art, but also to the appreciation of the relationship between the formal ordering of motifs and the overall shape of the individual stones. Herity published an alphabet of designs and motifs, which included decorative elements like rayed circles and arcs relating to the oculli. Other complex motifs from Sess Kilgreen may have represented naturalistic faces as well as their more abstract forms in Newgrange. In a third category there were symbols conjoined with arcs and spirals that could have formed into human faces. More recent research suggests that there are two basic stylistic approaches – based on the art at Knowth – that are also applicable to the carvings of Newgrange and Dowth. The first is a depictive style of motifs or elements in the form of spirals, circles, chevrons and lozenges, initially carved on the stones without attempting to produce an overall design. The other is a later plastic style where the design lines were boldly stated with ornamentation, and tending to fill the face of a stone. Both aspects are apparently not mutually exclusive, although the depictive styles seem to be contemporary with the construction of the main tumuli. The mature plastic style appears to have been applied later as some designs are superimposed on earlier carvings. At Knowth the carved surface area rarely extended to within 30cm of the bottom of the stones. This is an indication that the work was completed when they were in situ, after being placed at important turns of the passages and particularly in the right-hand side recess of the central chambers. Some of the important outside kerbstones at Newgrange and Knowth would appear to embody the essence of this style, as well as individual compositions from inside Knowth, Fourknocks and Barclodiad y Gawres in Ynys Môn. (O'Sullivan, 1986)

The geometric symbols of renewal in the tomb shrines on both sides of the Irish Sea are essentially abstract, not in the modern sense as devoid of visible meaning, but rather in the universal all-inclusive manner that is apparent from cave paintings and petroglyphs in Old Europe, Africa, America and Australia. It appears as if the geometric megalithic art first flowered here at a period in the mid-third millenium BC without obvious antecedents. It also seems to have ended as suddenly with the closure of the tombs. Hidden from view until recently, it remained in a time-warp without influencing the later Bronze Age petroglyphs. Before looking in detail at the Welsh carvings done towards the end of the period, as most commentators assert, it may be worthwhile to review earlier prehistoric decoration in Britain in order to ascertain if there were important lines of continuity from the Mesolithic period or earlier Upper Palaeolithic eras.

Cult of the Dead

The retreat and renewal of the ice sheets resulted in many topographical land changes through enormous shifts in sea levels. The wide Bristol Channel beyond the raised beaches of Penrhyn Gŵyr (Gower Peninsula) was once part of a great plain. The warm climate made the region like the savannahs of Africa, and the same kind of animals roamed the land. Bones of hippos, rhinos, elephants with straight tusks, lions and hyenas from the warm interglacial periods have been found in the caves of the limestone ridges that run from east to west and reappear at Ynys Bŷr (Caldey Island) and at Penfro (Pembroke). This carboniferous limestone indicates the region was once submerged and was formed by millions of small marine creatures. In the same area of caves are bones of creatures from colder periods, such as the mammoth, woolly rhino, reindeer and bear. It was in 1792, after quarrymen discovered extinct bones at Crawley Rocks, that geologists began to take an interest in Penrhyn Gŵyr and its extensive caves.

William Buckland was a flamboyant, eccentric and articulate Professor of Geology at Corpus Christi College in Oxford. A renowned and witty public speaker he often carried a large black bag from which he would produce his latest find or mimic the prehistoric animals that lived in his imagination, like the flying reptile he named the Pterodactyl. On being informed by some amateur geologists from Castell Pen-rhys (Penprice Castle) of the new finds from Goats Hole and Hounds Hole, almost as soon as he arrived he immediately began to dig up the hard floor of the former cave. Halfway up Goats Hole, amid the thick occupational deposits, he found a skeleton that had been buried in an extended position. The skull, vertebrae and parts of the right side were missing. However, close to the thigh there were two handfuls of perforated shells *(Nerita littoraia)*. They were piled so neat that they may have originally been in a pocket of a burial garment. In contact with the ribs were nearly fifty fragments of small cylindrical ivory rods and fragments of ivory rings. The shallow grave, the human bones and the ornaments had been powdered by a powerful red ochre dust. A mammoth skull and some flint tools were in the nearby deposits. Buckland decided that the animals and humans could not have occupied the cave at the same period and declared the burial and flints to be later intrusions. Because of the shells and ivory ornaments, he assumed the skeleton was female and named her the Red Lady of Paviland. No doubt the bones were labelled, placed in a sack and taken back to Oxford to be stored. It was one of his professorial successors in the same post, W.J. Sollas, who re-examined the site eighty years later. He found thousands of flints in the cave and declared that the body must have been a twenty-five year old man. Radio-14 carbon dating indicated that he lived twenty-six thousand years ago.

In a sense every burial is a singular activity whereby the living honour the voyage of the departed to whatever realms their society believes in. The fact that it remained relatively undisturbed and survived for so long in the cave amid its changing environmental conditions is extraordinary enough, but the care and preparation of the internment point to a variety of cultural factors prehistorians lightly call the cult of the dead. The body, complete with personal adornments and laid in a shallow grave that was covered with red powder, shows a marked degree of ritual intent we rarely equate with people of the Ice Age. It should make us pause about the assumptions that have been put forward about the dispersal of bones in the stone chambers by Neolithic society.

The young male with his personal possessions was laid out, full length on a shelf and perhaps wearing a simple garment. The final dusting of red ochre gravely pulling him back into the earth. There is a simplicity here! An acceptance of life in death and in after-life. He was probably a hunter and the tiny ivory sets he carried with him may have been symbiotically related to the tusks of the mammoth's head buried nearby. In fact one might surmise that since the skull was found in the cave, man and beast may have spiritually joined in the hunter's spirit world. In the manner that the red ochre – the favourite medium used in Palaeolithic cave burials and paintings – was sprinkled over the body, it would soak through to the bones and the surrounding earth. Perhaps this was in imitation of the lifeblood flowing away, and to symbolize that he is both inside the sacred cave and outside on the plains joining the ancestral spirit beast, directing its food to his family group. As a healing spirit mediating between his people and the realm of the animals, he could have been as much a shaman as those more graphic depictings in cave paintings. Two examples are a dancing man with a beast head around the cattle at Les Trois Freres in France, or the half-man half-beast dancer among the mammoths in Les Comberelles chapel in Spain.

In fact in terms of its date span of 26,000 years BP (before present) the latest find of sophisticated cave art at Chauvet was created five thousand years before. It makes the survival of the Paviland burial a rare ritual event, even in the broader European context. It shows that there were people in Britain at the climatic downturn of the last glacial maximum. Other finds in the cave were ivory workings dated around 21,000 BP and earlier bone spatulae that may represent schematic female figurines. It has been suggested that the continuation of visits at that period (when no other human evidence has been found in Britain) and particularly with the ritual objects and burial, that the cave and perhaps the hill itself that surrounds it, may have had religious or ancestral significance. For people approaching it from the south, the Gŵyr plateau at this point would have presented a high dominant land feature. Perhaps what this may represent is yet another variation on the sacred mountain, the abode of the goddess in her various guises from provident Mother to Winter Hag. (Aldhouse-Green, 2000)

In 1912 there was a flurry of renewed interest when it was thought that a unique prehistoric wall painting was discovered inside Bacon Hole, further east around the Gŵyr coast. However, recent research indicates what appears to be a series of reddish streaks covered with a thin layer of stalagmites on the rock face, as the natural formations of red oxide. Similarly at Madog rock shelter above the river Wysg (Usk) the reports of wall painting were later discounted. Other finds at Bacon Hole included a decorated clay bowl from the fifth century BC, and a tiny flute carved from a bird bone. It turned out to have been a child's toy lost during the Middle Ages!

Perhaps the most exciting and unequivocal carving of incised chevrons was found in Kendrick's Cave, near Llandudno in northern Wales during the 1880's. The zigzag patterns on the jaw-bone or mandible of a horse is the only example of such portable art from Wales. Dated to 10,000 BP, it falls on the cusp of the final cold phase and in a sense heralds the Mesolithic era. The cave was named after Thomas Kendrick, who dug out most of the deposits that included human bones, perforated bear canines, flint artifacts and a decorated badger's tooth. Four engraved and ochre stained tallys and nine perforated teeth of wild cattle and red deer with incised decoration on their roots were also found. Recent research and close dating indicates that rather than being grave goods with the four human skeletons in the cave, the burials occurred a few thousand years earlier than the decoration of the jaw-bone. In relation to the millennia of prolonged glaciation, the following warm phase is thought to have occurred quite quickly, in less than fifty years. During the early Mesolithic period, the coastline of Wales at 35 metres below the present sea levels was more rounded, without the familiar Bae Ceredigion (Cardigan Bay) and even Ynys Môn would have been seen as a plateau. This means that much of the territory of the hunting and scavenging groups is now under water, and it is the earlier cave sites where flint working and other evidence of culture is available.

From an open site at Prestatyn in Sir y Fflint (Flintshire), in Madog rock shelter, and in Rhuddlan cave hazel-nut shells have produced dates to 8,700 BP. Even earlier dates have been postulated for Nap Head now on the south Penfro (Pembrokeshire) coast. Although no settlements have been found, the range of finds at this important site shows that it was reoccupied at different later periods up to the early Neolithic. Six incised pebbles decorated with geometric lines and scratch marks from the Rhuddlan site are a rare example of Mesolithic art, although whether they can be classified as decoration, as art or even a sign language is an open question. The largest single design (5cm high x 3cm wide) on one stone could represent a house or a fish-basket – similar examples are found among the extensive rock carvings of the Camonica Valley in Italy. At Nap Head, among the stray finds of stone tools, a small shale smooth carving has been interpreted as a Venus figurine or a phallus. At different times, over five hundred shale perforated beads have been found here and at nearby sites. They may have been from earlier burials or as some are unfinished, locally made. Such finds of personal adornment are rare in Britain from this period. (Aldhouse- Green, 2000)

Carvings from Barclodiad y Gawres

Barclodiad y Gawres. Barclod 'apron' is a borrowing from Old English 'bearmclap', M. English 'barmcloth'. With the ending -aid 'full' we have barclodaid 'apronful'. The name of the site is therefore the apronful of the giantess' (cawres).

G. Melville Richards (1954)

The apronful, apron, or lap of outside ogres of Welsh lore in the form of giantess, goddess or hag were usually associated with earth mounds, heaps of stones or even glacial moraines. Barclodiad y Gawres was first recorded but not named in *A List of Cromlechau or Druidical Altars in Anglesey* in 1796, and was described as being partly demolished on Mynydd y Cnwc at Llanfaelog. It was described in much the same state in 1869, and in 1913 the RCAM(W) noted the ruined tumulus in rather cursory terms. Forty years later an archaeological excavation revealed (and recreated) the cruciform passage tumulus with its five decorated inner stones. As there are a number of passage tombs in Ireland with similar names and containing carved stones, such as on Slieve na Gaillighe at Loughcrew, a question that could be considered was if there were any connections? Or was it the folklore associated with the older structures that originally stimulated the popular imagination in this way? Or maybe other factors, now long since lost, that retained the place-names and the popular tales around them?

William Williams, in his 1802 *Observations on the Snowdon Mountains*, recounts a familiar tale about such a place-name at Bwlch y Ddeufaen, in Caerhun Parish in Conwy. A giant in the company of his wife was travelling towards Mona (Ynys Môn). Having been informed that a narrow channel separated it from the mainland, he carried two large stones, one under each arm, to form a bridge. His lady carried the smaller stones in her apron. However, on meeting a cobbler with a sack of worn-out shoes, he asked him how far was it to the island. On hearing that the man had worn out a sackful of shoes travelling from Mona, the giant dropped the stones where he stood. His wife opened her apron and the heap of stones between them has been since called Barclodiad y Gawres.

Thomas Pennant in his late nineteenth century *Tour of Wales* relates that a prodigious heap of stones lay on the summit of a conic shaped hill south-west of Llanaelhaearn in Pen Llŷn. The ruins were called Arffedogaid y Gawres, or the apronful of stones flung down by the

Giantess. 'Arffed' is another word for lap with 'arffedog' for apron and 'arffedogaid' for apronful. Edward Llwyd records Arffedogaid y Wrach (the Hag's Apronful) at Llanfor in Gwynedd, under Moel Fama at Cilcain in Sir y Fflint and at Estyn where the same place-name is used for a cairn put up by the wife of Gwrle the giant, where he is reputed to have been buried.

A shortened form 'ffedogaid' as in Ffedogaid y Forwyn (Apronful of the Maiden) is in the name of one of the three stones that lie in a meadow below the waterfall Pistyll Rhaeadr near Llanrhaeadr-ym-Mochnant. The other two stones were called Baich y Gawr a'r Gawres (the Giant's and Giantess's Burden). Apparently the trio were crossing the falls when the giant Beryn (the name of the nearby range of hills) heard a cock crow. One of the conditions of his sanctuary in the Pennant Valley was that if he left it he should be home before the cock sounded. So he dropped the stone over the waterfall and advised his companions to do likewise. (Melville Richards, 1956)

The Winter Hag as portrayed in Scottish folktales and in upland place-names was a more primordial shape-shifter and builder of mountains. Popularly known as the Cailleach Bheur (pronounced kaillich-ver) or Auld Wife, she forged the hills and lake-filled valleys. She was often the Hag of bad weather, wind and storms whose lightning thunder-stick or power wand equated her with the Mother of Creation. Her annual struggle with Bride the Goddess of Spring, who melted the ice, greened the land and brought forth new life, may be the remains of a cosmological drama that recalled the fearsome archetypical aspects of nature when the formidable uplands were being moulded into their present recognisable forms.

The hills of Rosshire were said to have been formed by the icy breath of the Cailleach Bheur passing overhead. Ben Nevis was kicked into shape by the Auld Wife and the rock of Alisa Craig fell through a hole in her apron. Her route westward was littered with the suggestive place-names she passed every year at the start of winter, to wash her hair in the sea. As a result her ablutions created the great maelstrom of the Corywrechan, between the Isles of Jura and Scarva. Perhaps it is no accident that the islands and western coastlands have the most extensive examples of petroglyphs in the whole of Britain, showing cupmarks, spirals and other rock carvings.

In Ireland she was associated with megalithic monuments such as the Hag's Chair (Loughcrew) on Sliabh-na-Caillighe, and with other mountains like Sliabh Gullion, Cairbe Heights and the Macgillycuddy

Carved stones
Barclodiad y Gawres, Anglesey

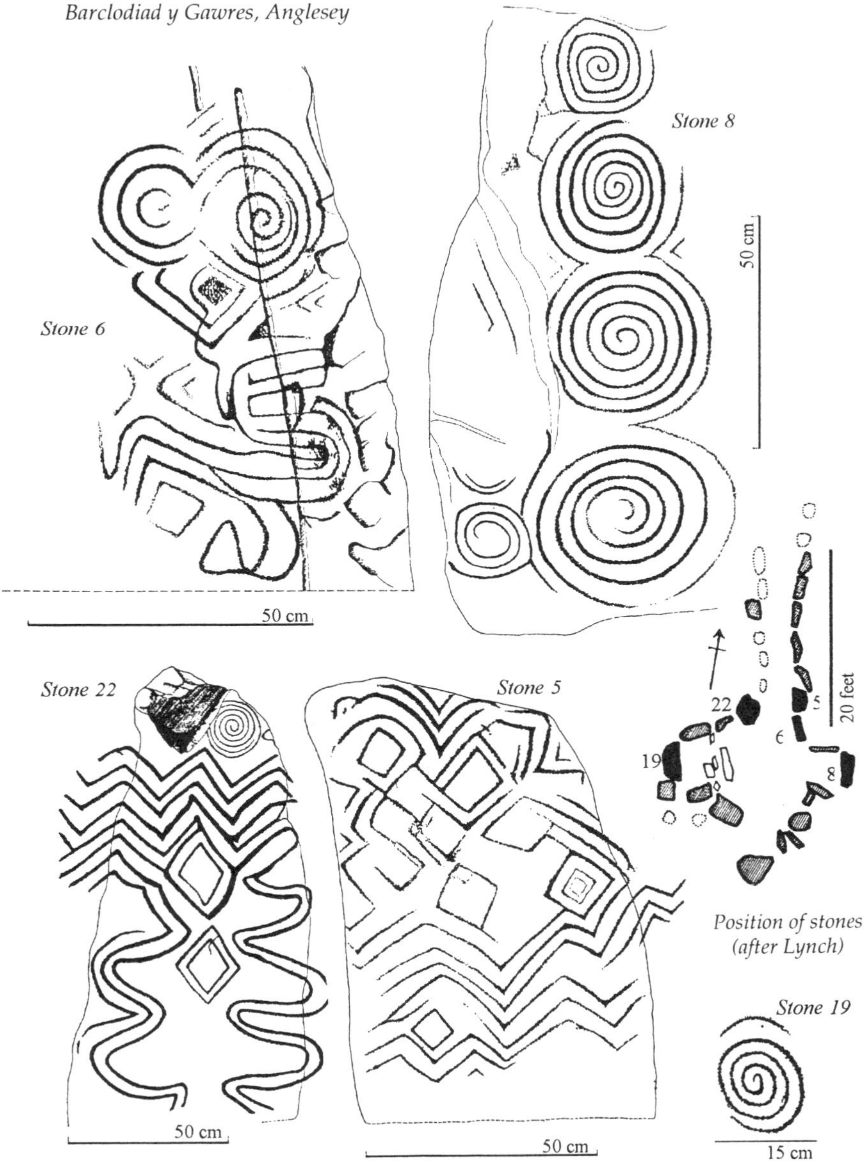

Reeks in the south-west. All were embroidered in folk memory with the creation of land forms or stone monuments.

There is an interesting anecdote from Irish lore, recorded by Jonathan Swift during a visit to Co. Meath with the antiquary Dr Thomas Sheridan to hear the local stories. He afterwards embellished the tale of a mythological giantess named Garbh Ogh with the traditions of the Hag, who is said to have dropped the stones from her apron to form the cairns along the ridge named after her at Carnbane West and Carnbane East, but she tripped and fell over the longstone at Patrickstown – named after the patron saint whose encounter with the old goddess on Croagh Patrick, the holy mountain above Clew Bay in Mayo, resulted in the *Devil's Mother* being confined in a nearby lake. She has had many folk variations in Ireland but none so parodied as the verse penned by the satirist who was then the Dean of St. Patrick's Cathedral in Dublin.

Determined now her tomb to build
Her ample skirts with stones she filled
Dropped a heap on Carnmore
She stepped one thousand yards to look
And dropped another goodly load;
And then with one prodigious leap
Gained Carnbeg, and on its height
Displayed the wonders of her might!
And when approached death's awful doom
Her chair was placed within the tomb
Of Hills whose tops with heather bloom.

The summits of Carnbane West and East contain over twenty tombs of varying sizes. More than a hundred carved stones have been recorded in the two largest passage graves, in cairn L and cairn T respectively. There are isolated examples from other parts of Ireland, but the majority of the carved stones are clustered in Co. Meath close to the rivers Boyne and Blackwater. Perhaps the group of carvings from Barclodiad y Gawres and Bryn Celli Ddu in Ynys Môn and the Calderstones originally from the estuary of the Mersey, may equally have been a significant focus for the artisans on the west coast of Britain. (O'Sullivan, 1993)

The Calderstones are six decorated sandstone flags of varying sizes that were originally part of a small megalithic chamber. The tumulus and other stones were removed early in the nineteenth century. The first mention of this site occurred in a boundary dispute between the Lord of

Allerton and the Queen's Steward of the Manor of Wavertree in 1568. Both mention the stones as being three in number and refered to as the 'Dojer, Rojer or Caldwage stones'. This may indicate that they were visible and not covered over by a cairn. Some were dug up in 1765 and one was named as a Robin Hood Stone. Correspondence in the *Liverpool Daily Post* during the last decade of the nineteenth century records that the tumulus was removed in 1814, with probably some of the original stones as well. The remainder were arranged in a circle by a Mr Walker in 1845, and surrounded by a low wall and iron railing. The site stood within two miles of the river Mersey, probably not far from its original position as marked on an early map. A century later, due to weathering, soot and pollution discolouring, the City Authorities had them moved to the Liverpool Museum. They are now to be seen in the greenhouse at Calderstone Park outside the city. The carvings include a bold open spiral design. A right and left-handed double spiral is bordered by two circular lines. There are six pecked out crude feet-shapes and seven outlines of boot graffiti from a more recent date. The pair of feet on a slab at Petit Mont in Brittany to which they are often compared, are in fact models of perfection. Other stones have spirals, concentric lines, broken circles, a picked triangle and irregular carved lines. (R. Cowell, undated)

A rough stone placed in a vertical position against the west wall of the parish church of Llanbedr in Gwynedd has a single spiral carved on its visible surface. The spiral covers an area 30cm in diameter at the top end of the metre high stone. Its groove is incised about 3cm wide and less in depth. The spiral runs clockwise in a seven-band expanding loop. There are seemingly no other carvings or lettering on the stone, which was found in 1866 in or around a ruined dolmen at Dyffryn Ardudwy, reputed to have a series of straight incisions on the edge of one upright. Brought down from the hills the carving was placed between the two pillar stones known as Meini Hirion at Llanbedr. The largest is 3.15m high and the other is 2m high. In 1915 the spiral stone was moved to the churchyard where it still stands. (RCAM(W), 1921)

This large complete spiral is exceptional among the very few known in Wales. Although impossible to date, it is often included along with others carved on large boulders of Rocky Valley in Cornwall, on the standing stones of Long Meg in Cumbria and Nether Largie in Argyll. These spirals along the western sea route may well have been done during the Bronze Age. They may indicate a tradition of pilgrimage that seems to have carried on into the late Christian period. Examples are on two cross slabs from old church sites at Llangaffo and Llangeinwen in

Ynys Môn and a small triple spiral found on the base of the Llanbadarn Fawr high cross when it was moved from the churchyard in 1916. The narrow 3m tall stone is extensively carved on all sides and now stands in a small display area of the church near Aberystwyth in Ceredigion.

The Passage Shrine-tomb

The sharp cultural demarcation between the later settled phase of the Mesolithic and the beginning of a primitive farming economy during the Neolithic may be less absolute than archaeological scenarios imply. If distribution site maps for the former suggest an empty quarter in the central upland region of Wales, the distribution of megalithic tombs of the latter are equally sparse. Apart from the incursion of the Cotswold-Severn cairn types into the south-eastern border region, it is among the south-west and north-west coastal areas where portal dolmens were situated, alongside a small scatter of passage graves. There would appear to be both architectural and symbolic differences between the two types. Those with a short passage of the dolmen box-like stone construction, named from their dramatic high H-doorway comprised 'a scattered group of seven small isolated monuments in west Wales'. The second, as represented on Ynys Môn with a long passage of stone orthostats, inner chamber with recesses and surrounded by a covering mound, are of a much later date. It is the corbelled cruciform passage tomb of Barclodiad y Gawres (and Bryn Celli Ddu to a lesser extent) that contains lightly carved stones, that have been compared with similar monuments of the Boyne Valley in Ireland. (Lynch, 2000)

The archaeological excavation at Barclodiad y Gawres in the early 1950's showed that the original walled passage was 6m long, and the only surviving roof slab which was extremely heavy had a diameter of 3m x 1.50m. According to the Rev. John Skinner on his ten day, *Tour of the Antiquities of Anglesey* in 1802, this coverstone was carved with the graffiti of personal names and was known locally as the Stone of Names. It is curious that there was no mention or comment of the ancient carvings previous to the excavation, by him or Rev. Hugh Prichard later in the 1860's or even by the Rev. Henry Rowlands, vicar of Llanidan, whose illustrated compendium of island monuments was published in 1723. Perhaps there may have been some old traditions associated with the place, that drew people to the large stone in order to carve their own personal marks on it.

Apart from the necessary archaeological details involved in the condition of the site and its subsequent reconstruction, the published report made some interesting observations at Barclodiad y Gawres. No evidence of human burial was found within the central structure although some cremation deposit was thinly spread in the western side chamber. Therefore the cruciform passage shrine seemed entirely given over to ritual purposes. In the central chamber a stone hearth, roughly a metre in diameter rested on an old turf floor which had been turned into a grey colour with red patches. In its centre was a thick deposit containing burnt grey earth with charcoal lumps, which was overlaid by a thin layer of small flat stones, smooth pebbles and quartzite bits.

When the content of this was professionally analysed, an extraordinary stew of sea creatures with two hundred bone fragments of small animals was revealed. These included oysters and limpets, wrasse, eel and whiting, frog, common toad and natterjack, grass snake, mouse shrew and rabbit. The ritual sequence that was suggested with this ceremonial brew – worthy of Macbeth's three witches – was equally amazing in its detailed action. First, a wood fire was lit. It was allowed to burn down until it was composed of hot ash and lumps of glowing embers. A special stew containing all the above had been prepared and as a libation was poured into the hot ashes. The fire was immediately quenched and then small pebbles and shells were thrown in. A large stone covered it all. (Powell & Daniel, 1956)

This makes an interesting comparison with the pit that had been discovered in the excavation of Bryn Celli Ddu during the late 1920's. Beneath a large slab of white schist that had been placed in the centre of the monument, fragments of charcoal, unburnt hazel-wood and a burnt bone from a child's right ear were found in scorched fire pit. This was covered with a mixture of clay, stones and pieces of jasper. A lump of purple clay that had been worked into a shallow hole, was placed into this filling prior to the final covering of the stone slab. (Hemp, 1931)

The published report on Barclodiad y Gawres does not elaborate on the finding or replacing of the five carved stones in reconstructing the monument. It gives a breakdown of the main motifs found to be lightly incised on the stones as spirals, conjoined circles, lozenges, chevrons and vertical zigzags. They view the context for this art as from Iberia, but note that few of the actual designs appear to be comparable with megalithic carvings elsewhere. A decade later a set of clear rubbings with comparative notes of the decorated stones was published. The author emphasized that they did not add any unexpected details to the previous photographs but provided a useful opportunity to take a new look at the relationship between the Welsh designs and those from Ireland and

Brittany. (Lynch, 1967)

It was a review of the outward aspect of the carvings, comparing them with a complement of other motifs to ascertain some obvious stylistic connections. She relied on the rather hazardous reproductions of Irish art at that time, when the major long-term excavations of Newgrange and Knowth had hardly begun. In fact, in her conclusion she states that no Irish tombs can show the integrity of the patterns and the interest displayed in the intricate working out of the designs. The recent work by O'Sullivan emphasizes that the finished stylistic forms on particular stones from Irish and Welsh monuments are a feature of what he terms mature megalithic art. The other stones at Barclodiad y Gawres certainly do not show anything like the same integration of forms and overall design on which to base some sort of chronology, in terms of a finished early or late art. In the main, a closer link with Ireland is postulated than the excavators were willing to admit. They thought that there had been a second spiral on stone 19 and that it had weathered leaving the small disjointed ovoid carving. Even if this were so, Lynch finds it the least impressive of the carvings. She described it as a disappointment and a waste of a stone which had a reasonably smooth surface! Even her response to 'this single miserable motif' (and recalling the spiral in Bryn Celli Ddu) is strangely likened to what she describes as a plethora of unrelated details on some carvings at Loughcrew. Then after comparing the work of the Welsh artists to that of the extraordinary sculptured entrance stone at Newgrange and the fine architectural lintels with extensive zigzags at Fourknocks, the writer began to doubt if her overtly subjective impressions were justified in deducing (any valid) comparisons (page 43).

There are other ways of looking at such carvings without the necessity of such a wide-eyed comparative approach. The long passage runs on a north-south axis which means that the inner cruciform chamber has clearly defined east and west compartments. Each have a decorated backstone. Stone 19 for instance, shows a broken four-looped spiral running clockwise out from the centre and anticlockwise inward. A right-hand energy flow could mean rebirth or reincarnation. A left-hand flow may indicate death and dissolution. The stone was placed in the right-hand recess, an important position in Irish passage graves and usually reserved for singular carved images. Rather than the weathering suggested by the excavators, the remains of another spiral may have been deliberately rubbed off in order to enhance the remaining one at the top of this stone.

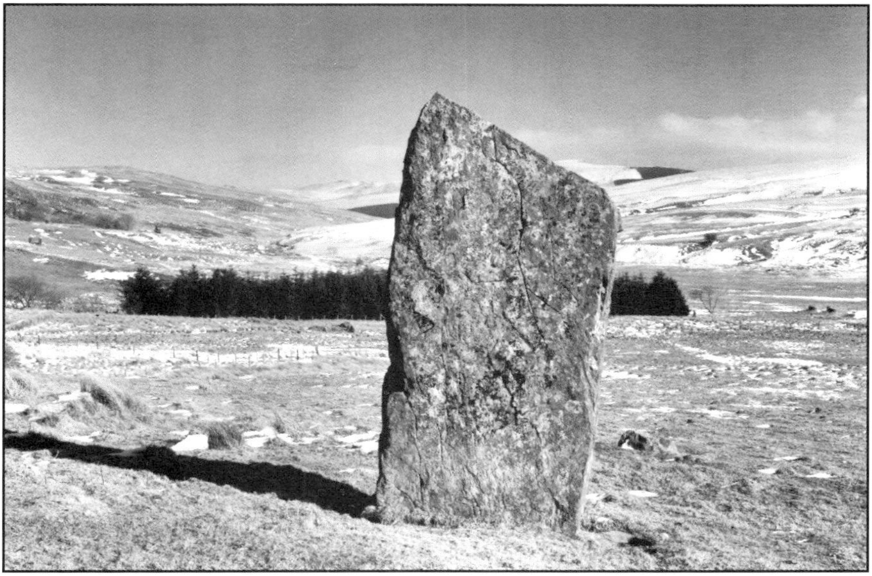

Llech Idris standing stone, nr Trawsfynydd, Gwynedd

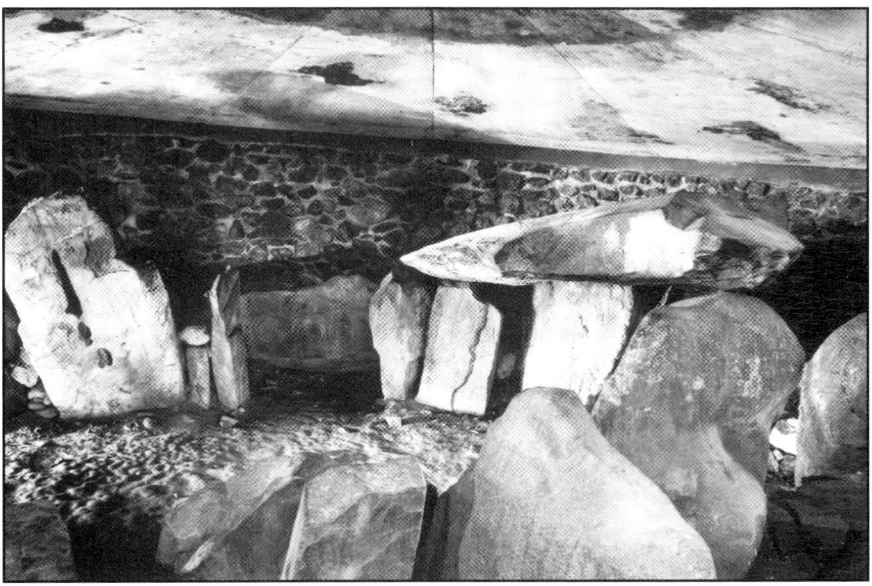

Barclodiad y Gawres passage grave, near Rhosneigr, Môn. (Mick Sharp)

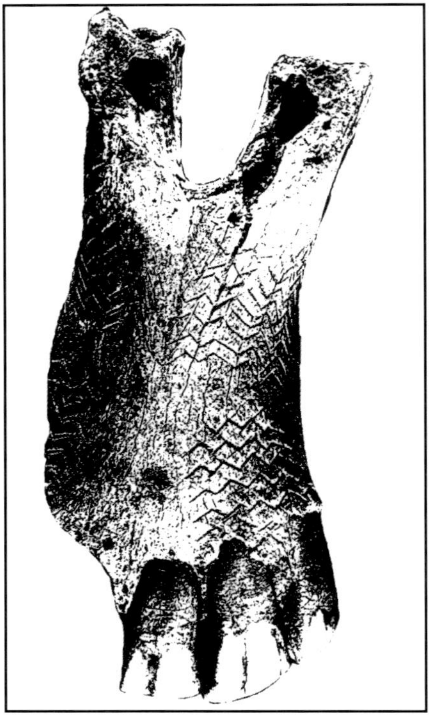

Decorated horse mandible from Kendrick's cave North Wales (after Barton).

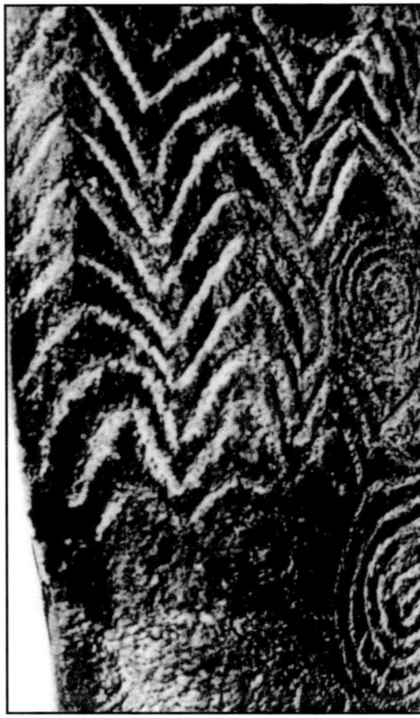

Details of passage stone from Newgrange (after Coffey)

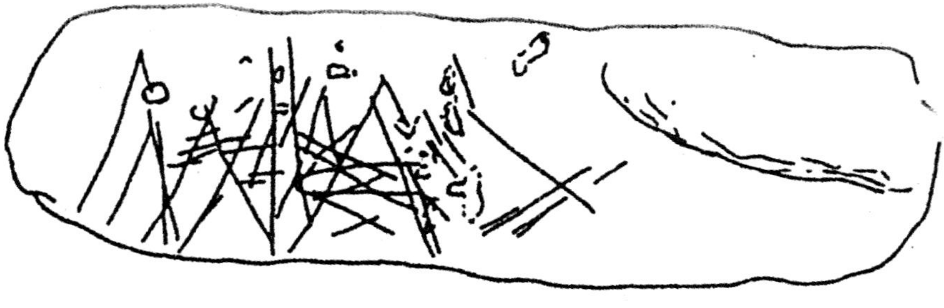

Markings scratched on passage stone of the Neolithic house complex at Scara Brae, Orkney (after Shee-Twohig).

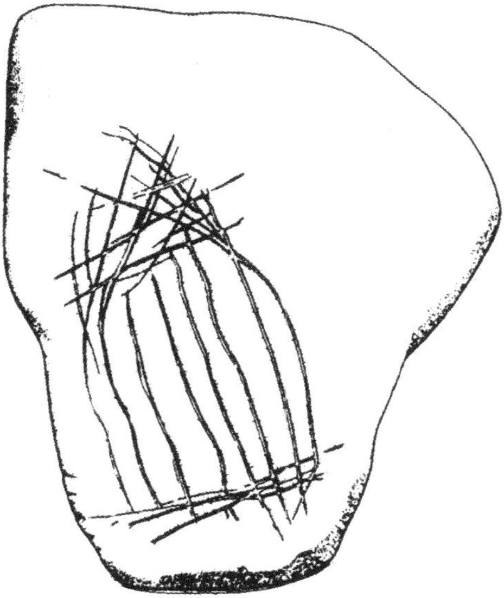

Decorated pebble from Mesolithic site at Rhuddlan, North Wales (after Aldhouse-Green)

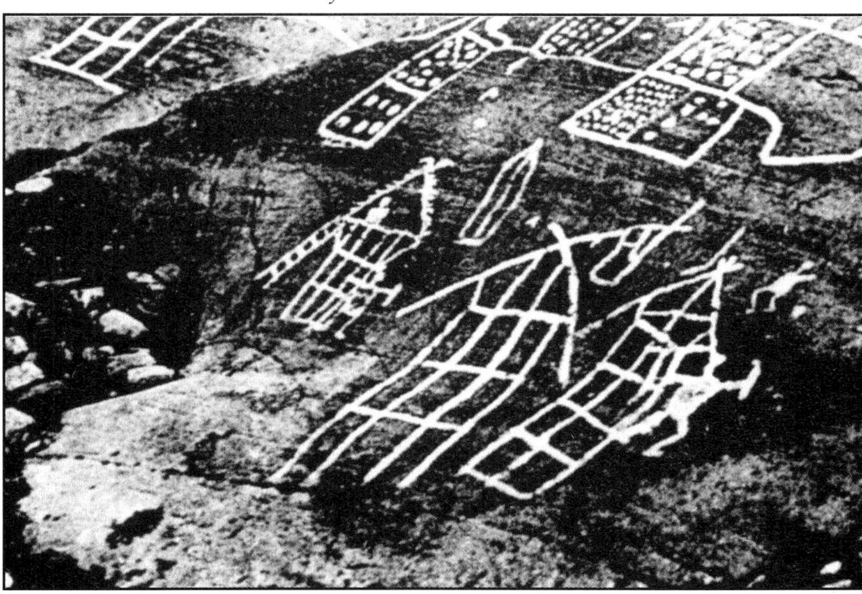

Detail of house designs on Bedoline rock in the Carmonica valley, Italian Alps Early Iron Age c750bc (after Anati)

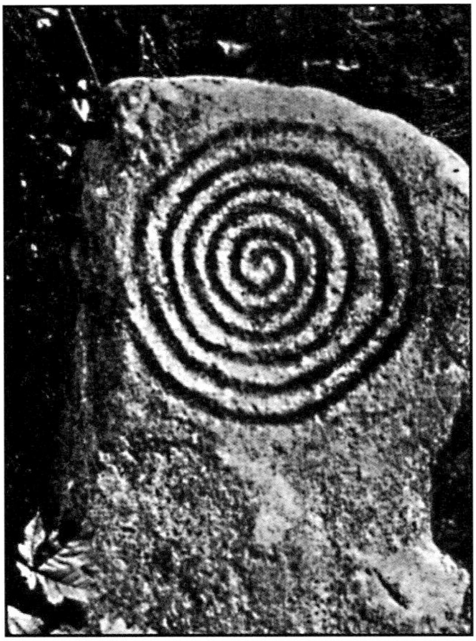

Spiral stone, now at Eglwys Pedr, Llanbedr, Gwynedd.

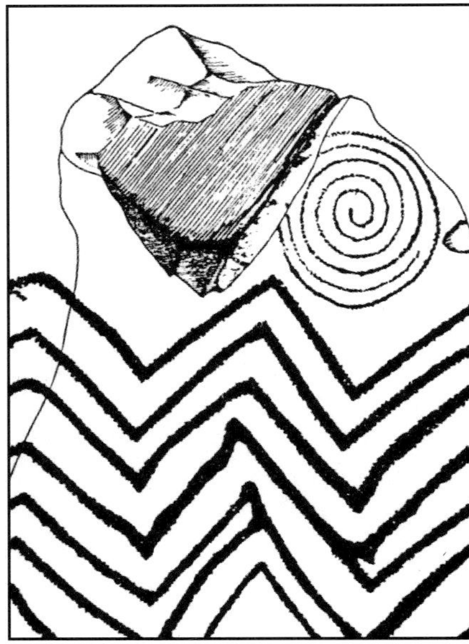

Passage stone, Barclodiad y Gawres, Ynys Môn.

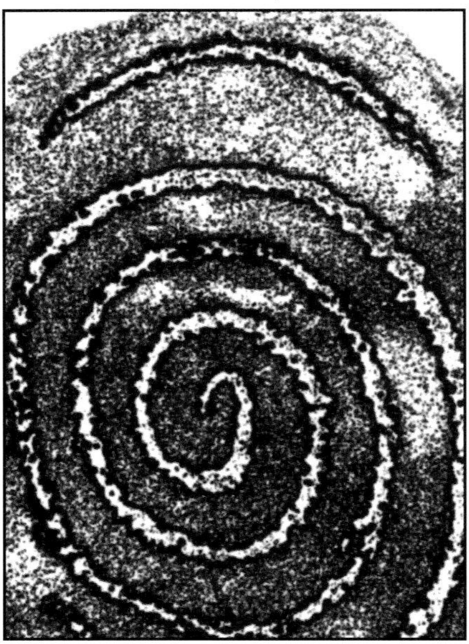

Spiral stone in chamber recess, Barclodiad y Gawres, Ynys Môn.

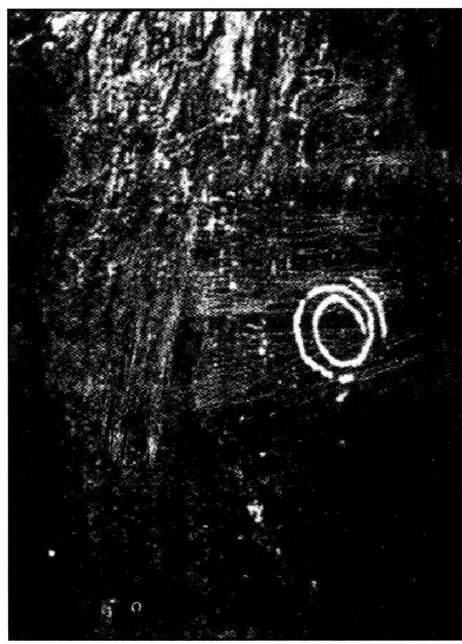

Spiral stone, Bryn Celli Ddu, Ynys Môn.

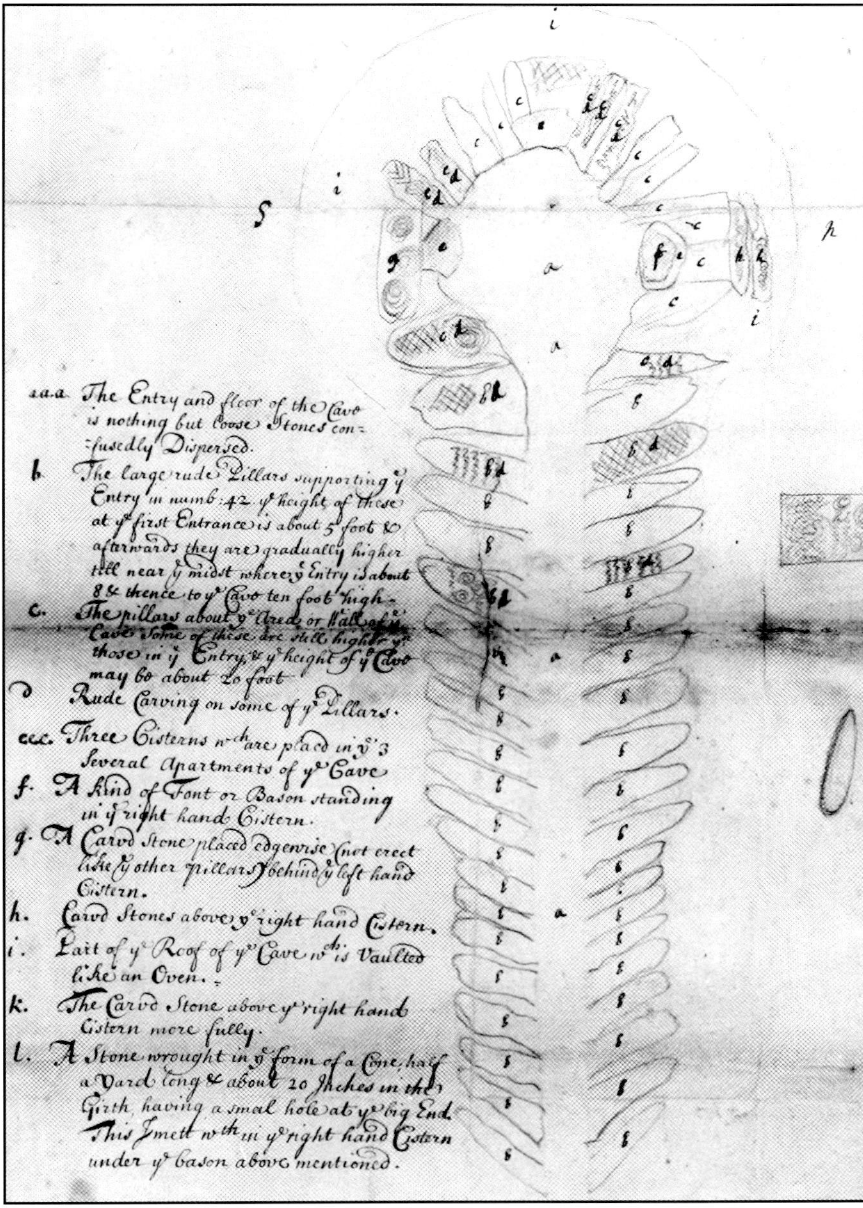

Plan of Newgrange made by William Jones for Edward Lhuyd, 1699 (by courtesy of the Board Trinity College, Dublin.)

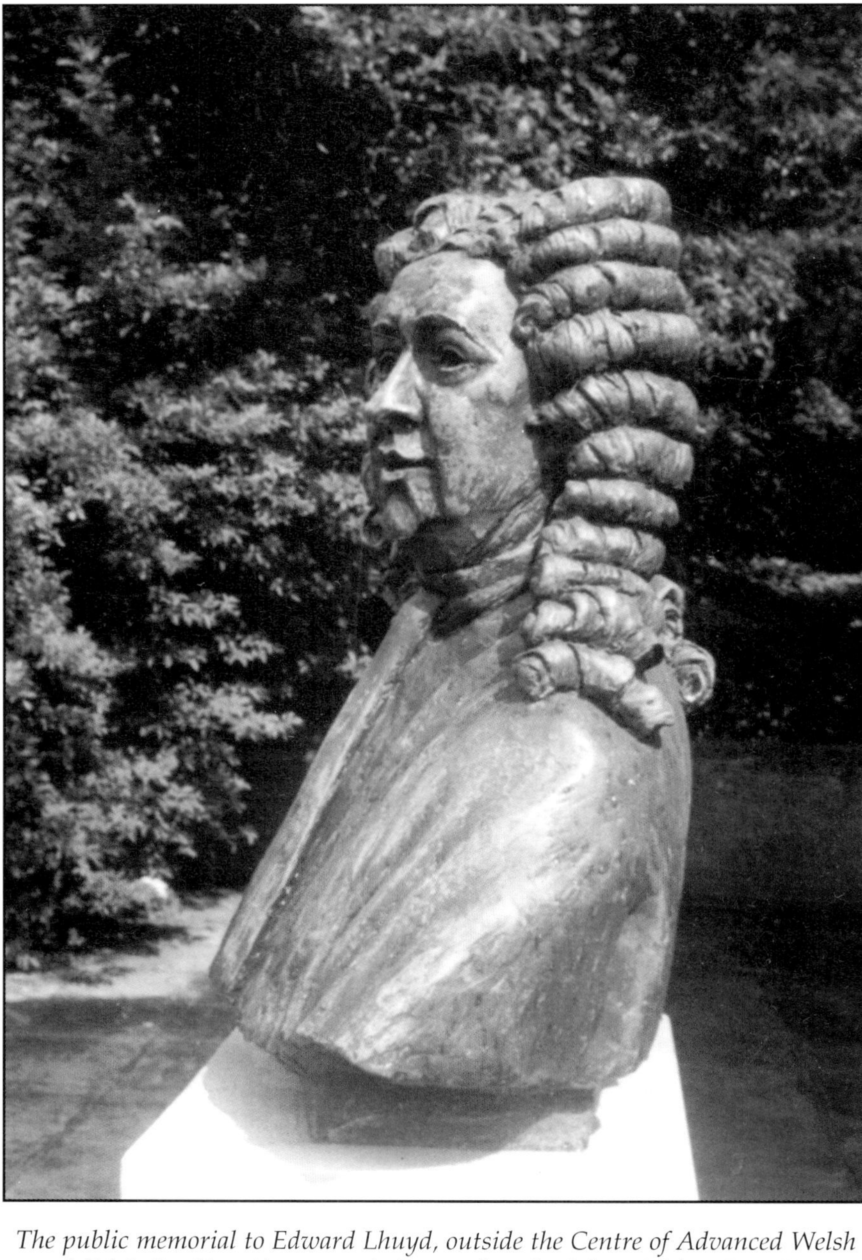

The public memorial to Edward Lhuyd, outside the Centre of Advanced Welsh and Celtic Studies, Aberystwyth, Bronze bust by John Meirion, June 2001.

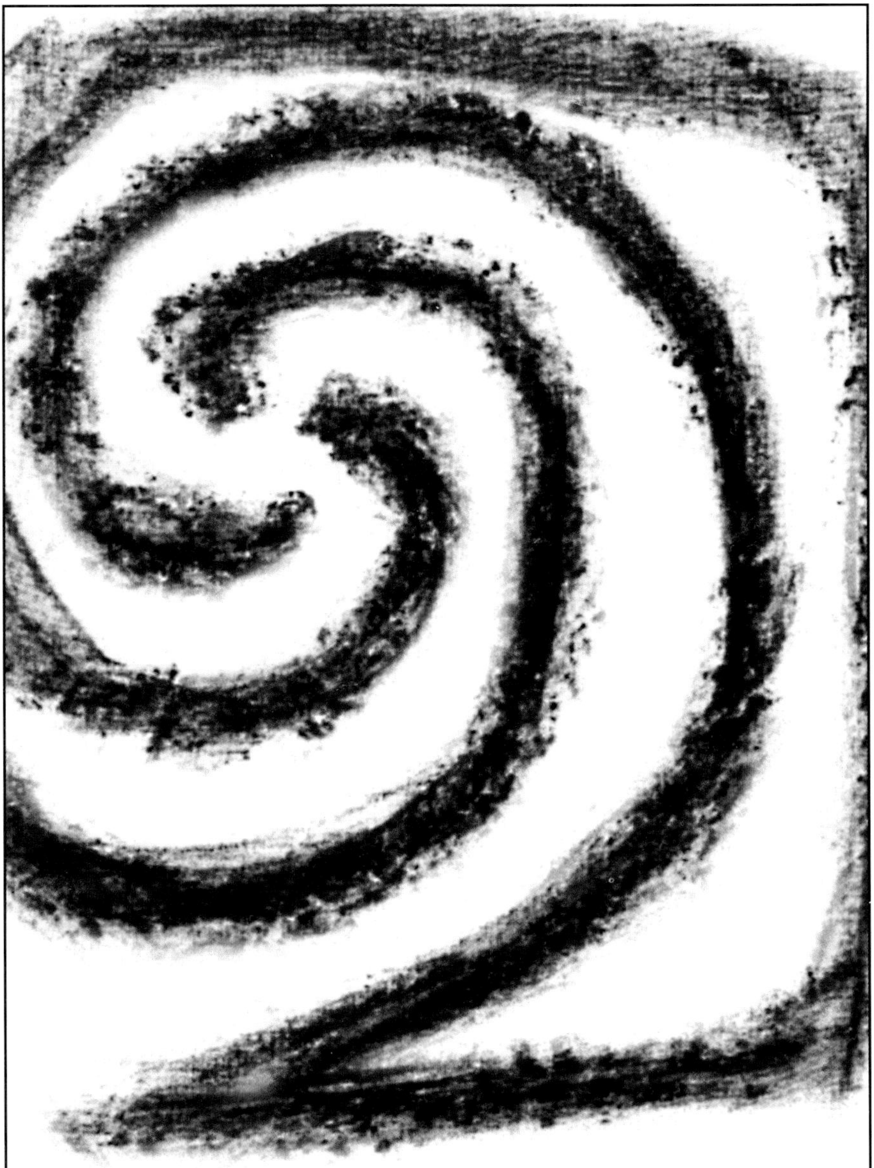

Triple spiral carved on the lowest panel of a 3m high, 10thC. free standing stone cross, Llanbadarn Fawr, Aberystwyth, Ceredigion. (From rubbing by J.S. actual size 28cm x 21cm)

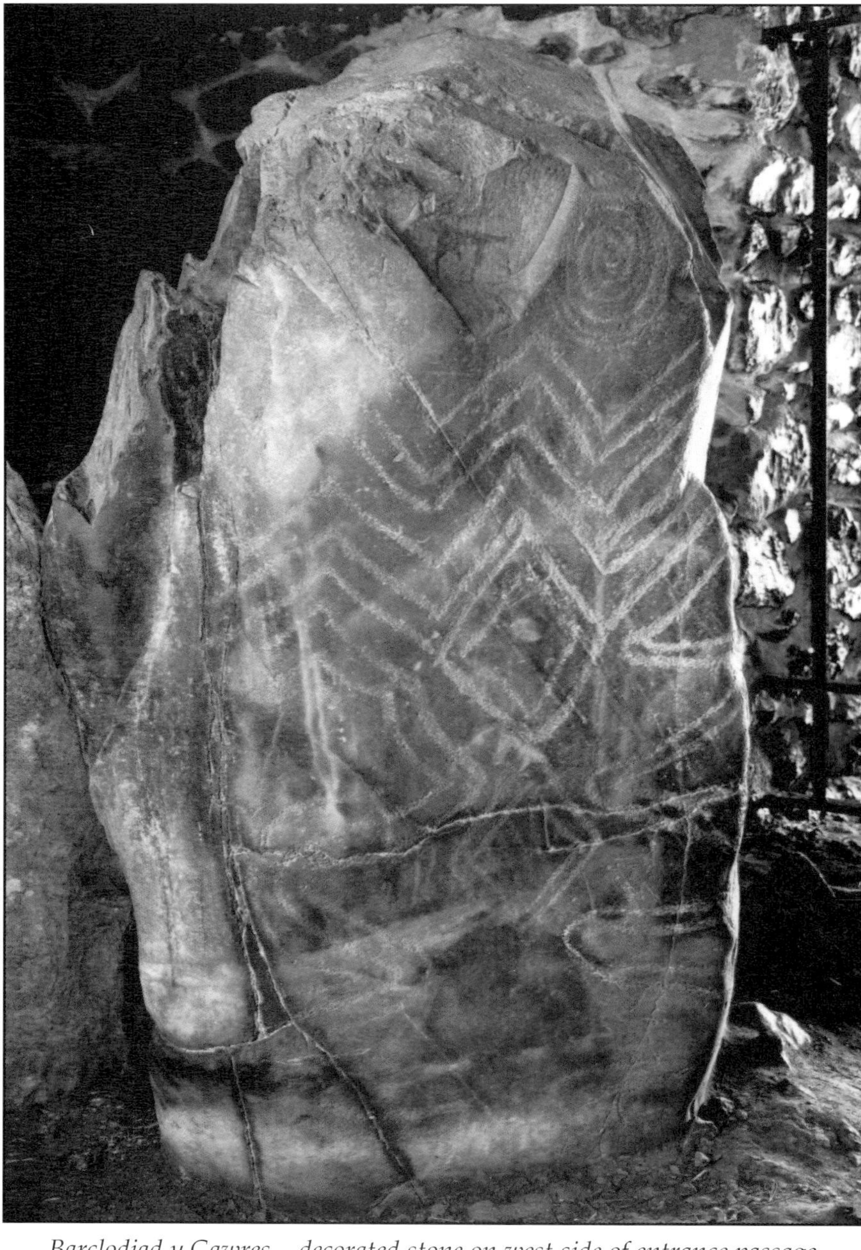

Barclodiad y Gawres – decorated stone on west side of entrance passage.
(Mike Sharp)

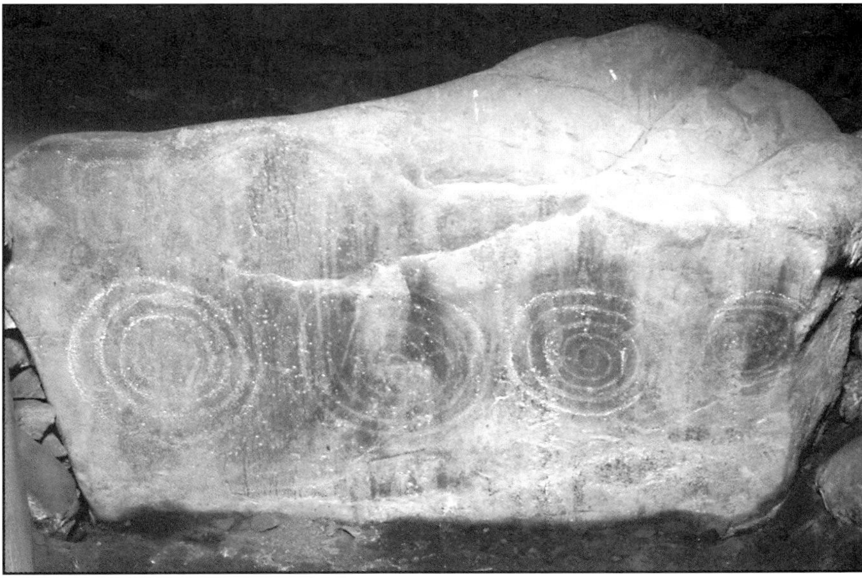

Barclodiad y Gawres – carvings on east chamber.

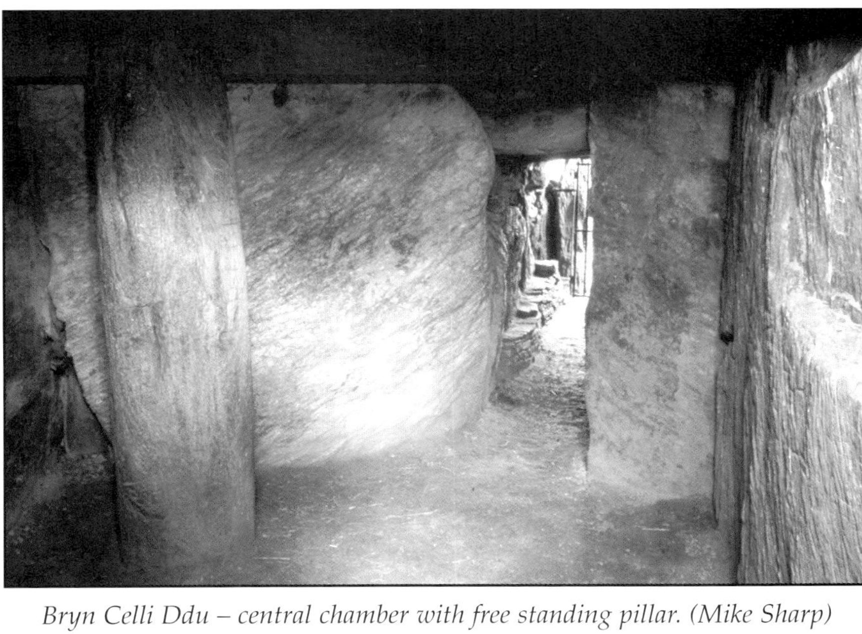

Bryn Celli Ddu – central chamber with free standing pillar. (Mike Sharp)

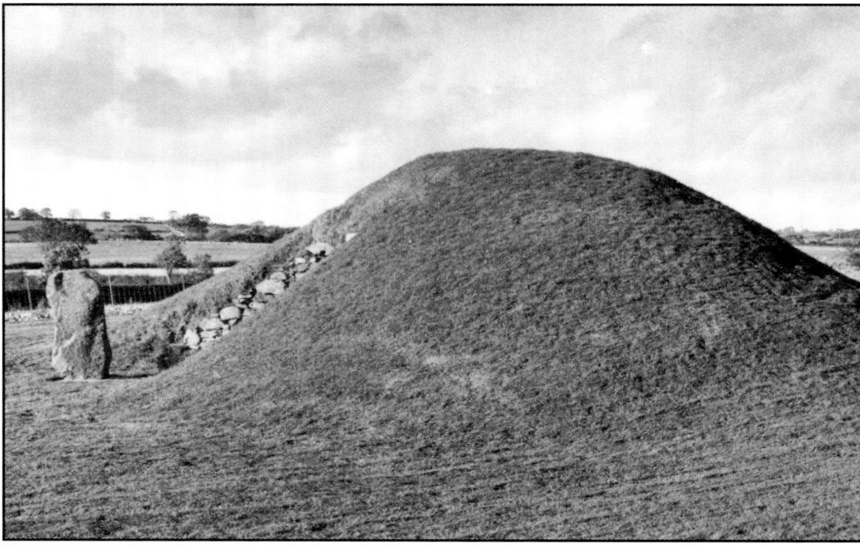

Bryn Celli Ddu passage Grave, Llanddaniel-fab, Môn. (Mike Sharp)

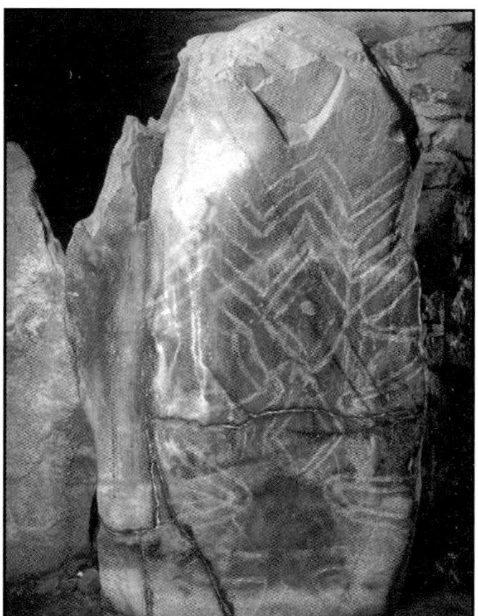

Barclodiad y Gawres passage grave, portal stone. Decorated stone at end of entrance passage

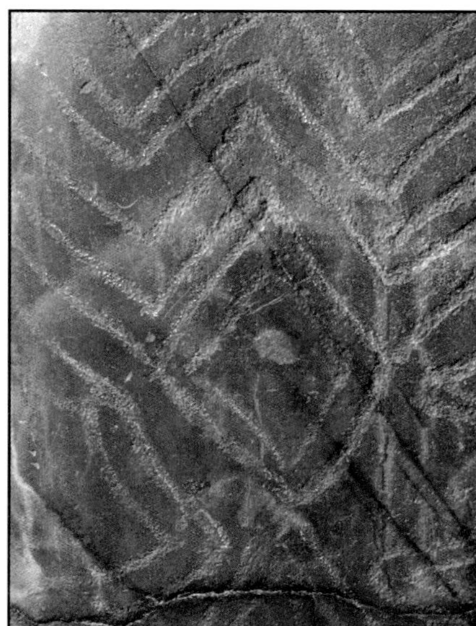

Barclodiad y Gawres passage grave, carving on portal stone

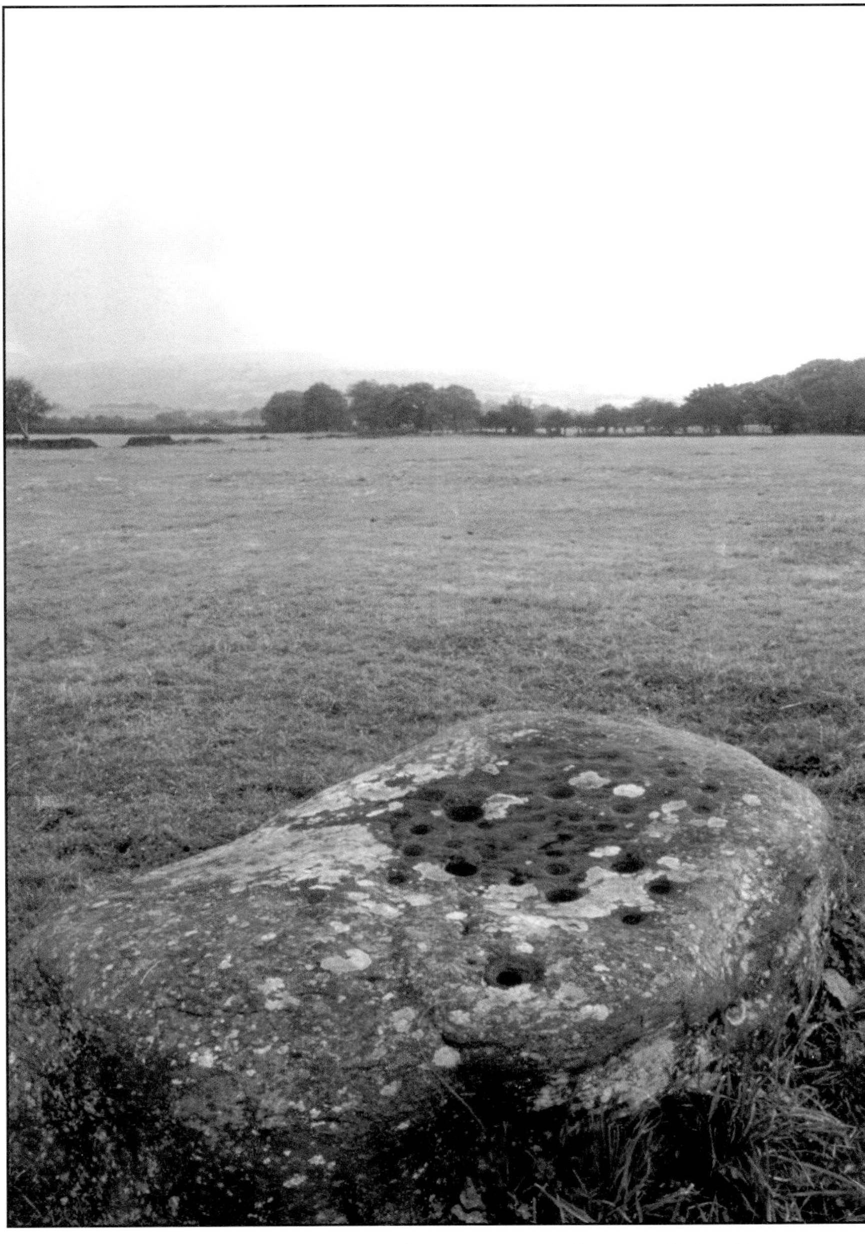

Maen Catwg, Gelligaer, Caerffili – cup marked stone. (Mike Sharp)

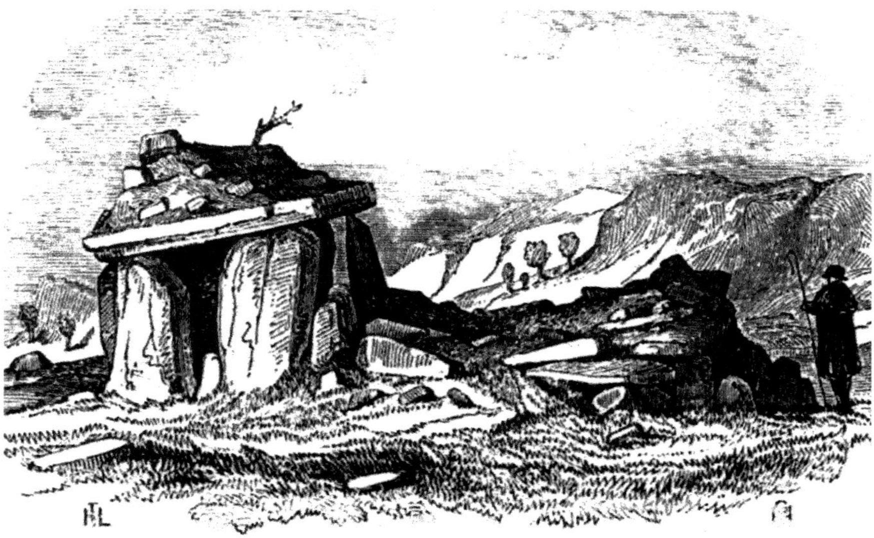

Bryn Celli Ddu engraving by Henry Longueville Jones, 1847
Schematic drawing of Turoe cult stone, Co. Galway, Ireland (after Duignan)
Schematic drawing of Pattern Stone, Bryn Celli Ddu (after Grimes) showing the north, top and south side of the stone (below right)

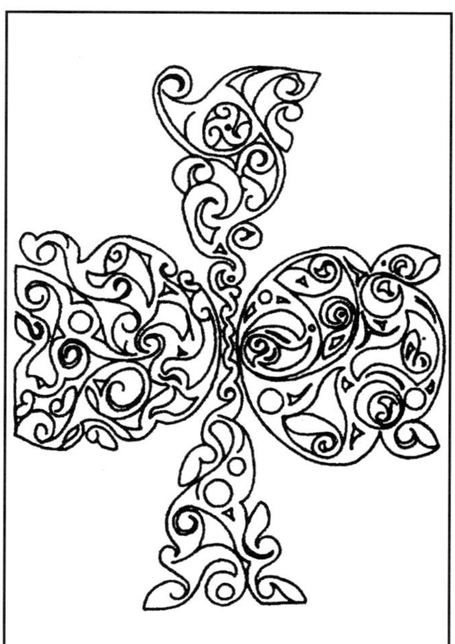

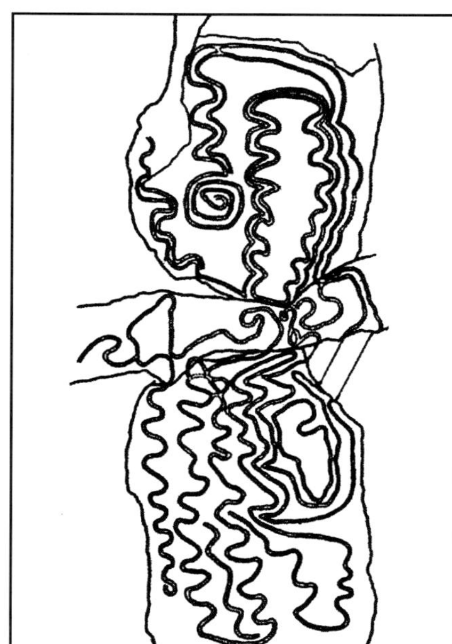

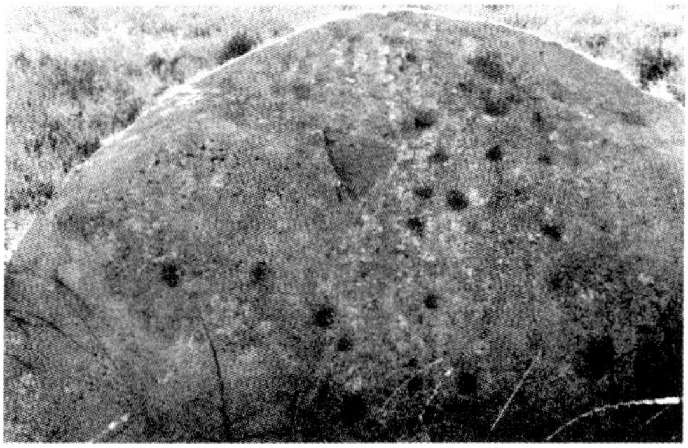

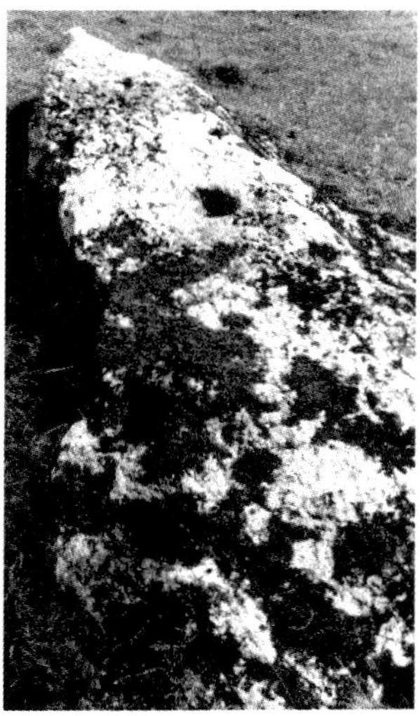

Cupmarks on what may have been the capstone of a dolmen at Trefoel (M.H.)

Cupmarks at Cerrig Y Gof (M.H.) left

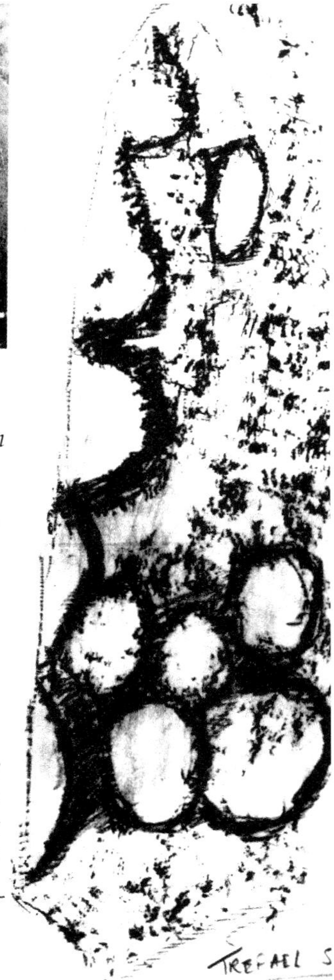

Paper rubbing by J.S. of cupmarks on a stone now lost at Trefoel, Nevern

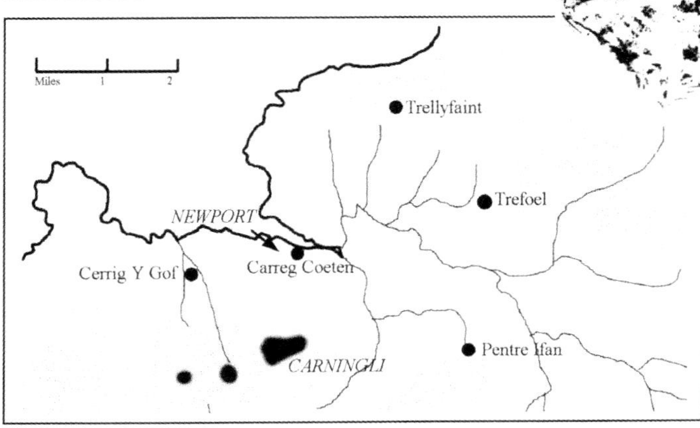

Map of cupmarked dolmens in the Preseli region of northeast Pembrokeshire (M.H.)

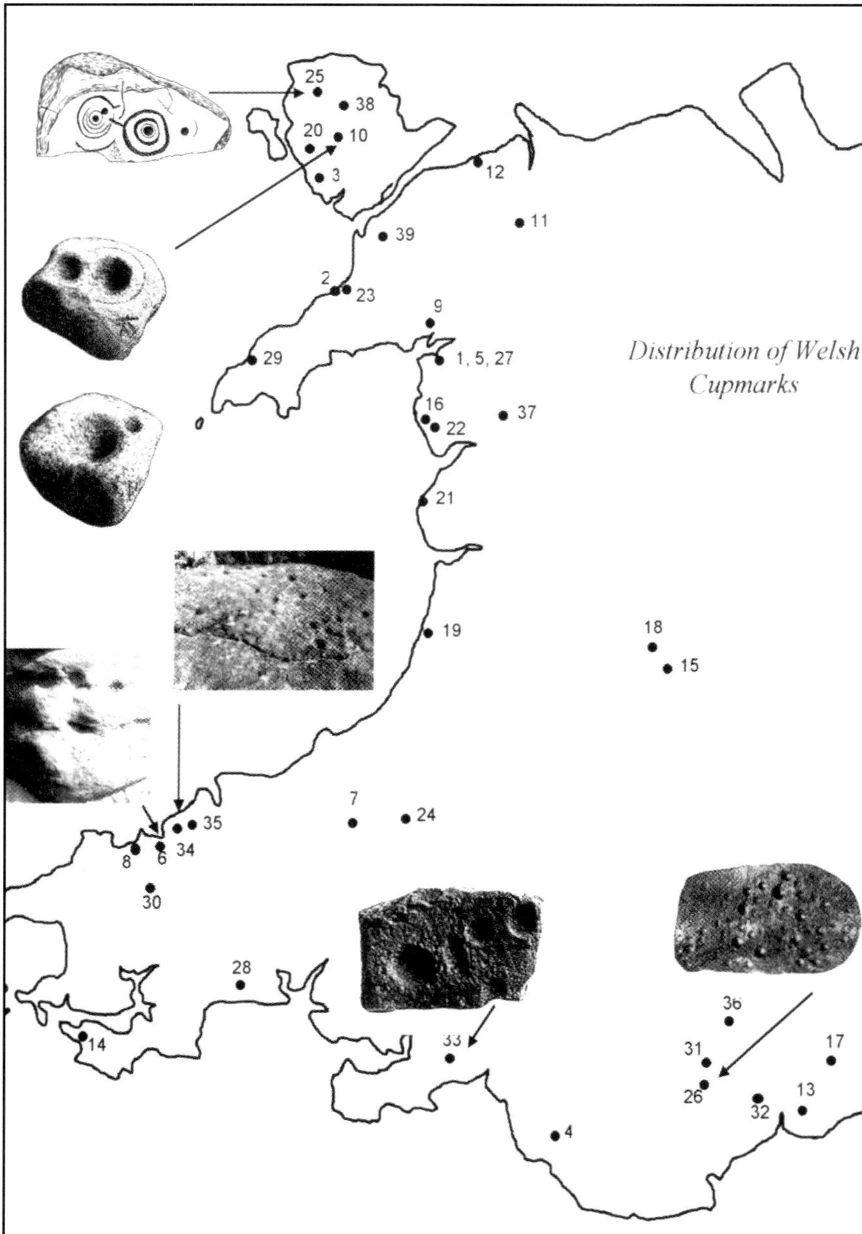

(See pages 94-98) Maura Hazelden

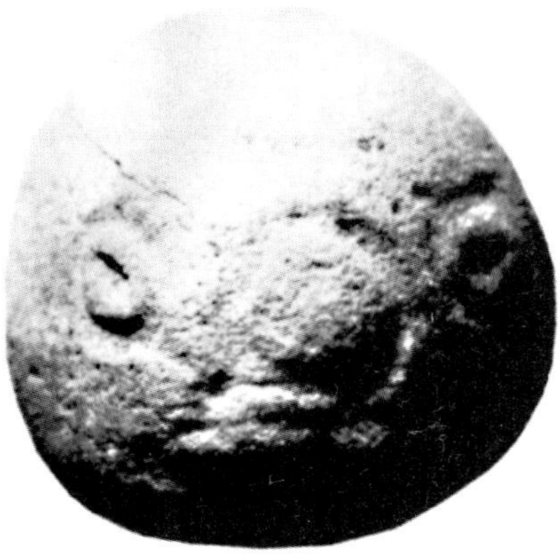

Face pocked out on a natural ovoid pebble with flat base (approx 8.5cm high). Found in Maentwrog churchyard wall, Merioneth (after Crewe)

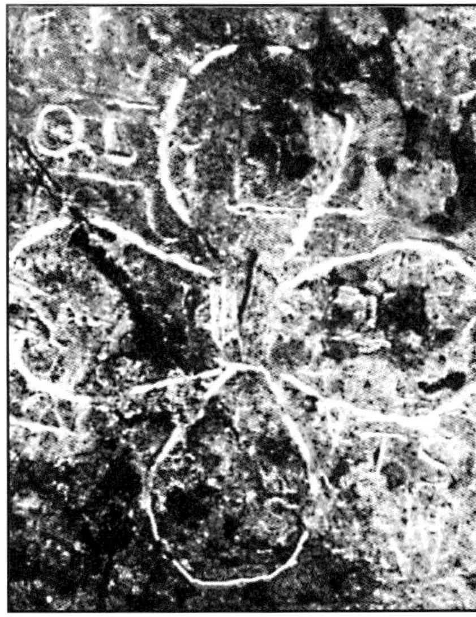

Graffiti on stone bench above Newport estuary, Pembrokeshire (M.H. – digitally enhanced photo)

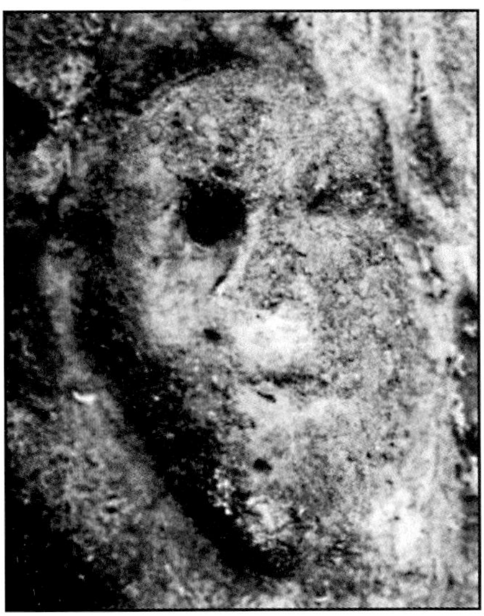

Cult head carved on rock face at Tarren Deusant, Llantrisant, Mid-Glamorgan (M.H.)

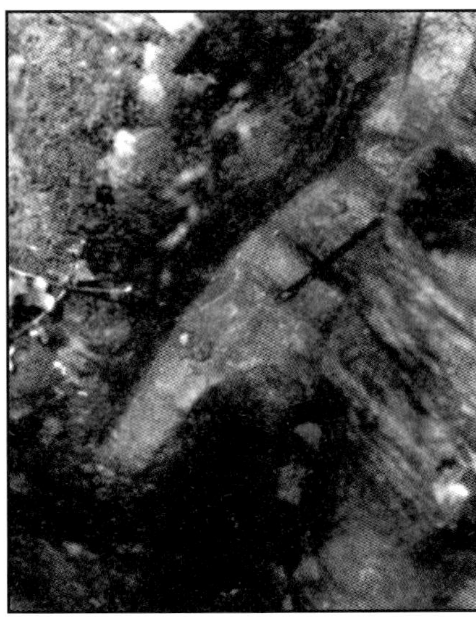

Graffiti cross in stone hollow beside the Pilgrim Cross at Nevern Pembrokeshire (M.H.)

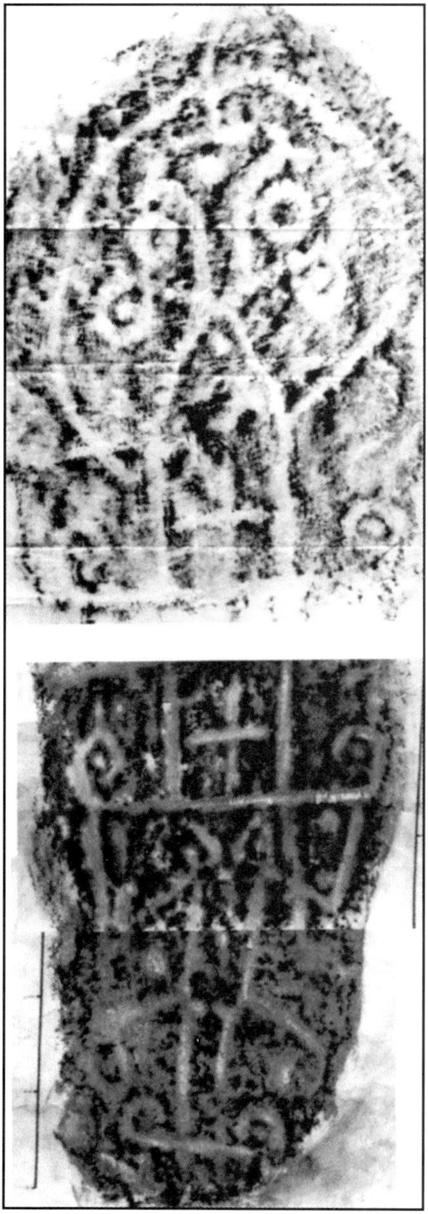

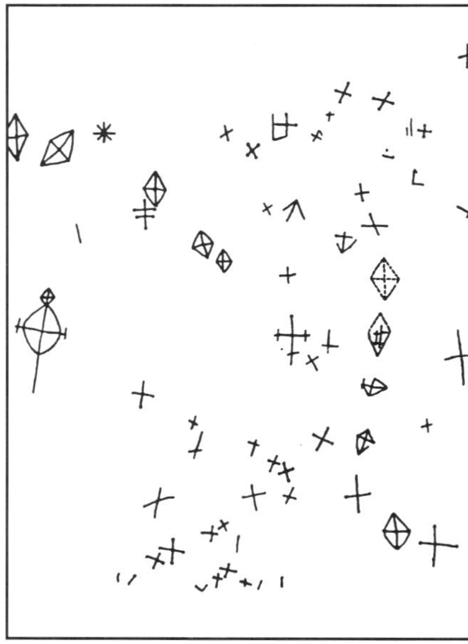

Detail of carvings inside the prehistoric chamber of Tŷ Illtud: (after Grinsell).

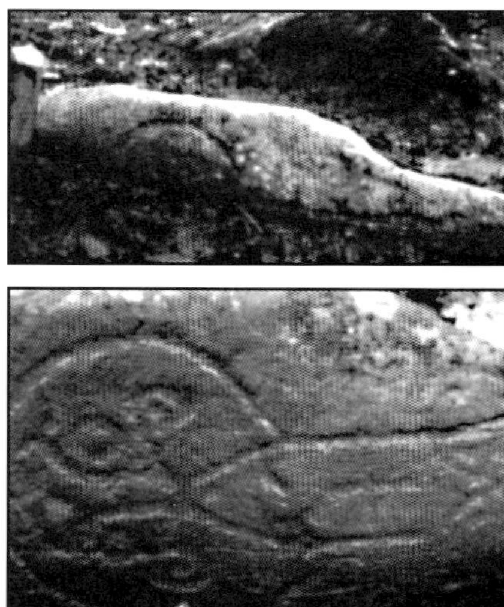

Individual rubbings from Blaenawen Stone by J.S.

Photographs of the emergence of the Blaenawen Stone by James Warburton

Perhaps this was a key stone placed here in order to read the others in the chamber, especially in relation to its opposite stone 8, set in the eastern recess. It has a set of four spirals descending in size from left to right along the 1.3m length of the slab. On top of the largest five-looped anticlockwise one is a much smaller triple-loop running clockwise, a mirroring of the opposite symbol. It impinges on the outer left-hand loop of the large spiral, that continues to underline the bottom of next two right-hand spirals. What this might mean is conjectural but repeating in a more visual manner the dynamic between rebirth and death, spiritual growth and physical decay. The outer left-hand curl of the large spiral continues to underline the bottom of the next two, while the end curl of the second spiral runs over the top of the third one. This is a series of dynamic interactions, perhaps bringing into the chamber of the goddess her cosmic and natural attributes. The four-looped spiral at the end of the sequence, and separate from it, is also left-handed to mirror the first great spiral. Perhaps these were carved as symbols of the waxing and waning moon.

This rather maze-like configuration is accentuated if run from the outside inward, while not altering the carved pattern. The small key spiral impinging on the largest may show the gradual decrease in size in the form of a spiral vortex. This is a dynamic interaction of shifting energies rather than an image of a linear configuration. In fact the faintly incised spiral on the right-hand corner of stone 22 – the most realised design of all the stones here – may also be a key symbol in this regard especially if a second spiral was intentionally erased.

At the right-hand junction of the passage and inner chamber the tall 1.5m stone 22 has often been described in anthropomorphic terms by many prehistorians. The top portion shows a series of deeply pocked angular bands running across the front and around both sides. They enjoin a large double lozenge, joining the outer corners on the left to continue down the stone in a double chevron. On the right corner of the outer lozenge a line turns into a second double chevron that actually curves around that edge. Both form a mirror image on either side of the stone and contained in its centre is an isolated double lozenge. This is an image of death housed within the path of life, or perhaps rebirth within the path of death. Since the carvings break off at the bottom, it has been suggested that the work was done after the stone was in situ, perhaps adopting to an existing floor-line. The excavators thought that a second spiral at the top may have been intentionally rubbed off or broken off as the stone is clearly damaged. The double spiral could have been an oculus representing the head of the goddess while the body below was formed by angular and curved chevrons along with the double lozenges. The question as to what could be seen in the semi-darkness of this chamber, even with candle light, was answered by the finding of carbonised shale pebbles that may have been used for rubbing on colour around the edges of the incised grooves.

There is clearly some interesting doubling of images represented on these stones. Two double lozenge shapes and chevron lines and the possible erasure of two spirals on stones 19 & 22. The clockwise and counter-clockwise motion of spirals on stone 8. And then on the left-hand junction of the passage and chamber the stones 5 & 6 seem to form a paired set containing all the above motifs but in a cacophony of violent movement. The angular forms of chevrons and lozenges on stone 5 may represent the natural world, while the rounded oculli contain two unequal but broken left-handed spirals, death and decay. The curving chevrons on the lower part of stone 6 could symbolise femininity and reincarnation. A central lozenge has been pecked out from the surface of the stone and its surrounding (almost squared) spiral joins up with the curving figuration that runs profusely over the bottom area. This perhaps shows how the dead can travel along the spirit path of life.

One writer who has invested these symbolic forms, suggests that stone 22 at Barclodiad y Gawres deserves the title of the Goddess Stone. For him the top lunar spiral stands for her birth-giving aspects. The chevrons signify her role in controlling lightning and hence the rain clouds transform into flowing streams on the lower part of the stone. She ruled the weather and nourished the sown fields, symbolised by the double lozenge which therefore represents the birth-giving capacity of Mother Earth. The two spirals on stone 6 and the fully pecked lozenge with its outer right-angled lines join with the celestial Goddess. It provides confirmation, for him, that the lozenge symbolises her Earth Goddess aspect. He points out that at Seefin in Ireland a stone is engraved with two double and one triple lozenge in a single configuration, reminiscent of the many triple spirals at Newgrange. Knowing what the lozenge represents, transforms a geometrical form to its true status. The representation of the Great Goddess herself. (Meaden, 1991)

The use of geometric symbolic signs are the oldest record we have of the spiritual journey. The lines of chevrons carved across the jawbone of a horse, found in the Kendrick's Cave on Penygogarth in Llandudno, have been dated to 10,000 years BP. More than five thousand years later, chevrons alongside the spiral and lozenge on the inner stones of the tomb, within its turf floor and stone mound, gives us a glimpse of the symbolic abode of the Earth Goddess. In relation to sacred architecture, Herbert Weaver maintains that certain configurations or symbolic signs can be classified in terms of their energy force-fields. For instance, if the spiral on stone 19 is a key to understanding the hidden language of Barclodiad y Gawres, it can be considered as a vital signalling sign to attract benign energies and the favour of the goddess. The form of the round inner chamber with its long stone passage pointing outwards as the dominant shape should help to locally suppress any potentially harmful sources within the enclosed space. Such monuments had specific effects according to their configuration. The carvings on the lap or apron of the goddess with their doubling of pairs of stones, and of twining symbols like the double lozenges and lines of chevrons are considered as wide-extent suppressers of harmful energies. They can evoke protection, as well as representing the power of the goddess, by containing her energy within the tomb. In relation to this way of describing symbols and the patterns they created, the comment of the excavators on finding no evidence for any burials, and that it was originally used for entirely ritual purposes, is quite enlightening. (Weaver, 1978)

The site for this monument above the deep water entrance to the sacred island of Mona may have been carefully chosen for this very purpose. This is what we might term as an experimental model within a Neolithic cemetery or isle of the dead. It may also have included the other passage chamber of Bryn Celli Ddu, 15km away by the Afon Menai. Both tombs are in fact on an east-west alignment with the latter 3km to the nearest waters of the Menai channel facing the rising sun on the equinox and the former by the sea at its setting. Recent commentators place the building of the Welsh passage tombs to the Late Neolithic or Early Bronze Age, when new religious concepts based on the economy of metallurgy were becoming important. Society clearly needed a different kind of ancestral architecture. Hilltop burial cairns, ceremonial stone circles and alignments of standing stones reflected the power of the sun, rather than the goddess. Or perhaps in terms of the reuse of sacred sites, as at Bryn Celli Ddu, it was to incorporate the ancestral earth goddess into the new priestly dominated and communal religion rather than the family oriented burial rituals of the Neolithic era.

Bryn Celli Ddu – a Welsh omphalos!

In the religion of some primitive societies this might have corresponded to a local 'Centre of the World'.

G.T. Meaden (1991)

The casual visitor walking though its narrow stone-walled entrance might be forgiven for thinking that tomb building in the prehistoric era was not only neat and tidy but decidedly airy. This is probably the best known of the few passage-type monuments in Wales, situated at Llanddaniel-fab above Afon Menai (Menai Straits). Beyond the roofed portal, at the end of a narrow 7.5m long passageway is a polygonal shaped inner chamber. It contains a smooth round tall stone amid the wall slabs roofed over by two large coverstones. The rebuilt grass topped cairn is bounded by a stone kerb and a ditch. Prior to reconstruction in the late 1920's the site was surrounded by trees hence its name – mound of the dark wood.

There is a rough spiral cut on the first stone on the left as you enter the chamber but its authenticity has been doubted. Like much else in this renewed version of Bryn Celli Ddu, there is doubt among archaeologists about the actual nature of the reconstruction by Walter Hemp. By 1930 he was, I am sure, convinced he had done a good job with the scatter of uncovered stones that he started out with. When the owner, the Marquess of Anglesey, handed it over to the H.M. Office of Works in 1923, the original mound – with the exception of its edging stones – was almost depleted. The passage and chamber stones were exposed. The walls stood just above ground level. What remained of the ancient structure was in a ruinous state and generally obscured by the trees grown up around the site.

A visiting group from the Cambrian Archaeological Association, after it had been formally opened, were told by Mr Hemp that the chambered tomb was originally an Early Bronze Age memorial constructed between 1800-1500 BC. It then had consisted of a circular cairn of earth and stones over 12 ft high and about 160 ft in diameter. It was probably surrounded by a ring of large upright stones. Two circles of stones were found to have been sunk into the ditch 6 ft deep and 18 ft wide. Within the area enclosed by the ditch was an irregular circle of stones of varying sizes, some inclined outwards and having deposits of cremated bone under them. Lines drawn to connect these stones diametrically crossed at the same spot in the centre of the monument, just behind the chamber. Here was a flat stone that covered a pit with traces of burning and ritual filling. Against it lay another with incised wavy spiral patterns. This is not a typical example of megalithic tomb art, according to Hemp, though the style was familiar from sites in Brittany and Ireland. Its meaning was unknown and it may have been some form of magic. The expanded spiral schema – drawn by F.T. Grimes director of the National Museum after it was taken to Cardiff – has been so often reproduced we need reminding that the abstract carving is actually incised on both sides and across the top of the 2m high stone of local coarse grit. Quite an extraordinary feat if indeed this was the intention of the artist who carved it. At the back of the mound a cast of what has become known as the Pattern Stone was placed near to the centre.

A visitor from the Cambrian Association seventy years before had stated that the ruin had been surrounded by a wall to protect it, but unfortunately the enclosed space was so choked up with briars and shrubs that access to it was not very pleasant and examination not easy. Of particular interest was the gallery leading into the chamber that was described as nearly perfect with only one or two of the stones at the narrow entrance having been dislodged. The then secretary of the Association in 1846 measured the passage as 18 ft long by 3 ft high and 2½ ft wide. H.L. Jones reported that all traces of the cairn had disappeared except for the earth and stones that still lay on the cromlech, where a tree had taken root. It was withered and dead. His published engraving shows an old tree on the top of the passage leading to the chamber.

The earliest written account was by the Rev. Henry Rowlands (1655-1723), an antiquarian and a native of Ynys Môn. His *Mons Antiqua Restuanta,* also included Edward Lhuyd's 1700 letter of the entry into Newgrange tumulus. Rowlands stated that there was in Llanddaniel parish, at a place formally called Llwyn Llwyd (the grey grove), the remains of two carneddau (cairns) within a few paces of each other. One was somewhat broken and pitted into its side where the stones had been carried off, and the other had its stones almost all taken away into the walls and hedges. Two standing pillars were erect between the cairns. By the time of Thomas Pennant's visit in 1784, the larger of the mounds had recently been opened and the smaller one entirely disappeared together with the Meini Hirion upright stones outside, mentioned by Rowlands. Pennant wrote that the mound was nearly 100 ft in diameter and that the passage led into an irregular hexagram shaped room 7 ft high, composed of six rude slabs. In the middle was a pillar that supported the roof slab which was 10 ft in diameter. Along the sides of the walls was a stone bench on which were human bones that (when handled) fell to dust. The Rev. J. Skinner visited the site in 1802. He described his entry holding a lantern and crawling along a narrow twelve foot passage to get into the more capricious chamber. His companions followed close at his heels and the six of them assembled together in this singular sepulchre. The narrow passage was about 3 ft high and 'a little more in breath with flat stones stuck edgeways and covered with others of still greater magnitude laid across'. He also mentioned that a gold wedge covered by an earthen pan had been discovered twenty years previously and recounted the story of the first intruder in the chamber sometime in the year 1777.

A farmer was employed with removing some of the stones from the north-east side of the large cairn. He came to the mouth of a passage covered with a square stone. Anxious to reap the fruits of his discovery he procured a light and crept forward on his hands and knees along the dreary vault. He said that in a chamber at the further end, a figure in white seemed to forbid his approach. The poor man had scarcely sufficient power to crawl backwards and out of this den of spirits, as he imagined it to be. However a few days later, instigated by the hope of riches and the presence of many assistants, he made his second entry into the cavern. And finding the white figure did not move, he boldly went forward and discovered the object of his apprehension was no other than a stone pillar about 6 ft in height standing in the centre of the chamber. His former consternation could now only be exceeded by his eagerness to see what was contained beneath the stone which he overturned. There was no treasure! Some large human bones were lying near the pillar, sufficiently testifying the purpose for which the structure was intended. This was the substance of an account received from the young man whose father was one of Colonel Peacock's labourers and on the premises at the time of the discovery.

Hemp's list of the chamber's contents included the human bones found in 1777, small fragments of burnt and unburnt human bones, a broken flint knife, a javelin head, limpet shells and charcoal from 1865, the fragments of burnt and unburnt human bones and teeth, cockle, mussel and limpet shells and a broken chert scraper uncovered by him. He also made some interesting observations on his excavations there. The smooth pillar stone was semi-prostrate and in much the same position when it was overturned by the farmer. It was reset in its original packing stones and the 8 ft long stone tapering at both ends projected 5½ ft above floor level. The maximum circumference was 4½ ft at about two thirds of its length. The top part of the stone was damaged, upsetting its original symmetry. A number of the entrance and upright stones had been dressed – smoothed by hammering or picking – to make them fit into position. He removed the mound material on the covering stones to see if any cups or other marks were on the upper surfaces. Then he replaced the original material on the stones. A 5 inch diameter spiral was found to be incised on the inner face of upright number four. The inner line of the spiral shape faded away into the central turn but the outer line was free. A low wall of flat stones was built on clay, perhaps it was the stone bench mentioned by Pennant. There were two small pointed stones standing in a niche such as the baetyls that are found in Irish tombs, but nothing more seemed to have been heard about them. A purple coloured clay was spread over the floor of the chamber and covered the pit on which the Pattern Stone lay. He thought this may have been a ritual act. The outer passage was originally blocked by stones mixed with earth and cremated bones. A layer of water-worn stones and broken quartz pebbles had been laid down. An amount of cremated burnt bones had been placed in a basin of clay 1 ft deep and 3 ft x 1½ ft across. This may have represented the last rites before the final closure of the monument. Five post holes were found in a round arc beyond the forecourt with a pit containing an ox burial. Perhaps one of the most interesting and unexpected finds was that of a large slab of schist measuring 3½ ft by 2½ ft when the old floor was lowered. It appeared to have been placed as neatly as possible in the centre of the monument, near the Pattern Stone. When it was lifted a sequence of ritual events were revealed. A pit had been sunk in the natural gravel and the bottom was scorched and hardened by fire. On it were fragments of charcoal and unburnt wood with bark still attached that was identified as hazel. Most extraordinary, there was a burnt human right ear bone of a child. The cochlea, or the spiral cavity bone of the ear would have been among the smallest in the body. The pit had been filled with a mixture of clay and stones resting on a layer of brown clay that contained two large pieces of jasper. Into this filling a lump of purple clay roundly made into a 6 inch inverted cone was inserted. The stone had been placed as a cover over the pit and its ritual contents. (Hemp, 1931)

A potent brew indeed especially as the White Lady – a Goddess of Death in many folk traditions – revealed itself to the first visitor. A purple floor in the chamber discovered by the excavator, along with a spiral ear bone, a hazel branch and two lumps of quartz stone with coloured surface veins, had been placed ceremoniously in a pit at the centre of the monument and finally covered by a slab of crystalline rock. The fact that the hazel branch was unburnt is clearly significant. This tree is often associated with divination, and the oracular or hidden knowledge in Celtic lore. It was especially associated with Cormac in the Land of Promise and the sacred berries of wisdom.

The distinctively shaped standing stones clearly paid some important part in the ancient rituals at Bryn Celli Ddu. The long smooth stone narrowed at both ends and placed in the centre of the chamber seems related to fertility, and brings to mind the equally tall and slim stone that stands in the central chamber of cairn L on Carnbrae West at Loughcrew and a stone that is thought to have stood under the main mound at Knowth. Unlike the worked smooth stone that was standing in the chamber, the possible relationship of the Pattern Stone is difficult to fathom. Hemp thought it to have been laid alongside the flat stone – over the ritual deposit – and therefore in a central place of the original passage tomb. He considered the whole structure with its three surrounding circles of stones were set, 'in the shape of a gigantic spiral with the chamber forming a loop in it'. Its position as he found it seemed due to that particular ritual augmentation. However the reconstruction brought into question my feeling that the Pattern Stone – like the one on top of the mound of Newgrange reported by Lhuyd but never mentioned again – may also have stood here before falling inward during its gradual demolition. The placing of the stone on the top of the original mound, after being carved with a meandering spiral across and around the top of it, could have represented an omphalos. The tall stone as the visible link between the inner realms of the passage chamber and the elements outside to become the sacred pole between earth and sky. That traditional omphalic shape of a hill with a peak on top can be seen carved on an orthostat at Petit Mont, along with feet and other symbols of the Goddess. (Gimbutas, 1989)

Even the proposition of an earlier henge monument on the site with the later expansion of the enclosing mound, makes it hard to relate the stone to either form of construction except as a symbolic omphalos. The very particular flowing meandering style of its carving on both sides and across the top part of the 1.20m long stone indicates that it was originally meant to be upright and visible. If it had been in the centre of the old henge, with a rededication it may have been reset inside the central chamber as part of the final ceremony beneath the enlarged mound, before being removed and then ritually placed on top. Such a high profile connection with the newer and more symbolically realised fertility stone hidden within the centre of the tomb-shrine would have linked both old and new structures into a symbolic wholeness. Taking on a new religious lease of life within the ancestral island of the dead, the visible carved stone would be significant. It could explain why such a site was chosen for a passage grave in western Britain if, as Lynch maintains, that this tradition of tomb building, 'represents a late restricted entry into Wales'.

In relation to a possible phallic, totemesque or religious significance of the Pattern Stone there are interesting similarities with other stones elsewhere. On the Hill of Tara in Co. Meath are a number of phallic stones. The 1.5m high Lia Fail or stone penis as it was known in Irish literature – possibly because of its suggestive shape – was traditionally associated with the inauguration ceremonies of the Kings of Ireland. Prior to its present position, it formally stood near the Mound of the Hostages with its small simple type of passage tomb covered with two massive capstones. One of the seven orthostats of the inner chamber had been carved, recalling the single spiral decorated pillar stone inside Bryn Celli Ddu. The nearby Adamnan's Stone is a four-sided granite pillar that has a small figure carved in relief near the bottom of one face which may be a Sheela-na-Gig or even a Cernunnos figure, as Macalister suggested. The top of this stone has been damaged so it could have been larger when originally dressed or even carved. Near it is a small rounded domed stone. None of these can be dated with any certainty. However, there are rounded stones in the west of Ireland that on stylistic grounds are thought to be carved as late as the Iron Age. The earliest may be the Killycluggin shaped stone fragment, now in the National Museum in Dublin. It has flowing curvilinear lines around its base and spiral patterns on the top. It had been set outside the round kerb of a ruined megalithic structure in Co. Cavan. The Castlegrange stone is an egg-shaped granite boulder, 60cm high by 90cm long, and completely covered in the curving patterns associated with the La Tène style. Now inside an iron railing by the Castlestrange Demesne, Roscommon, it probably came from the immediate neighbourhood. The decoration has been engraved on it rather than in relief, as on the more famous Turoe cult-stone, near Loughrea in Co. Galway. It also innocuously now stands inside an iron railing but originally came from not far away, outside the rath of Feerwore.

The first centuries BC & AD artifacts found in Ireland are mostly imports or based on European La Tène culture. However the Turoe Stone, like the other two rounded ones, are of native stone and decorated by local craftsmen. It was carefully shaped and smoothed, with the carving working into the surface leaving the large tendrils and open trumpet shapes standing out in relief. The top part is completely covered in the La Tène style of decoration and below is a band of Greek key ornament. The Turoe stone, as one of the earliest examples of Irish three-dimensional sculpture, has often been likened to the Greek omphalos the Navel Stone in the Temple of Apollo at Delphi. (Weir, 1980)

The schematic drawing of the Turoe shows that its design was composed of two rounded and two elongated series of interrelated variations joined across the top of the stone. The Bryn Celli Ddu drawing shows a series of seemingly unrelated lines carved on the upper part of both sides of the standing stone, but when joined together appears to be a series of meandering spirals. The former, in the fully developed insular style of La Tène art, certainly differs from the simpler, earlier decorative carving of the tall standing stone. Yet it would be a mistake to take comparisons of their decorative aspects too far. Each carving is an integral part of the overall visual symmetry. The stones were consciously carved in terms of a completed design running around and over the top areas. But a significant part of the original stone was left unadorned which accentuates their fertility, magical or totem aspects. These decorated stones, as well as those standing on the Hill of Tara, have a common ancestry in the fact that they have been found to be originally associated with prehistoric sites. The positioning of the decorated Entrance Stone placed outside the Newgrange tumulus and the worked but uncarved smooth fertility stone inside the chamber of the Welsh passage tomb, were deliberately chosen to accentuate their sacred magical qualities.

A cat amongst the pigeons

A paper by Claire O'Kelly published in 1969 and entitled *A Reinterpretation* kindled interest in the reconstruction by Walter Hemp, causing a stir that still ripples among British and Irish archaeologists. Basically her thesis came to the conclusion that the monument had been a two-part construction.

Phase 1: A henge, an open-air sanctuary for religious ceremonies. The ditch – originally with a bank outside it – the ring of stones and possibly some central feature belonging to the original henge setting.

Phase 2: As the stratigraphy and the style of building fits best with the passage grave, she suggested that such features related to the later and final structure, with perhaps a rededication of the site when the tomb was built.

The juxtaposition of the two monuments – the later one built within or above the first – resulted in the passage grave obliterating the earlier one. This suggested to her a certain antagonism between different religious beliefs. One related to the ancient world order and the wider community while the newer was more closed, family orientated and temple based. The burial mound had a classic passage grave with a high polygonal chamber, clearly differentiated from the lower entrance passage. She also claimed that the purple clay found over the interior and the inner slope, which was thought to be a ritual covering, was due to shifting levels and - as known from elsewhere – was the result of the decay of the original turf surface. For her, it demonstrated that the ditch was already silted over and grass had grown before the passage tomb with its cairn and kerb was built. It also meant that the Pattern Stone had been laid down flat then, rather than dragged in at a later date. (O'Kelly, 1969)

The time separation between the two monuments, which could be centuries or even millennia apart, was not postulated as essentially Kelly's was a paper exercise. It was based on Hemp's published work and the earlier accounts, and on the projected height or slippage of an original mound that was a shadow of its former shape, even in the earliest reports. There seemed to be no recognition that the modern covering, in the words of the HMSO guidebook 'had been constructed over the chamber for its protection and only covers a small part of the area; the original cairn covered nearly the whole of the ground inside the fence'. Curiously enough she made no mention of the remains of the other original mound as noted by Rowlands, and its possible relation to her thesis or its absence in regard to the modern structure.

The decorated passage tomb of Fourknocks in Co. Meath, within its large mound covering, was excavated in 1950 and a year later a second mound 50m to the east was also excavated by Hartnett but it was not a single construction like the former tomb. There were no carved stones found in Fourknocks 2 and it appeared to contain Neolithic cremated human remains of children. Later in time a stone passage was reconstructed to face in the same direction as that in Fourknocks 1 and with an identical covering mound to create what appeared to be a pair of identical tumuli. However this aspect of twinning shows that the rebuilding or reconstruction of a ceremonial site often belies its seemingly simplistic alterations and that it is not a modern phenomenon. (Cooney, 1997)

A year after the O'Kelly publication, Frances Lynch in her prehistory of Ynys Môn reiterated the two-phase construction theme. She deduced that Bryn Celli Ddu must be recognised as one of the latest Welsh megalithic tombs to be built, and repeated much the same words in terms of an explanation, that the destruction of the henge and rebuilding of the passage tomb represented an antagonism and conflict between two different religious systems. However she did not even begin to approach the question of why the later builders should have chosen this particular site for the passage-type tumulus. (Lynch, 1976)

A. Burl in his 1979 opus on the stone circles of Britain describes Bryn Celli Ddu as 'the passage grave that was built on a ravaged circle-henge'. In fact for him the two-phased construction of this monument is like a lief motif that crops up time and again throughout his work. Twenty years later, in a collection of essays as a homage to Burl, Richard Bradley looks at the issue in terms of a number of major sites in Scotland, Ireland and Wales. As regards to Bryn Celli Ddu he states that the problems of Hemp's excavation and the original two-phased building, as witnessed by changes to its kerb, were already addressed by O'Kelly. And it appears to support Burl's view that stone circles originated alongside henge monuments during the Neolithic era. Equally a close link between passage graves and standing stones – evident at Newgrange – was a point emphasized in her 1969 paper. She had been closely involved with Michael O'Kelly the archaeologist, who spent twenty years excavating and reconstructing that monument and she had also written on the art of the Boyne Valley. But Bradley points out that George Eogan, who was similarly engaged at Knowth, had drawn attention to the two separate phases of one of the smaller tombs at Newgrange. This involved a mound with a passage grave surrounded by a ditch. At a later stage the mound was enlarged, the passage itself extended and a new kerb of stones built beyond the original earthwork. Eogan suggested that a similar sequence could have taken place at Bryn Celli Ddu. Bradley reminds us this view would entail a significant revision of O'Kelly's interpretation and would, in fact, question the prior existence of a henge on the site. He presented the schematic diagrams of their ideas alongside his own, which seems to favour a smaller passage grave and a covering mound within a stone circle, that would eventually be enlarged into the generally accepted final version. (Bradley, 1997)

An interesting sidelight on the two-phased monument debate illuminates the philosophic outlook of the informed modern archaeologist. This is their ease and ability to pick up on some obscure detail and to use it like a thread to weave a colourful variety of themes and examples from professional papers, standard works and articles in obscure journals. These are brought out in references to an equally varied set of major monuments that their colleagues have worked on, written about or even sourced in their writings. Since it seems that the ideal reader should have a full panoply of such references, there is no need of being site specific or going into detail with regards to previous revisions of interpretation, nor especially having to dip into the chronological depths of prehistory. To make sense of the minimal diagrams used to illustrate the two-phased building, a descriptive key based on some of the above is necessary.

With the notion of a key to make some sense of ancient carvings, we may have to try to differentiate between one symbol and another of the same kind, and often on the same block of stone. Or as in the case of the small broken spiral carved on the orthostat at Bryn Celli Ddu, to view it almost as a comment – a symbol of lost energy carved on that particular stone before entry into the inner chamber. A symbolic re-enactment of regeneration within the body of the earth.

The form of energy expressed by the spiral vortex can sometimes be experienced in a physical way, although generally such subjective and often momentarily alterations are hard to pin down. It is one of the unfortunate tribulations of field archaeology that not only is the evidence within the earth itself destroyed in the undertaking, but often only that which can be visually perceived or examined is worth preserving. However, a number of new geophysical techniques are available and being applied that include magnetic gradiometry, ground radar and digital terrain imaging, which do not require the destruction of a buried site. Perhaps one of the latest additions to the archaeological portfolio is acoustic, although there has been relatively little consideration of such understanding with regards to megalithic monuments in Britain. A number of researchers have been testing the possibilities inherent in both passage tombs and more open stone configurations. At Camster Round in Caithness they induced a standing wave phenomena, by emitting two waves of equal frequencies travelling in opposite directions within its solid walls. This resulted in sounds being audible in different parts of the central chamber and from both inside and outside the central passage. Electronic tone generators produced a continuous low note, and vocalizing and drumming were used in group experiments, as these were unlikely to have been beyond the ability of people in the Neolithic. One of the most startling effects was that the sound of drumming was heard in a second cairn 190m away, but not by those directly outside the main monument. Helmholtz Resonance occurs in passage grave chambers when the oscillation within causes sound waves to increase in magnitude. The results in Camster Round showed that the frequency produced was about 4 Hertz, which is below conventional human hearing. However, many of the listeners within did complain of some unfamiliar sensations of pulse and breathing patterns, and of speech becoming distorted to create some extraordinary harmonics. In order to test these and other results in the field, they created models of the internal volumes from a range of tombs in Britain and Ireland. This indicated that the larger ones, like Newgrange and Knowth were in the region of between 1 and 2 Hz. Bryn Celli Ddu had the highest range of 6 to 7 Hz. This infrasonic rate would be less than half the lowest range that cathedral organs can achieve. At Bryn Celli Ddu the estimated frequencies allowed for a two-phase construction. The change in passage length had relatively little impact, nor was the density of the covering mound material an issue for Heimholtz Resonance. The problem with the monument was that the apertures in the (reconstructed) chamber walls make any direct measurement impossible. (Watson – personal correspondence)

The conclusions reached was that prehistoric monuments may not have been so peaceful in their uses, as they are today. Although it could not be shown that the architecture of passage graves was deliberately built to incorporate such phenomena, the behaviour of sound both above and below the conventional audible ranges would have been a noticeable factor, and especially during ritual events. Therefore they concluded that acoustics should be considered alongside the structural, spatial and visual attributes of ancient monuments. (Watson & Keating, 1999)

Capstones and Cupmarks

For over a hundred years archaeologists have been trying to solve the puzzle which these petroglyphs present – 'Who carved them?' 'When?' 'Why?' and 'What do they mean?'

Ronald W.B. Morris (1977)

R.E.M. Wheeler, when Director of the National Museum in Cardiff (and whom later was better known as Sir Mortimer for his archaeological excavations in post-war London, and as media commentator on the ancient world), published what was probably the earliest popular overview of prehistoric Wales. In it he wrote that two monuments were notable for the presence of small cupmarks on the upper surface of dolmens. At Trellyffaint in Sir Benfro the cover-slab had about twenty-two shallow cupmarks and at Clynnog Fawr in Gwynedd the dolmen's capstone was literally pock-marked with them. He also included a rather interesting illustration of a cast of Maen Catwg, the cupmarked stone at Gelligaer, Morgannwg. Instead of the usual hollow intrusions it showed them as smoothly rounded protrusions. It was artificial and probably made by constantly rotating a small stone or tool around the surface of the boulder. (Wheeler, 1925)

His successor at the museum, W.F. Grimes, noted in 1929 the multiple depressions on the capstone at Trefoel farm near Nanhyfer (Nevern) in Sir Benfro as cupmarks. Perhaps due to changes in archaeological fashion, there seems to be a strong reluctance by modern writers to concern themselves with the cupmarks found on dolmens, standing stones and movable boulders. In fact the most recent survey of Wales from the Palaeolithic to the Iron Age does not even index them. It may be due in part to the similarity of many minute marks to natural weathering in certain rock formations. And even if accepted as artifactual on earlier authority, there is the obvious difficulty in not only dating them to a specific period, but in relating them to a definite archaeological context. (Lynch, 2000)

It seems to be accepted that cupmarks and cup-and-ring carvings in Britain and Ireland are generally consigned to the mid-second millennium BC onwards. This is based on the context of the many such carved stones that covered the stone box in cist burials of that period, especially those in the north of England and on the Borders. One rare example was excavated from the Simondston cairn in Morgannwg, prior to its destruction. In 1957 Sir Cyril Fox found some pottery vessels, flints and a nodule of marcasite – a type of iron ore – shaped in the form of a cup. One of the side slabs of the stone cist had five shallow cupmarks on its inner face. However, there has been serious doubts about the dating of such artifacts. From the uneven edges of many of the coffin stones, Richard Bradley, professor of archaeology and a prolific writer on the ritual landscape, considers that they may have been broken off from original rock-sites and reused to enhance religious or ancestral significance. The inference here is that the petroglyphs were carved much earlier in time than the actual burials. In fact the earliest known example of a cist burial with cupmarks has been dated as far back as the Neanderthal era. A slab stone with at least fifteen cups was found in a rock shelter known as La Ferrassie in the Dordogne. (Hadingham, 1980)

The cupmark on the Trecastell stone – now on display in the British Museum – is usually ignored because it is in the midst of a sixth century Latin inscription. Even the pictoglyph carved on the other face, to which it may have been related (if the long slab was originally the cover of a cist burial), is considered to have been carved during the Christian period. In the current climate of archaeology as a scientific business, small round hollows on isolated stones appear to have a limited value. Yet for many like myself who partake on the fringes of the science and are immersed in data peripheral to academic history making, the ancient carvings on rocks speak clearly about the ritual mindset of the individual marker, as the large megalithic structures can show the collective consciousness of the builders. Enough topographical research has been carried out over the past centuries to indicate that the original positioning of ancient monuments – from the megalithic collective burials to the high crosses of the Christian era – was never merely a haphazardous undertaking. Nor their carvings just meaningless decoration or graffiti!

The cupmarks found in Wales can be grouped by area and by their application to different kinds of stone monuments, and specifically on dolmens, on standing stones and on movable, broken or earthfast boulders. The small hollows carved on the capstones of portal dolmens are from two distinct coastal regions, on the edge of the Preseli Hills in Sir Benfro and Pen Llŷn in Gwynedd. Current evidence shows that such ritual activity only took place on a small number of the dolmens in each area.

The Bachwen Dolmen at Clynnog Fawr is exceptional in regard to its historical and artistic record, because until quite recently little attention has been paid to the decorative aspect of other monuments. For the

Cupmarks prior to 30,000 BC during the Middle Palaeolithic, on slab covering a Neanderthal child. Found in the cave site at La Ferrassie, Dordogne, France (after Hadingham)

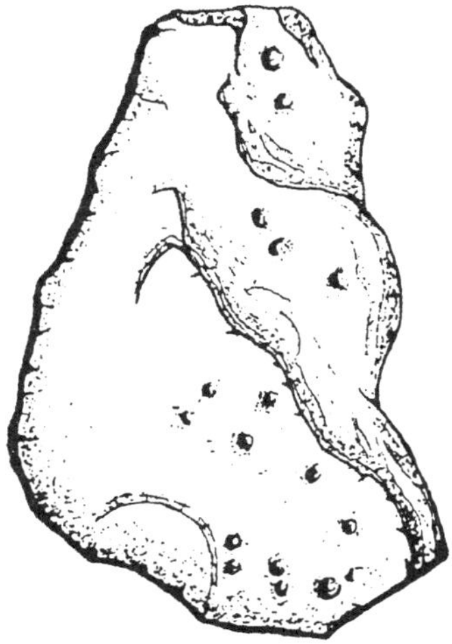

A cupmarked circular stone 1.7m in diameter, reused as the base of a mediaeval cross at Corwen in Denbighshire (after Westwood)

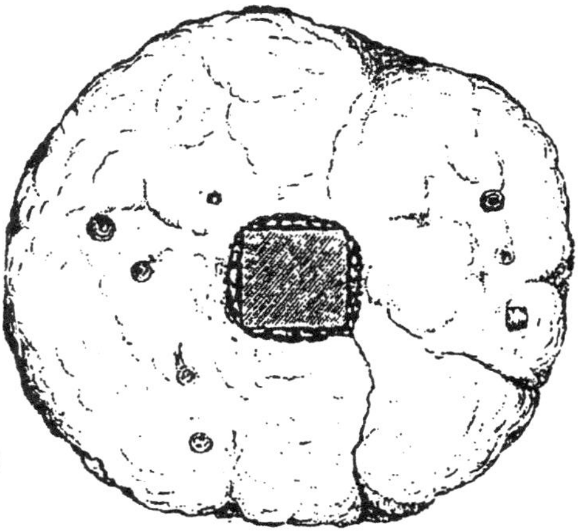

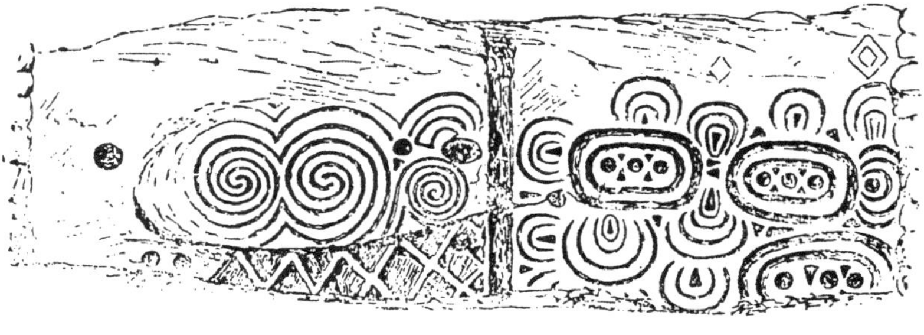

Triple cartouche motifs with three cupmarks and single examples on the left side of kerbstone K52 at Newgrange, Co. Meath, Ireland (after Coffey)

context of the earliest illustrations of this dolmen, one has to go back to the late eighteenth century and to a very significant Welsh painting entitled The Bard. Below a blasted oak and clutching a harp at the edge of a rocky precipice, the wind-swept biblical clad figure with the other arm raised looks behind him as if to ward off some dark elemental force. Birds of prey hover above a few stricken figures lying prone amid the rocks. They may have represented the murder of the bards by the army of Edward I marching off in the distance. It was the central episode in an epic poem of the same title written by Thomas Gray. The sole surviving Welsh bard is about to leap from a cliff in despair. The painter Thomas Jones of Pencerrig, had visited Salesbury Plain and was so impressed by the grandeur of the stones at Stonehenge that he transposed it amid the symbols of the decline of the old bardic order. It is visible in the background as a stark version of the monument with its trilithons high among the stone ruins. Swirling clouds hover over the brooding scene amid patches of dramatic light and dark set against the still mountainous presence of Eryri. The painting now hangs in the National Museum of Wales. Thomas Jones painted this symbolic work in 1774 when the popularity of the druids in wild romantic landscapes like northern Wales was at its height.

A more characteristic work of the period is Moses Griffith's 1778 watercolour of the Bachwen dolmen at Clynnog Fawr. It was commissioned by his patron Thomas Pennant (1726-1798) as an extra illustration to his *Journey around North Wales*. It shows an imaginary figure of an ancient bard with a flowing cloak, who is standing by a massive capstone that rests on three stone uprights with a fourth on ground. The bard has his hands clasped as if he is uttering a fearsome oracular inspired prophecy. On the right-hand side of the picture is an oak in leaf, and in the left background are more trees against a series of gentle mountain peaks. No two representations of Welsh bards executed within a short span of years could appear to be so dissimilar. Yet both partake of the romantic feelings of their period. One is in the summertime of the bardic revival with the officiating vatic at the druidic altar stone. The other is amid the cold desolate mountains, where the only surviving bard stands above the abyss with a final horrified glance at the remains of a shattered world order. The elements of light and the shades of dark! The romance and its shadow doppelganger permeated the creative landscapes of the mind as much as the wild landscapes in nature portrayed in Romantic literature, music and the fine arts.

Pennant had already gained a distinguished reputation as a writer of natural history before setting out on his topographical tours. When commenting on the popularity of druids' altar stones he remarked that those who were interested in druidical antiquities may see a very uncommon cromlech on the field of Bachwen. He suggested that a nearby upright stone – presumably Maen Dylan – was placed to mark the (keep-off) limits of the people while rites were performed by the priestly druid. The question is what kind of rites was he thinking about and why at this particular stone setting? Did the bright watercolour he specially commissioned from Moses Griffith have a hidden meaning for his literate readers interested in the dark side? Perhaps it was the mass of hollows on the sloping capstone seemingly designed to capture the life-blood of a victim that he had in mind when referring to this druidic altar. Caesar in his *Gallic Wars* had written on the bloody auguries of the druids and burning of prisoners in massive wickerworks. After the Restoration, plays such as *Boudica* by Fletcher and Baumont, based on the classical texts, were popular in London theatres. So a common link had grown around the ancient British druids and the cutting of mistletoe with golden sickles in natural oak groves and their rites of flowing blood in wild desolate places. If this was what Pennant was referring to, it would have certainly appealed to his romantically inclined readers especially as the locus of the Tour was his home patch in northern Wales, one of the favoured areas for painters in search of the picturesque. Sir Richard Colt Hoare (1758-1838), a patron of artists and antiquarians as well as a competent water-colourist, did a delicate wash drawing of Bachwen at the turn of the century. The long coverstone sits on its uprights but without any emotional charge. The centrepiece of three cromlechs from Gwynedd, it is still in the romantic style of sketching, but more concerned with recording the ancient monuments from a single viewpoint of the traveller. And without a druid in sight!

The Contemporary Record

Standing in a field next to the sea, surrounded by an iron railing, photographs of the small dolmen usually present it in clear daylight. It is smoother, slimmer and certainly lacking the grandeur of earlier reproductions. The archaeologist Mortimer Wheeler in considering the large number of cupmarks on this very dolmen – one hundred and ten on top and eight on the side of the capstone – noted the then common view that they were associated with some form of sun-worship. The bright orb in a vast clear sky at sunrise or sunset can be reminiscent of a round cupmark on a stone. Less likely is that they were soul-houses or the dwelling places of spirits due to their symbolic primitive roundness. He also pointed out the similarity of cupmarked stones to those used for holy water in certain parts of Europe with perhaps a similar kind of ritual use to hold rainwater or milk in prehistoric times. Some well defined cupmarks have been noted on the capstone of Tŷ Newydd chamber on Ynys Môn.

Of the five remaining portal dolmens built around the coastal area of Pen Llŷn, cupmarks have been recorded on an outcrop close to Cist Cerrig and on the large stone originally found some distance from Mynydd Cefn Amlwch, near Tudweiliog in 1947. It stood 1.25m above the ground with nearly twenty cupmarks on its flat surface. Most of the hollows are between 5cm and 8cm in diameter and 1.5cm deep. The igneous stone now stands up as a gatepost to a farm building near St. Mary's Church, Penllech. Some of the cupmarks are apparently below ground level.

All that remains of a ruined burial chamber called Cist Cerrig near Borth-y-Gest are three tall wide stones. The dolmen stood on the south-western slopes of Moel-y-Gest, below Porthmadog, at the narrowed estuary on the extreme edge of Bae Ceredigion. A group of cupmarks are on the smooth face of rock outcrop due east of the large stones. Ten cups run in an irregular line about 1.6m along the face of the outcrop with an outlier cup at the top and the bottom of the row. A further five hollows are below the ground level and it was clear that they were made by pecking with some small tool rather than grinding. Some of the smallest ones in the row would be classed as doubtful were it not for the five larger cups that are roughly 1cm deep. This linear collection of cupmarks could be said to have been a representation of one of the major constellations in the night sky. Walter Hemp, who recorded this find, was the archaeologist who reconstructed Bryn Celli Ddu in Ynys Môn. He specifically states that during that excavation he removed and then replaced the original mound material on the main coverstones to ascertain if there were any cups or markings on the upper surface. He also checked the other large stones but found no evidence of carvings on any of them apart from the Pattern Stone and the small spiral inside the passageway. (Hemp, 1931)

While reconstructing Barclodiad y Gawres in the early 1950's, archaeologists suggested that there was a possible cupmark to the left of the spiral on stone 19. In her study of the island's archaeology Francis Lynch recorded the only example of a cup and ring carving to have been discovered in Wales to date, on a metre long boulder in the garden of

Llwydiarth Esgob near Llannerch-y-medd. This was the home of a notable collector of antiquities and the fact that the stone was composed of a rare horneblende picrite only found locally suggests that the broken boulder originally came from somewhere in the vicinity. Another unusual stone artifact was found during the demolition of an ancient hedge at Clegyrdy Bach near Llangefni, also in Ynys Môn. It was a well rounded stone – 32cm x 30cm x 17cm – with two deep hollows on one side. One had a ring cut around the top of the larger hole. It was thought originally to be a quern but from the illustration it appears to be more like a worn ballaun stone. Because of the natural hollows they were prized in Ireland and are commonly associated with early churches. This example may have been reused as a holy water font in an ancient chapel which may account for it ending up in the old stone hedge. However, the authors are certain that the stone is cupmarked, and they state that Professor Bradley of Reading University confirmed their opinion, but from his quoted reply he appears to be quite diffident and unsure if its hollows were man-made. However, similar types of rounded boulder stones with hollows are recorded at Selkirk in Scotland and at Fowberry in Northumberland. (Chapman & Roberts, 1996)

A large circular stone at Corwen in Sir Ddinbych (Denbighshire) has a definite religious association which makes it difficult to account for its cupmarks. At present it forms the base of the churchyard cross and looks as if it may have previously been a mill stone. There are two rows of three and four clear hollows on the 2m wide round stone. The five large hollows on a stone stump of Carreg Llanpumsaint in Sir Gaerfyrddin had its name from the story of the five saints on pilgrimage to Tyddewi (St David's) who used it as a pillow in a hailstorm so fierce that the five weary pilgrims left the impressions, which are still visible on the stone. Another suggestion is that the stone was used as a mortar during Roman times to crush gold bearing ore from the nearby Dolaucothi mine. (Worsley, 1987)

The Devil's Quoit stone on the extreme south-west coast of Sir Benfro at Sain Pedrog (St Petroc in Pembrokeshire) has two circular hollows 30cm apart. The larger is 8cm diameter and 2cm deep, the lower cup slightly smaller. (Lewis, 1966) The boulder known as Maen Catwg – St Catwg's stone – is in a field near Gelligaer, Morgannwg. It has a group of nine cupmarks up to 12cm in diameter carved in distinctive conical and circular shapes. (Barber, 1987)

On the south side of the centre stone of a triple alignment of tall standing stones called Harold's Stones at Tryleg in Sir Fynwy, are two large cupmarks. All three stones now lean in different directions, the largest being 2m tall. The south-western of the Four Stones near Walton in Powys is cupmarked. This site was first reported by Camden as a stone circle ruined in the reign of King John. However, it has been considered to be a rare example of a small four-poster, a type of stone setting more commonly found in north-east Scotland. Also mentioned is a boulder in the Llugwy valley, at Llanarch Farm, 'one of the few cupmarked stones in Wales', with thirty-one cupmarks in four rows. (Burl, 1976)

At Rhiwderin an earthfast boulder of millstone grit was found to have twelve well defined cupmarks, 3cm – 5cm in diameter. It was discovered in 1895 but it had not been verified since. During recent excavations at Castell Trostre also in Sir Fynwy, a stone was recovered from a post-mediaeval field drain. It was a fragment but on the coarse sandstone surface, a triangular set of thirteen cupmarks were pecked out in a checkerboard fashion. The triangle, with its base about 10cm. wide had been marked out and recessed prior to the decoration. The bottom part of the stone is gone so there may have been more hollow cups there originally. The find spot of the stone was in close proximity to a stone circle and what may prove to be a Bronze Age ring cairn. (Meins', 1998)

I recently found a group of possible cupmarks on the underside of a smooth boulder in the estuary of the Nanhyfer (river Nevern), below the town of Trefdraeth (Newport). There are about ten well-worn hollows on the landward side with the largest 9cm x 7cm x 3cm deep. It has the appearance of a capstone and is less than a half-a-mile due north of the Carreg Coetan Arthur dolmen now standing in a small housing estate in Trefdraeth.

By a car park at the foot of Hay Bluff is the large incomplete Blaenau Stone Circle with a diameter of 30m. One of the stones has a single cupmark 3cm deep and 7cm in diameter, located below a modern S benchmark. A 2.6m high by 1.20m wide standing stone called Carreg Waun Llech at Llangynidr, also in Powys, has a series of pitted holes on its eastern face. They may be artificial or due to the weathering of the limestone block. (Children & Nash, 2002)

At the embanked Llecheiddior stone circle, in Dyffryn Ardudwy, Gwynedd, is a single shallow cupmark 35mm in diameter that is quite difficult to make out. In the same region, at Arthog is a cupmarked stone north west of a small stone circle at Maes Pan y Llan. Lying on a raised mound the flat stone has eight hollows, about 3cm in diameter. At Arthog, at least three other sites have been recorded. The most definite is a large squarish block of stone at Bron Llety-Ifan, with five cupmarks

5cm in diameter, carved in an arc on the top face. (SMR – Gwynedd Arch. Trust)

Two cupmarked stones were discovered during the excavation of a ring barrow by the stone circle at Crucywel in Sir Fynwy. In different parts of the surrounding ditch one measuring 1.60m by 1.10m had twenty-three cups on its top face, and the other slightly longer stone had a group of smaller cups on top of it. (Savory, 1940)

Hill of the Angels

Circumambulating a prominent Sir Benfro landmark like Carn Ingli from the vantage points of its megalithic monuments would not appear to be a difficult or even a long term undertaking. The dolmens, built on the skirts of the hill as it were, are easily accessible and located roughly clockwise about two to five miles from the central rocky upthrust which is an old volcanic cone that aeons ago was separated from Mynydd Preseli. Glacial action cut out the deep river valley of the Gwaun from the crescent curve of low hills and single outcrops running north-east to south-west from Frenni Fawr and Foel Drygarn to its highest point at Foel Cwmcerwyn (Preseli Top) at 536m above sea level. The name of the bare coloured upland, now within the Pembrokeshire Coast National Park, did not originally refer to the range of hills but to a specific unknown place. It hardly changed from the Preseli as written down by Gerallt Gymro in the twelfth century to Bresselau, Breselecly, Pressely, Precele, Percelley, Percellye, Parcley and Parcelly. It was an unusual combination linking its original coreform 'pres', as in thicket or brushwood with the personal nomen 'Seleau', 'Selyf' or 'Sely', an archaic form of Solomon. It was a vivid combination as mysteriously aloof as the hills themselves. (Charles, 1992)

The surviving monuments around Carn Ingli have been recorded over the past four hundred years by antiquarians, travellers, churchmen and more recently by archaeologists. From the old descriptions of Pentre Ifan, Llech y Dribedd, Carreg Coetan Arthur and Carreg y Gof near the seaside town of Trefdraeth, their condition does not appear to have changed much through the centuries. However, the once vivid accounts of the surrounding landscapes, particularly of unrecorded circles of stones or menhirs have become more prosaic. This is in keeping with the manner in which the individual structures have become isolated from their environment. They are fenced off as singular monuments at the behest of the heritage industry for the benefit of an increasing number of tourists who can quite happily spend a few minutes taking photographs before driving off to the next ancient site.

For instance, Pentre Ifan, the largest and best known was sketched by George Owen of Henllys in the mid-sixteenth century. Drawn from a south-western vantage his sketch included the cardinal directions and each stone was lettered for ease of reference. If some of the uprights are now missing, the general accuracy was well captured by the self-styled Lord of Cemaes, even the sense of the long tapering capstone seemingly lifting off from its uprights. Although Owen's work was not published until the late nineteenth century, his account was known to Edward Lhuyd who included it in his Welsh additions to *Camden's Britannia*. It was also copied by travellers interested in antiquities and by the Pembrokeshire historian Richard Fenton who had a copy of the manuscript in his possession. On it Fenton added 'a crescent of seven stones that doe stand circlewise like in form to the new moon'. Another early observer was John Jones, vicar of Nanhyfer Church in the 1840's. Under the druidic name of Tegid he reaffirmed Fenton's surrounding circle of stones and also mentioned a recumbrant capstone and a causeway of large boulders from Tŷ Canol woods to the cromlech itself. None of these were observable or could be traced by the writers of the Royal Commission of Ancient Monuments published in 1925. It was suggested that this was due to the shifting and displacement of large fieldstones.

During the past decades there have been further extensive stone displacements in the immediate environment. A massive standing stone became 'lost' in the field to the south-west – it was almost certainly an outlier, a common feature in the area like that at Trellyffaint. While Pentre Ifan was recently re-fenced by Cadw, Welsh Historic Monuments, a virtual wholesale clearance of its surrounding large stones into the fieldbanks took place. Even the old footpath to the dolmen was covered over by huge boulders that added to the general confusion. Behind its neat information board, it is now presented to the public as a single isolated burial chamber. There is no indication of earlier landscape associations or indeed that there ever had been any drastic changes made to the surrounding area. For most visitors, young and old, it confirms the stark and familiar iconic representation on tourist brochures and heritage guides as Wales' largest prehistoric monument.

When I first began the survey of the dolmens around Carn Ingli I did not expect any surprise revelations. This was especially in relation to then recorded cupmarks like the hollows on the broken coverstones of the Trellyffaint double-chambered dolmen and those carved on the embedded stone at Trefoel farm in Nanhyfer. I had lived locally for more than a decade and visited most of the sites on many occasions whenever I was in the mood or happened to be nearby. However, as the strange notion of notating how the form of the hilltop looked from each of the dolmens with a line-of-sight on Carn Ingli took root, it seemed a good idea to be more systematic. This was a way of getting through a long winter, and the right season for such a madcap scheme, as the intervening tree foliage was minimal. From my own observations amid this undulating terrain with its small farms and odd patchwork fields, the surviving dolmens were fairly close to the sea. As a composite group within a wide-spread riverain system they are quite differently situated from the manner that the Nevern Valley tombs have been alluded to in the archaeological literature. (Lynch, 1972)

With compass, notebook and camera I began at Llech y Dribedd in the corner of a field near the village of Trewyddel (Moylegrove). It is an immensely bulky capstone, now resting on two of the three points that the Welsh name suggests. Since the time of Edward Lhuyd many have commented on its bulk, its unwieldy boulders or dumpy uprights. But it has almost a classic portal dolmen coherence with its uplifted enormous wedge about 3m long. Sitting in the lee of it, the summit of Carn Ingli almost mimics its structure appearing as a chunky cone in the south-west. From its other seaward side, the sun on the evening of the summer solstice shines inside the stone chamber. The axis of the monument is aligned to this particular celestial event. (Heath, 1993)

Its massive capstone, once known as the Altar Stone, was thought to have been wrenched from the Preseli Hills by St Samson and thrown into place here. Such hyperbole and exaggeration were usually part of popular storytelling. Yet as at Carreg Samson and Ffust Samson near Sain Nicholas, he and Illtud are the only Welsh saints specifically associated with megalithic monuments. The Tŷ Illtud chambered cairn and Bedd Gŵyl Illtud, said to have been once a rounded cairn, but now a single metre long narrow sandstone hidden amid ferns with the nearby pool, overgrown from the holy well, are both in the vicinity of Aberhonddu. Samson's Jack stone in the Gŵyr is 3.2m high.

From the double-chambered dolmen Trellyffaint, the shape of Carn Ingli is unchanged. Trellyffaint is a low-lying collection of brown coloured stones whose name in Welsh means town of the toads. It has spawned a series of onomastic tales from Gerallt Gymro (Giraldus Cambrensis) in the late twelfth century to the present. He recounts the story of Susillus Longshanks or Cyril Long Legs who was buried here and had a fear of toads. He became so ill his friends tied him into a blanket hanging from the nearby tree. However, they still managed to gnaw him to death. When Richard Fenton visited Trellyffaint House he noted a well sculpted carving of a toad in black marble on the mantlepiece. It was behind glass. Perhaps it was a talismanic object of some power and renown, and that it had been covered over. More recently a local author recounted the story of how a toadman acquired power over animals. The ritual initiation began with ants eating the fleshy parts of a toad. Its bones were cleaned and thrown into a nearby stream. The man waited and grabbed the one that turned tide, screaming as it went. He then carried this bone in his pocket for three days and as he walked around the cromlech at midnight on each of the three nights. In this manner he became a proper toadman, like his father before him, with an uncanny power over animals. A strange story that brings the place-name, ritual magic and the ancient cromlech into a timeless symbiosis. (Worsley, 1987)

The double stone chambers may have been much higher when originally built, but the broken capstone resting on three low uprights does not quite cover the larger intact chamber. On the 2m round coverstone is a scattering of over thirty shallow depressions, about 5cm in diameter. A smaller stone nearby with a deep oval hollow appears to have broken off from it.

At Trefoel farm on the road to Nanhyfer is the other cupmarked stone that was recorded in 1929 by W.F. Grimes, then Director of the NMW. The exposed oval with nearly thirty 5cm hollows, a larger 10cm one and smaller depressions is now embedded in the earth at an angle of forty-five degrees. It may have once been a capstone to a dolmen of which there is no record. The flatish 2m wide slope gives a comfortable leaning position for an excellent view of Carn Ingli that is spread supine on the horizon to the south-west.

In the nearby bank were a number of boulders and beyond that in the next field, at the end of an ancient hedgerow, a group of stones. Late in 1994 I noticed that one of the small uprights, 45cm long x 15cm wide, had a series of incomplete cupmarks 4cm deep x 6cm long on a broken jagged edge. It had also had a clump of five hollows conjoined measuring from 3cm to 6cm in diameter with a 4cm oval cupmark above them. When I visited the site during the following summer the field had been plowed over and the line of stones gone. The largest of the group had been pushed into a nearby hedge. The smaller cupmarked stone could not be found anywhere in the vicinity. Fortunately I had made a rubbing from it when the stone was still in situ. This brings up a number of complex issues in relation to the conservation of field monuments. The cupmarked oval-shaped stone that had been known and recorded still remains in place. Yet the fact that it may have been the capstone to the remains of its substructure in the next field, can never now be ascertained. Nor can the significance of the cupmarks and the possible link to the newly found group on the disturbed stone ever be known. It seems to be part of an unfortunate trend by the state guardians to isolate monuments from their immediate surroundings. The wholesale removal of large stones from around Pentre Ifan over the past decades is an example of the manner in which the tourist gaze becomes focused on a denuded structure rather than on the ritual landscape it once adorned.

There seems to be some contention among archaeologists about a possible cupmark on one of the uprights of Pentre Ifan. It may seem odd to most people that experts – whose self-appointed function is the preservation and conservation of such ancient monuments, especially the most well-known one in Wales – cannot ascertain whether a single hollow is artificial or natural or if it actually constitutes a cupmark! Perhaps it was the discovery as late as 1960 of the carvings of some Mycenaean-type axes on the south trilithon at Stonehenge on what is possibly the most observed and written about man-made structure in Britain. The publicity of the axe carvings may have brought about a closer examination of the Preseli dolmen! Lynch in 1972, quoting Alcock, wrote that a single cupmark surrounded by a ring had been recognised on the outer face of the portal blocking stone. This feature had been interpreted five years previously by Morris – the foremost authority on the Scottish rock petroglyphs – as a spiral. However the re-examination of the several depressions present on the surface of this stone failed to convince the verity of either of the alleged (carved) identifications. (Barker, 1992)

Abrasions would be a better term to use and they look as if they were deliberate, perhaps to remove some of the graffiti that is currently evident on the other side of this stone. However a shallow depression about 10cm in diameter and 0.5m from ground level on the left inner side of the rear support stone, has the appearance of a possible cupmark.

Cromlech, or the Welsh plural cromlechau are common on old maps although during the premodern era tumuli or carneddau, sepulchral and druid altars were often used indiscriminately. The Breton word dolmen, meaning stone table, is the current archaeological term for these denuded single-chambered polygonal large stone structures, formed by a number of uprights holding up a heavy massive boulder called a capstone. There appears to be some depressions on the thick wedge of stone covering Carreg Coetan Arthur that rests on some of the 1.5m high front uprights. Its traditional name suggests it was playfully pegged by Arthur who left it as it is after a game of giant-sized quoits. In 1775 the landlord of a hovel here showed the antiquarian traveller Wyndham the stones and doubted not, that upon digging, the very skeleton of a giant would be discovered. When it was finally excavated in 1979 all that was found were pottery shards and bones from a cremation dated to the mid-third millennium BC.

The dolmen is now almost hidden in the midst of a housing complex in Trefdraeth. Even though it is somewhat obscured by trees, the view of Carn Ingli southwards shows a deep indentation in the centre of the summit. It is possible to see nearby stretches of water from where it was built, not far above the low lying river estuary of the Nanhyfer. Due north, almost directly across from here is a weathered stone on the other side of the estuary above the high water mark. It is roughly 1.5m long x 45cm wide x 45cm deep. It looks as it may have been part of an ancient structure, perhaps even a dolmen as there are other large stones nearby including a quartz boulder. On the innerside of the stone, away from the water, are a series of nine cupmarks ranging up to 7cm in diameter and 3cm deep (page 61).

Due east of the town – in a field by the road to Abergwaun (Fishguard) – is the group of five stone chambers known as Cerrig y Gof, the rock of the blacksmith. The indentations on the skyline of Carn Ingli have a more pronounced female shape that curves down to the hump of Carn Ffoi. Perhaps, this is the anvil of a celestial smith! George Owen in the sixteenth century remarked that locally this feature was said to be named after a giant whose form can best be seen on the road across the moor to Bedd Morris – a tall standing stone on the parish boundary. The earliest recorded account of Cerrig y Gof by Edward Lhuyd mentions two stones standing near to the cluster of its five tables or altars. All subsequent accounts omit any reference to outliers although both large stones are plainly visible lying in the western end of the field. We know from Fenton's actions that when he removed the lid coverings of the five circular chambers and dug down into the mould, that he was singularly unimpressed by the trifling variation of their contents. Charcoal, rude pottery shards, particles of bones and a quantity of black sea pebbles were found. A veritable treasure by today's scientific standards!

The group of five stone boxes, one of which remains structurally intact, were raised around an open centre in a 10m diameter circle. On two of the remaining four capstones are some small indentations. A group are visible on the north north-west stone with one kidney-shaped depression, 12 x 7 x 4cm deep on the southern chamber. A nearby recumbent stone at the end of the field also has a large kidney-shape and rounded cups.

Whatever good intentions I started off with in my original itinerary, the sheer physicality of the rock strewn landscape and the protracted amount of time involved turned it into a rather piecemeal effort. It was not just a question of going from one monument to the next, but at every turn there were seemingly endless numbers of significantly looking clusters of large boulders piled up in fields and around the hedgebanks to be checked out. Tramping the hills I was surprised at how often Carn Ingli would disappear from view or undergo yet another extraordinary change of shape from wherever I travelled. I am totally dyslexic about compass directions and lack any kind of spatial awareness. So the geography of its conical shape from the numerous country roads around it, and its furthest presence up to twenty miles away from many points of the Preseli Hills, meant that it was never the entity that appeared to be a constant on the map or from my disjointed and often illegible notes. Even over the years, in the very trying weather conditions of this area when revisiting the mainly intact dolmens, the hilltop would look different from previous occasions. It often was as frustrating checking the hill from the many structures marked possible or doubtful in archaeological surveys, as it was from those places where I felt sure that a cromlech must have once existed on a particular spot. Sometimes it was as if the hill itself was pointing them to my overworked imagination. The actual shape of the hill and the residue of folk traditions attached to it, had been tied into an obsessive conceit. A scenario that the early farmers and builders of the first dolmens on its slopes nearly six thousand years ago, had modelled their covered stone chambers on the goddess hill itself. Local folklore claimed that her form could be seen in the shape of south side of the summit and that from the north side when changed into a winged angel. It was a form embedded in the inner space between sacred time, ancient place and hidden power. Needless to say I was often overwhelmed by this transpersonal encounter with its shift between the seemingly old and current modes of consciousness.

The influence of a visible mountain on the siting or situation of monuments, in a sense of creating an esoteric and exoteric totality within the known physical landscape, has been noted by a number of modern archaeologists. The collection of eighteen dolmens of the Severn-Cotswold group in Powys and Swydd Henffordd (Herefordshire)that face the dominant rising escarpment of the Mynydd Du (Black Mountain), seems to exhibit somewhat of the same ancestral relationship. (Children & Nash, 2001)

Site List of Welsh Cupmarks

1 **Arthog**, Gwynedd. (SH 66241323)
3 cupmarks, with others possibly hidden by the turf, are on an area of exposed bedrock, south of the summit of a low ridge. A massive rounded boulder to the north, has some hollows that may not be actual cupmarks. (SMR – Gwynedd Arch. Trust)
2 **Bachwen**, Clynnog Fawr, Gwynedd. (SH 407495)
The capstone of the dolmen has at least 110 cupmarks, with 8 others on a side stone. (Wheeler)
3 **Barclodiad y Gawres,** Llanfaelog, Ynys Môn. (SH 329707)
At its excavation a possible cupmark was said to be on the left of the spiral on stone 19. (Daniel)
4 **Pen-y-bont Standing Stone,** by Leisure Centre, Pen-y-bont ar Ogwr (Bridgend). (SS 902795)
Natural grooves on the north side of the 1.8m high standing stone has some cupmarks. When it was moved from its original site, burnt bones of an adult were found beneath it. (SMR – Glam. Gwent Arch. Trust)
5 **Bron Llety-Ifan,** Arthog, Gwynedd. (SN 63341263)
Five cupmarks are set in an arc with another outlying, on the top face of a seat-shaped block of stone. Each one roughly 5cm in diameter. (SMR – Gwynedd Arch. Trust)
6 **Carreg Coetan Arthur,** Trefdraeth, Sir Benfro. (SN 061359)
A number of depressions on the capstone of the dolmen may be cupmarks. Half-a-mile to the north on the tidal estuary is a well worn round boulder. 10 cupmarks are on the landward side. The largest is 9cm cross and 3cm deep.
7 **Carreg Pumsant**, Pumsaint, Llanymddyfri, Sir Gaerfyrddin.
A short standing stone has five large hollows on one face
8 **Cerrig y Gof,** Trefdraeth, Sir Benfro. (SN 037389)
Small groups of cupmarks on two of the remaining coverstones of this five-chambered dolmen site. Four deep depressions and a kidney-shaped one on the recumbent stone in the western end of the field.
9 **Cist Cerrig,** Borth-y-Gest, Porthmadog, Gwynedd. (SH 54363839)

A straight line of 10 cupmarks run down the 1.6m face of an earthfast stone east of the ruined dolmen with others below the ground. (Hemp)

10 Clegyrdy Bach, Llangefni, Ynys Môn.

A rounded stone (32cm x 30cm x 17cm) has two deep hollows, the larger with a circular cut around the top. (Chapman & Roberts)

11 Corwen, Sir Ddinbych.

A 2m round stone base of the churchyard cross, has seven cupmarks in two rows. (Westwood)

12 Craig Hafodwen, Penmaenmawr, Conwy. (SH 72827578)

A cupmarked stone, recorded in 1995 with no details. (SMR – Gwynedd Arch. Trust)

13 Crucywel, Caer-went, Sir Fynwy.

Two of the flat stones embedded in the ditch of a bell-barrow near Crick House are cupmarked. (Savory)

14 Devil's Quoit stone, Sain Pedrog, Sir Benfro. (SR 96229637)

The stone has 2 cupmarks about 30cm apart. The larger is 8cm in diameter and 2cm deep. (Lewis) (SMR – Cambria Archaeology)

15 Four Stones, Old Radnor, Powys. (SO 24576080)

The south-western stone of this four-poster site is cupmarked. (Burl). The four stones are aligned to the cardinal points, the three shallow cup marks may be natural, & the name first appeared in a will of 1652. (CPAT)

16 Gwerncaernyddion, Dyffryn Ardudwy, Gwynedd. (SH 59402543)

Several cupmarks are on the flat top of a massive boulder by the side of the road. There are also extended straight grooves that may be due to glacial action. (SMR – Gwynedd Arch. Trust)

17 Harold Stones, Tryleg, Sir Fynwy. (SO 496052)

The centre stone of the row of three standing stones has two large cupmarks. (Whittle)

18 Llanarch, New Radnor, Llugwy Valley, Powys. (SO 15785858)

A stone on the farm has 32 cupmarks carved in four rows on its flat surface (Burl), (CPAT).

19 Llanbadarn Fawr, Aberystwyth. Ceredigion. (SN 599810)

Three marked hollows on the front of a 1.4m high block of sandstone with deeply incised moulding. It may have represented a goddess figure that was crudely reshaped into the form of a cross. A curious phallic carving is visible at the rear.

20 Llanfaelog, Ynys Môn. (SH 356746)

In the centre of the east face of the inscribed Cunogusi stone is a single cupmark. (Arch. in Wales, 21)

21 Llangelynnin, Gwynedd. (SH 64951393)
7 irregular patterned cupmarks, about 5cm in diameter, are on the topmost part of a large stone block that is amid the boulders of a field clearance. (SMR – Gwynedd Arch. Trust)

22 Llecheiddior, Dyffryn Ardudwy, Gwynedd. (SH 61112174)
A single shallow cupmark on one of the stones of the embanked stone circle. It is 35mm diameter and difficult to see. (SMR – Gwynedd Arch .Trust)

23 Llannerch, Clynnog, Gwynedd. (SH 55953799)
Four large slabs, the possible remains of a cromlech, are built into a wall near the road to Llannerch Farm. Two of the stones are thought to have cupmarks. (SMR – Gwynedd Arch. Trust)

24 Llywel, Trecastell, Powys.
A tall inscribed slab with a possible single cupmark. Now in the British Museum.

25 Llwydiarth Esgob, Llannerch-y-medd, Ynys Môn. (SH 436844)
A double cup and ring marking connected by a groove and with two further cups on a metre long boulder in the garden of the house. (Lynch)

26 Maen Catwg, Gelligaer, Cwm Rhymni, Morgannwg. (ST 127974)
The stone is 2.6m long (NE-SW) x 1.7m wide x 0.6m thick. On the top are 33 cupmarks from 40-115 mm diameter and 5-60mm deep depending on the degree of weathering. A further 17 other hollows are imprecise.

27 Maes Pan y Llan, Arthog, Gwynedd. (SH 65101400)
A flat stone on a mound, NW of the small stone circle, has 8 shallow cupmarks, 3cm in diameter. (SMR – Gwynedd Arch. Trust)

28 Morfa Bychan, Pendine, Eglwys Gymyn, Sir Gaerfyrddin. (SN 221075)
Three flat stones with possible cupmarks on the outcrop above the four chambered tombs. (SMR – Cambria Archaeology)

29 Penllech, Tudweiliog, Gwynedd. (SH 22263449)
Now standing up in a hedge by St. Mary's church gate with crude and faint cupmarks. Recorded (1964) as a gatepost 1.25m above the ground with nearly 20 cupmarks on its flat surface – roughly 7cm in diameter and 2cm deep. Some years later was uprooted and lay in a nearby field with its flat cupmarked surface visible and upright. (SMR – Gwynedd Arch. Trust)

30 Pentre Ifan, Nanhyfer, Sir Benfro. (SN 099370)
A possible cupmark on the inner side of the rear support stone of the cromlech.

31 Pen Twyn, near Bargoed, Morgannwg. (SO 141004)
Cupmarks were recorded here but the stone could not be found by RCAM(W).

32 Rhiwderin, Sir Fynwy.
Earthfast boulder with 12 cupmarks 3-5cm diameter. Recorded in 1898 but location unknown.
33 Simondston, south of Coety, Morgannwg .
Excavation of a cairn in 1957 revealed a stone cist 1m x 0.8m. The inner slab of the cist burial had 5 shallow cupmarks. Stone and artifacts now in NMW. (Grimes)
34 Trefoel, Nanhyfer, Sir Benfro.
An earthbound 2m round capstone of a possible dolmen has over 30 cupmarks. It is in a large field at Cwmgloyne Farm, off the main road. (Grimes) A number of other stones had been cleared from an old field hedge in 1994. One of the upright stones had a set of visible cupmarks.
35 Trellyffaint, Nanhyfer, Sir Benfro. (SN 083426)
The cover stone of a ruined dolmen had twenty-two shallow cupmarks. A broken off stone fragment has a small group of hollows. (Wheeler)
36. Trostre, Castell Trostre, Sir Fynwy. (SO 359143)
Stone fragment with a triangular set of 13 cupmarks on a base 10cm wide. (Meins')
37 Tyddyn Du, Brithdir and Llanfachreth, Gwynedd. (SH 73481643)
5 hollow indentations, known as cupmarks, may be modern drill marks. (SMR – Gwynedd Arch. Trust)
38 Tŷ Newydd, Llanfaelog, Ynys Môn. (SH 344738)
Five well-defined cupmarks are on the capstone of the damaged dolmen. (Arch. in Wales, 21)
39 Waun Oer, Gwynedd. (SH 617112)
A short stone row with a cupmark on its furthest pillar. (Burl)

The Clwyd-Powys Archaeological Trust (CPAT) provided the following cupmarked sites that are not numbered on the map (page 62).

40 Beili Onnen Stone, Yscir, Powys. (SN 98203225)
Recumbent stone (0.9m x 0.4m) near local summit has a possible cupmark on its upper surface. (CPAT)
41 Brynmelys Stone, Glasgwm, Powys. (SO 13355731)
A standing stone, cut and used as a mounting block, had five cupmarks, 5cm across. Whereabouts unknown at present. (CPAT)
42 Court Farm Boulder, Old Radnor, Powys. (SO 25676230)
A possible cupmark, 2cm across x 1cm deep, on the upper surface of a weathered stone lying in a hedgerow. (CPAT)

43 Court Stone Row, Glasgwm, Powys. (SO 08485683)
One of the four stones, 2.1m high x 1.1m square standing in a pool of water has been noted as cupmarked. No such depressions noted on recent site visits. (CPAT)
44 Maen Hirion Stone, Cerrigdrudion, Conwy. (SH 94504776)
In a field, called Dol y Fawydd, a large irregular boulder has a single cup mark and an inscribed circle. An oval figure is on the east end of the stone. (CPAT)
45 Owain Glyndŵr's Moat Cupstone, Corwen, Sir Ddinbych. (SJ 12784309)
Up to twenty cupmarks have been recorded on a large stone embedded in the southeast edge of the moat . Recent visit noted twelve genuine cupmarks with an average size of 4cm and the largest cup 6cm diameter by 2cm deep. (CPAT)

Tŷ Illtud

> The crosses and other figures of caprice are irregularly placed on the inside of one of the side stones and may have been made with a tenpenny or a twopenny nail.
>
> Theophilus Jones (1809)

The saintly attribution in the name for the monument is not as unusual as the sixty-odd small carvings that have been variously suggested to have been done as far back as the prehistoric era to the mediaeval period and beyond. Along with the graffiti dates carved on the outside stones, the combination of all three elements are a rarity unique to Wales.

In 1696, Edward Lhuyd in *Camden's Britannia,* wrote that the ancient chamber was composed of four large stones somewhat of a flat form, altogether rude and unpolished. Three of them were so pitched in the ground, and the fourth laid on the top for a cover, that they made an oblong square hut. It was open at one end, about eight foot long, four wide, and near the same height. Having entered it, he found the two side stones inscribed with a variety of crosses. He supposed that this cell 'notwithstanding the crosses and the saint's name, to have been erected in the time of Paganism'. The early nineteenth century Breckonshire historian Theophilus Jones remarked that the venerable relic of antiquity so renowned in topography, was nothing more than a very small cromlech. Merely an idle fable that it was the dwelling place of the saint.

John Aubrey, the Royal topographer to Charles II, wrote that Tŷ Illtud was first mentioned in englynion from the Grammar of a sixteenth century Welsh doctor, Siôn Dafydd Rhys in connection with a hidden treasure. The doctor had the cairn dug out but there arose such a horrid tempest of thunder and lightening that the workmen would dig no longer. They said they saw strange apparitions there but also appeared to have found a cake of gold which was of considerable value. Dr John Davies had studied at Oxford but left England at twenty-one to eventually read medicine at the University of Sienna, graduating as Doctor of Physic. He had published two grammatical treatises as well as a guide to Italian pronunciation, before returning home in 1571 to be headmaster at a school in northern Wales. Ten years later he set up a practice in Cardiff. It was during this time that he began his best known work, a Latin treatise on Welsh grammar. It was completed at his retreat in the Bannau Brycheiniog (Brecon Beacons) and published in 1592.

Unusually for his time, he was a professed Catholic and may have known that the saint's hermitage was or had been a place of pilgrimage. The casual manner in which Tŷ Illtud was introduced in the *Itinerary* of Gerallt Gymro who was then Dean of Brecknock (Brecon), by way of a curious bit of folklore of St Illtud, suggests that by the twelfth century, the saint's association with the stone chamber was commonplace locally. The saint with his half-horse and half-stag had led the life of a hermit at Llanhamlach as, gleaned from ancient and authentic records.

Aubrey, whose *Monumenta Brittanica* was never published until almost three centuries after his death, was probably one of the first writers to place the druids as the priests of Stonehenge. He also had strong connections with this area and referred to 'the Carn at Cravannesh in the parish of Llansandfred as a heape of stanes', as high and as long as a garden wall of the Inner Temple in London. As well as the crosses on the internal faces of the uprights, two of the stones outside the chamber have dates carved on them – mcccxi(i?) 1311 or 1312 on the long stone and 15110, probably for 1510, on the one to the west. These are thought to have been cut during pre-Reformation perambulations for the stone chamber is on the boundary of Llanhamlach and Llansanffraid parishes, 5km south-east of Aberhonddu and located within the ancient borderlands of two parishes in what was probably a wild place or a liminal abode of the dead and the elementals.

Yet such a wild area was probably conceived also as a source of hidden power. It was popularly centred around the haunts of tree or water spirits and religiously around the cult of a renowned saint. So an annual perambulation or pardon to Tŷ Illtud on the saint's day would be a grandiose affair, perhaps led by a bishop, carrying a holy relic, accompanied by local dignitaries and a great concourse of the people. It was an all-inclusive affair. The rituals held around the nearby standing stone Maen Illtud and the holy well would have been an equally important means of health and good fortune as the overtly religious trappings of the saintly source of power. The presence of a horse with its symbolic stag antlers – mentioned by Gerallt – would have been seen as a good omen or augury connected with the saint and his hermitage. All we have now are stories to indicate this universal belief in the power of place and its portents. (Wilson. 2000)

It is within such a sacred and secular context that the practice of incising the small graffiti crosses inside the walls of Tŷ Illtud becomes intelligible. In fact the closest mixture of such small Christian and pagan carvings are to be found in the old pilgrimage caves in Western Scotland and at Knockmore cave in Northern Ireland.

The Carvings

Apart from the weathered and lichen-covered north-east and north-west slabs with the incised graffiti dates, that may have once formed part of a forecourt of the original structure, the three inner walls of the chamber were used for the carvings. According to the last and most comprehensive survey, the south facing slab is incised with what appears to be a lyre measuring 6cm by 3.5cm. The south-east slab or the east wall has at least eight crosses with a weathered inscription first noted in the nineteenth century. The south-west slab or the west wall has the south end of its face more or less covered with a variety of over sixty incised carvings. Whatever kinds of decoration that was carved on the north end had then weathered away. The carvings were incised rather than pecked and a small hole was first punched into the stone from which the carvers could complete their work. Perhaps it was using 'a two or tenpenny nail' as Jones suggested in the early nineteenth century to scratch their marks on the stones. Comparing a photograph of the most definite carving of a cross-in-diamond taken in 1925 with one of the same area fifty years later, the author remarked that the original had become obliterated during that period. (Grinsell, 1981)

The stones are of Old Red Sandstone and prone to flaking from winter frosts and being rubbed by sheep sheltering inside. A breakdown of the most common motifs that have been recorded on the west wall is as follows:

A The varieties of simple open crosses numbering about forty. There are another eight on the east wall.
B Sixteen crosses enclosed in diamonds or lozenges.
C Another category of cross with five barred or crossleted ends.
D The two eight-rayed star symbols.
E The five stringed lyre carved on the south wall with its ends curving above the top of the frame thought to represent a Roman type of musical instrument.

Without going into detailed comparisons with relevant examples, the above may be grouped in terms of possible datable periods: B & D could represent motifs as have been found on Irish megalithic carvings. In terms of style C have been compared with the crossletted crosses of the seventh to early tenth century. The small graffiti crosses (A) could have been made at any time up to the pre-Reformation 1510 date that is carved just above ground level on the outside north-west stone.

This essentially reflects the consensus of opinion by those who have studied the Tŷ Illtud carvings. L' Abbe Breuil, the French prehistorian in a 1934 lecture, thought the marks on the south-west stone to be prehistoric. In an early 1925 publication Crawford, before he founded and edited the journal *Antiquity*, considered them to be late Christian. However, in a 1951 paper when he was writing *The Eye Goddess*, he placed them earlier in the prehistoric period. In the same year N.H. Savory, the then director of the NMW published a paper on prehistoric Brycheiniog and suggested that the crosses might belong to the Early Middle Ages. G.E. Daniel in his 1950 survey of the prehistoric chambers of England and Wales whilst considering the published accounts thought them to be probably mediaeval. L.V. Grinsell in 1981 concluded the carvings to have been made by pilgrims and 'other devotees of the cult of St Illtud'. The range of dates he postulated were from the crossletted crosses in an Early Christian style, to the inscribed dates of the periodic perambulations of the parish boundaries, when at least some of the crosses may have been carved. However, from the time of the Reformation onwards such customs were regarded as Popish beliefs and saints pilgrimages tended to lapse. So by the time Lhuyd visited in the late seventeenth century, the practice and even the purpose of the carvings had become forgotten, until Theophilus Jones could write in 1809 that such an idea was in fact an idle fable.

If one looks closely for comparisons between the carvings and those of the prehistoric and early historical eras, an extensive time-scenario over thousands of years seems untenable. At Newgrange, diamond forms are present on some stones but they are always part of a larger design. Even though we may not be able to decode their meanings there seems no doubt that the continuous run of joined lozenges, often with blanket picking, or like those placed above and below the intersection of two spirals, were essentially part of an overall scheme. At Loughcrew starbursts are visible but are not isolated as at Tŷ Illtud, as again they are part of a larger picture that we cannot read now. A most important factor that mitigates against such comparisons is the compositional or pictorial and obviously symbolic aspects of passage grave art. The small carvings in the Welsh tomb were apparently done intermittently over time and on an *ad hoc* basis.

Equally they show little comparison to the formal designs on the large incised stone crosses from the region, such as from Reynoldston, Llanmadog or Gelligaer in Morgannwg which are usually dated between the seventh and ninth centuries. They bear even less comparison when details are isolated from them, such as the crossletted motifs. The Christian crosses carved on stones were certainly diverse in form but they had a clear religious and iconic meaning for the original carvers, the monks and lay people who venerated them. In fact there is only one stone from Pont-rhyd-y-pen with an equal-armed cross complete with crosslets on the top corner that has the appearance of a graffiti cross. However the 24cm x 18cm dimensions of it on the metre tall weathered stone are greater than the largest similar looking cross of Tŷ Illtud at 7cm x 10cm long. So it appears that the lack of a contextual design and of any formal arrangement in the mass of Tŷ Illtud carvings would rule out many of the comparisons that have been put forward by previous commentators. (Nash-Williams, 1950)

The anomaly here seems to be the so-called harp. Some carvings of five-stringed Roman lyres are known from the Temple of Sulis-Minerva in Bath – but are now in Compton Dando church 11km. to the west – and from Cirencester. Tŷ Illtud is quite close to a Roman road between Aberhonddu and Abergafenni (Abergavenny). It could equally be that of a boat which brings to mind the obscure incisions on a stone by the right hand side of the main recess in Newgrange. This too has been debated in terms of a possible inscription, a mason's mark or even if it was genuine, but there seems to be no doubt that it represented a boat or a galley. (Coffey, 1912)

Considered as graffiti marks of popular devotion carved in homage to Saint Illtud, they can be appreciated in their own right. The repetition of limited images on the inside of his ancient hermitage and the discrete markings over a long period of time are specific attributes of such individual signings. Whether one wants to call them popular art or aesthetic forms of carving is irrelevant to the popular religious context and devout intention of the carvers. They could in all probability have been carved by ordinary people finishing a pilgrimage. Their mark done with care and attention may have been the final act of a spiritual journey around the major cult sites, as Grinsell suggested, from Ynys Bŷr to Llanilltud Fawr and through Bannau Brycheiniog to the saint's Bedd and Hermitage.

The Pilgrim Round

If one considers some very different Welsh saintly cult sites, it may be possible to appreciate the need of repeating similar forms of carvings that somehow became formally associated with a particular holy place. Each mark is essentially responsive but one that retains a certain mystery. In a sense nothing could be simpler than making the sign of a graffiti cross. The result of a vertical and horizontal cut on stone interacting as they intersect. Each one is thus a copy of the others, yet the question remains of who made the first mark and equally when or why the practice ceased. It was like the cuts on certain trees that almost invite people to carve their own initials into the bark, year after year and often over centuries. So it is not why do people do it, but why the need to copy others' initials, or love-hearts, small diamonds, crosses or even the deep outlines of human heads. It is interesting to note that the capstone now buried in the reconstructed mound of Barclodiad y Gawres – the only megalithic structure to have passage grave art in Britain – was so covered with personal graffiti that it was once known as the Stone of Names.

A spring by the base of a mudstone cliff near Llantrisant is the site of an ongoing head cult. One of Edward Lhuyd's informants to the questionnaire he sent out in the 1690's noted that there were two carvings of human heads at Tarrent Deusant, which literally means the Rock of the Two Saints. With incised eyebrows and slit eyes typical of Celtic heads, they are now difficult to pick out from at least eight stylised heads that have been carved in the soft rock since then. The carvings are on either side of a light coloured boulder protruding out beneath a natural ledge like a large phallic teardrop. Here, as at Tŷ Illtud, the human need to imitate the primal symbols of an old shrine makes it hard to establish any chronology or even when the initial two heads of the saints were first carved. Standing alone at the rockface by the spring amid the noise of the surrounding trees gives one a strong feeling of intruding at an ancient pagan or certainly a pre-Christian cult site (page 63).

When I first climbed the steep track to view the Pilgrim Cross cut into the rockface at Nanhyfer in Sir Benfro many years ago, there was much the same mixture of curiosity and awe. I was almost like an intruder into such an ancient place, in which I could no more pray below the cross with my knees on the small graffiti crosses carved in the hollows of the pilgrim rocks beneath, than touch the fearsome outlines of the almost inhuman heads in Morgannwg. Now of course the site is very much changed with signposts and wooden benches. There is a wide track remade by the Pembrokeshire National Coastal Park, that has almost eradicated any sense of numinous that was formally enclosed in what remained of the natural grotto. The nearby St. Brynach's church nestles below the tree-covered hill. Some way up the steep hill is the Pilgrim Cross. Carved in relief – half-a-metre in length – it stands out boldly from the rough rockface. The smooth rocks below had been hollowed out, it was said, by pilgrims kneeling in prayer for a safe journey to Tyddewi, the final destination of their pilgrimage thirty miles away. Scratched inside the hollows are tiny graffiti crosses. It is probable that this was once a natural grotto with water falling from the cliff above, which hollowed out the smooth rocks. Perhaps it is one of the many holy wells dedicated to Brynach, a saint who also had strong connections with the area of Tŷ Illtud – as the soul-friend or spiritual instructor to Brychan – and commemorated in local placenames such as the 629m high peak south of Aberhonddu, known as Fan Frynach.

Below the Fan on the north-western flank is a high ridge known as Mynydd Illtud. Near the present Mountain Centre was a Bronze Age stone monument called Bedd Gŵyl Illtud, meaning the Grave of Illtud's Eve. There was an ancient custom here for the pilgrims to keep a night vigil before the saint's feast day. Held around bonfire night perhaps what occurred since was a secularisation and a shift of the older Hallowe'en rituals on the Night of All Hallows, when the spirits of the dead were once thought to roam the world. We might think that the idea of staying awake all night in or around an ancient stone chamber would be too creepy for words and not for the faint hearted. However, it was common practice for large crowds of people to spend the night out near a holy well or a popular pilgrimage site, waiting for the dawn to precede with the ritual walk sunwise trice around the well and a mass at the site of what became Capel Illtud. The next stage of the saint's round might well have been a perambulation along the Mynydd Illtud and onto the other side of the Wysg below Aberhonddu, to Tŷ Illtud with his nearby holy well and standing stone. The mark of a small cross carved on the inside of the saint's hermitage could have been an indication that the person had walked the complete pilgrimage of the major Illtud's church sites along the south coast, to end the round from his grave site to his heavenly house.

This kind of perambulation is still common in Ireland at many old pilgrim sites associated with its premier saints. At Cruach Patrick in Mayo, pilgrims in their hundreds still walk up the mountain barefooted on the evening before. At Glencolmcille in Donegal they walk around a series of standing stones and holy wells dedicated to Columba. It is still possible to see women praying and moving around the outside grotto at Lascannor Well in Clare on St Brigid's Day. They pick up a handful of small stones to mark one at the seven stations, or put it on the ground in front of them while reciting a short prayer. So it is not unreasonable to suggest that part of the cult to one of the most important of the early Welsh saints would have been an equally popular pilgrimage round. (Harbison, 1991)

An enigmatic Llywel stone

> It depicts a 'walking man' with a crooked staff walking away from a pyramid and an animal which looks like the Great Sphinx. Another pictogram shows a man crossing the sea.
>
> T. Breverton (1999)

Standing stones, according to popular folklore, were the playthings of giants or heroes like Arthur who littered the Welsh landscapes with the remains of his quoits. Saints, as in the case of the one named after the biblical giant Samson, were fond of tossing them around like ninepins. However, some stones were reputed to move on their own under the cover of darkness to go down to a stream for a drink. In the case of the so-called devil or dancing stones, they were thought to have been unfortunate people solidified for indulging in joyful play on the sabbath. More recently the standing stones with Christian crosses or the combination of Latin and Ogham inscriptions, often had holes bored into them as farm gate-posts before eventually ending inside nearby churches for safer keeping. Even the free-standing decorative high crosses placed on the south-western side of important ecclesiastical buildings have been moved. In fact the eleventh century St Brynach cross in Nanhyfer churchyard is probably one of the few still in situ. It seems that it was saved from the common fate by the length of its shaft inside the ground. Baronet Colt Hoare, who visited Nanhyfer in the late eighteenth century had workmen dig down for at least seven feet without reaching its base before filling in the hole again. When the decorated visible shaft is added to the unadorned part below ground, the original stone was nearly six metres in length. Such long columns of dolerite, like the bluestones at Stonehenge, were hewed from the outcrops that form the dominant visible aspect of the Preseli Hills in Sir Benfro.

The presently named Trecastell Stone from the edge of Bannau Brycheiniog was bought for the princely sum of ten pounds by the British Museum in 1882. It had not only moved since first recorded in the seventeenth century but it also had a frequent name change in the process. It may be the stone mentioned by Edward Lhuyd as at Capel y Fynwent, that turned up a century later at Pentre-Poeth farm near Capel Llanilltud. It was an old red sandstone oblong slab about 6 ft long and less than 2 ft wide that appeared to have been rubbed smooth prior to the carving of the inscriptions. The farmer thought its broad shape would make an excellent gate-post so he had it moved from the pile of stones that may have been an old cairn. The Rev. Lewis Price, vicar of the adjoining parish of Llywel, saw the stone by the side of the road and tried to prevail on the owner to allow him to have it in the church as he recognised that its carvings were important. He thought the rude attempts at a human figure might have significance beyond its association with the rest of the work that was obscured by lichen on the lower part of the stone.

It was more than a quarter of a century ago when I first came across this stone. I then lived in Covent Garden, a ten minute stroll from the British Museum where I spent far too much time in the domed central reading room. Still lined with books as a museum piece, it is now in the centre of the Great Court designed by Norman Foster, and spacious with bookshops and cafes. I often wandered around the museum itself which was constantly full of surprise revelations. This was long before the renovation of the main galleries, and the display of works had not the same educational brief that is so obvious at present. Scholars from different departments were readily available and seemed eager to talk about their specialities. There were also intimations of strange cultish events beyond its walls. There were secret meeting corners like one special section of the Egyptian galleries, or by the black obsidian Aztec mirror that Dr John Dee, the sixteenth century Welsh magus used in his scrying experiments. Such emotive places at special times, especially on a Wednesday afternoon, drew oddly dressed people who never needed to say much but their presence was usually sufficiently telling.

Meandering through the King Edward VII long gallery was not exactly off-limits, but felt like a private basement cluttered with the most diverse collection of sculptural works from all ages placed higgledy-piggledy in no special order. It was more like exploring a large monumental mason's yard than a public gallery. The single round cupmark in the centre of the broad face of the tall reddish pillar slab caught my eye. Since the small hollow was next to a line of large horizontal Latin lettering, I was immediately interested. A tiny cardboard notice informed me that it came from Trecastell in Wales and that an Ogham inscription of strokes had been carved on the right-hand side of the pillar. This was unusual as most ogham marks began at the bottom left and continued upwards, occasionally over the top of the stone. Translated into Old Irish – Maqutreni Saliciduni – as a commemoration of the same person as in the Latin. It was while looking closely at the incisions on the side of the stone that I poked my head around the back and noticed some deep incised lines and curves. The broad base of the pillar stood in a dull concrete base but was wedged into a corner. Pushing my head around the stone I realised the carvings were upside-down and trying to make sense of them was like seeing the Holy Grail. The excitement of any hidden knowledge was a powerful incentive then. I could just make out a distorted picture of what looked like mountains and rivers with funny men dancing or running between. Each time I went into the museum I would nip along to have another peep at it. I even talked to one of the keepers, who informed me that it was a late mediaeval Christian carving, hundreds of years after the sixth century inscriptions. He did not appear to be interested in my opinion that such an unique work could be equally if not more important than the inscriptions and should be allowed to be seen by the general public.

Eventually I managed to get a photographer along with me to visit the gallery. She was an old friend, and looking at my sketches, was as curious as myself about the carvings faced inward into a corner. The light was not that good but by shifting the plinth around a bit she was able to slip in behind and photograph it. Her prints contained all the details of the carving very clearly. I was so excited by this stone that I decided it should be reproduced in the forthcoming book I was working on. Its incised narrative and cupmark were probably much earlier than the Latin or ogham but it seemed to fit in with another Welsh visual and linguistic work I had noticed in the Sain Ffagan Folk Museum on the outskirts of Caerdydd. The *Y Wyddor* (The Alphabet) was a nineteenth century pictorial bilingual school hanging, that also had illustrations of the beth-luis-nion or Ogham alphabet, the Coelbren y Beirdd or the Welsh rune-type alphabet, and examples of lettering from early monumental stones in Wales. Eventually the London publisher had a professional photographer take a decent reproduction of the Trecastell Stone which was the final illustration in my *Celtic Mysteries*, one of the first reasonably priced large format paperbacks devoted to the subject. Before publication I wrote to the Keeper asking if they had any intention of removing the plinth and exhibiting this important Welsh carving in a manner that people could actually see and appreciate it, rather than tucked into the wall. I never received any answer. Over the years I kept track of the stone as it was moved from the ground floor to the Romano-British section on the first floor, and to other galleries where it was on its side propped up by the plinth at one end next to a large glass case, and then it was moved again. While writing this I paid a visit to the museum but found it wrapped in polythene and awaiting transportation to a new installation.

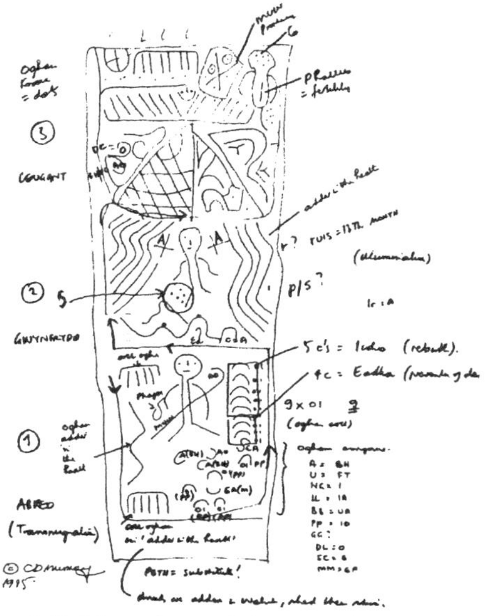

Colin Murray's ogamic interpretation of the Llywel pictogram (1985)

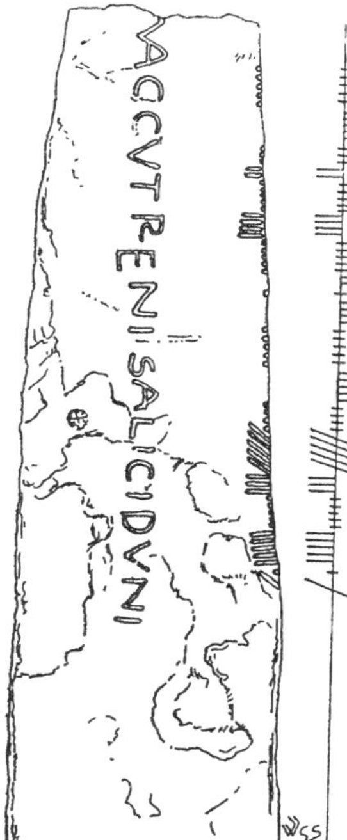

5th/6th century Latin and Ogham inscribed stone, Llywel, Powys (ECMW No. 71)

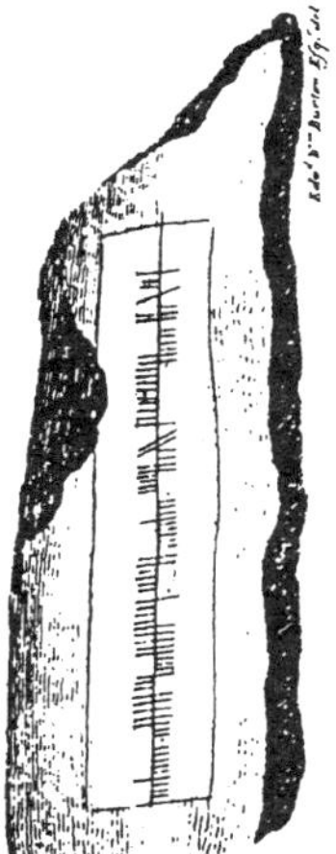

Ogham inscription, Mount Callan, Co. Clare by Theophilus O'Flanagan (1785)

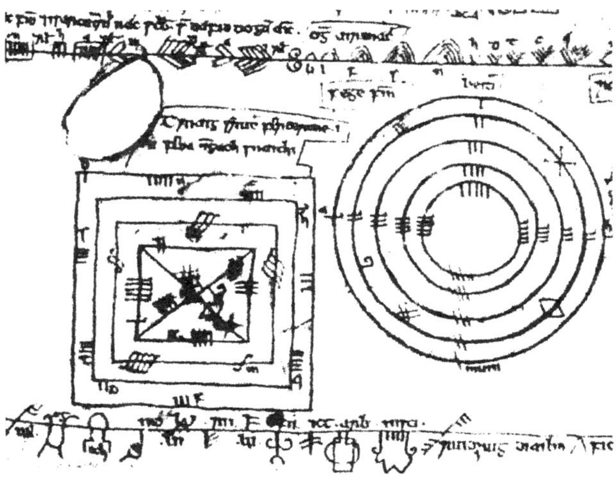

Fionn's Window, divinatory ogam from the Book of Ballymote, 14th century

Since then I find that the cover has been removed but it is still upside-down in its cleaned concrete plinth which hides the top of the work as seen from the floor up. The surface of the inscribed face of stone seems to be in a poor state with parts of the sandstone missing. Unlike the smooth plaster casts that were made in the 1950's and are on display in the church at Trecastell, in the Brecknock Museum in Aberhonddu and in the National Museum of Wales in Caerdydd. It may have looked better to the nineteenth century eye with the broad end as the base but reversing the stone now would not make much difference to ascertaining the actual inscriptions if one could read Latin or old Irish. The Llywel monument is unique. That name should be retained after its general findspot near Trecastell. It ought to have a pride of place in the Brecknock Museum rather than in London where, from my own observations, the recent history of its shift from pillar to post shows that it has not been appreciated or properly valued. Perhaps a campaign to have it returned to Wales would be in order!

A Rosetta Stone

The 2m long slab is incised with a cupmark, prehistoric motifs, and two quite different memorial inscriptions. The cup is a simple mnemonic outline, vaguely reminiscent of an object it may refer to but whose reference was clear to those who carved it. The symbolic value or meaning of such cupmarks would be available to others at that time. The carvings are ideographic, representing a story by pictures in three clearly delineated areas of the stone. I would suggest that this is a narrative device using three related ideograms. There is no doubt several meanings are involved if we could possibly interpret them. The ogham inscription is stylized. It uses regular groups of lines defined across the edge of the stone that allude precisely to a single letter. Each Irish letter has a given sound which is the hidden basis of this alphabet. Again there is a process of transposition, but one that now extends from a collection of definite cyphers to a word. The Latin inscription moves this a stage further by visually incorporating the phonemes or sounds of the written Latin language. Reading it as an unique stone, rather than a representative of a class of monuments, may provide insight into an ancient object of power with ritual or magical markings of different eras from four different cultural perspectives.

Formal inscriptions as memorials to the dead were common among the legions in Britain before AD 400. The plaques were carved horizontally in standard Roman lettering. The memorial style with

Three sections of the pictograph from the Llywel Stone, now in the British Museum, London

Roman glass dish, 1st c. AD, Boulogne, illustrating the sacrifice of Isaac with the Christian chi-rho *and pagan symbols of the sun and moon below. 'Tumbling down from heaven are clusters of berried rosettes thought to be symbols of an award from God' (after Kilbride)*

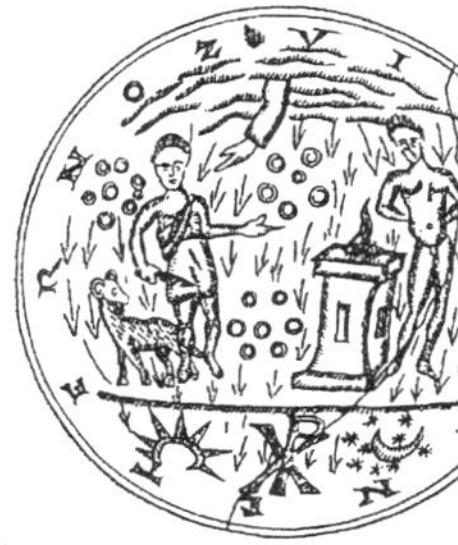

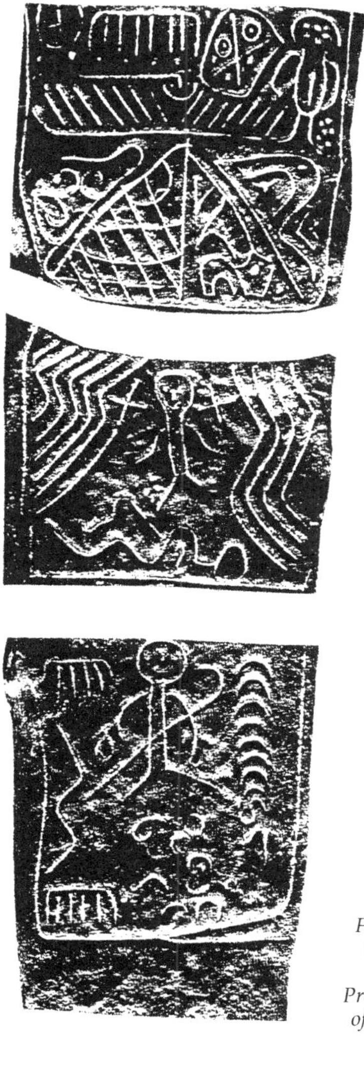

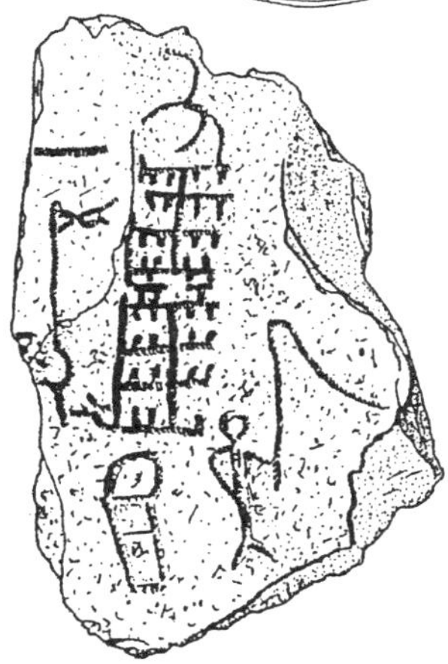

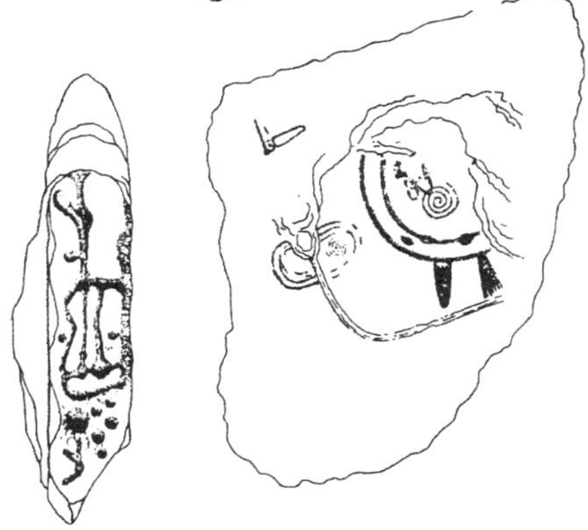

Fragment of slate decorated on both sides, Carreg Bank, Montgomeryshire (after Guilbert) centre

Prehistoric carvings on left side and front of stone B of the 6 Calderstones, Calderstone Park, Liverpool (after Cowell)

significant and regional modifications continued in use in Wales during the following centuries, and throughout the Early Christian period. By the end of the fifth or early sixth century, inscriptions to the dead on slabs or pillars were usually cut vertically along the length of the stone, and often included a formulaic prefix such as *HIC IACET* or *IACIT* (he or she lies here) followed by the name of the person or the parentage as 'x' son of 'y'. The prefix, like the first stroke of the initial 'M', may have broken off from the top of the stone. The two Latin words are in the genitive with an understood introductory word for the memorial stone of *MACCVTRENI* (Maccutrenus) and *SALICIDVNI* (Salicidunus). They are divided by a small cross to show the person was a Christian. Perhaps he was a priest of a noble family, or chief of a Christian community. At this period only those from the upper echelons of society would have been so honoured in stone. Wooden plaques on graves could have been the more plebeian form. The stone may also have indicated the boundary of land or territorial influence, for such permanent markers were usually so placed as *termini,* to use the old Roman word. The repetition of the name in ogham shows that Irish incomers into south-west Wales had moved across from Dyfed – where bilingual memorials are particularly numerous – into Brycheiniog where there are less than five examples. So this stone probably commemorates the local chief of an Irish Christian dynasty in Wales. Both Irish and Dyfed regal lines list rulers of the same or similar names, spanning many generations from the chiefs of the Deisi tribe who migrated there from Leinster. (Thomas, 1994)

Ogham in the nineteenth century was a lively intellectual topic among scholars and antiquarians in relation to uncovering the semantic links between it and the Latin inscriptions on British stones. Bishop Graves – grandfather of the poet Robert Graves – had published seminal papers showing that the cyphers carved on standing stones were based on the Old Irish. In fact the first publication was in 1784 by Theophilis O'Flanagan, written whilst still a student at Trinity College, Dublin. It was this same scholar two years later who listed the Selbright collection of Edward Lhuyd's manuscripts that had been given to the College library. O'Flanagan's claims for the inscription on Mount Callan in Co. Clare are still disputed, as the word-groups were separated by dots, as in the later mediaeval manuscripts, but unlike the stokes on the earlier monumental ogham stones. His suggestion that it marked the grave of Conan, a warrior of the Fianna, certainly made an impression in the gullible circles of Irish nationalistic scholarship. Curiously enough it also caused some local disturbances. One man had a dream that a legendary key was buried beneath it, which if recovered would open the door to a drowned city full of treasure, by the Atlantic Ocean. This was on a magic island in Liscannor Bay that was thought to have been sunk in an earthquake, but whose golden domes could be seen beneath the waves. It was reputed to rise to the surface every seven years, but those who saw it would never see its next appearance. The key would also magically green the boggy slopes of Mount Callan that rose above Lough Boolnagreine, the lake of the milking-place of the sun. However, in the scramble of diggings under the stone all that was found were bones and some old iron. (Westropp, 2000)

Irish tribal groups in Wales may have first used monumental ogham on burial stones, although there is a school of thought that it originated here or in Gaul and subsequently, along with the Latin upon which this sign language is based, was introduced by early British missionaries. Over 300 examples have been recorded, mainly in the south-west of Ireland, but none have any accompanying Latin on the stones. The language is the earliest known form of Gaelic although with the demise of ogham cyphers on memorial stones in the eighth century, it was already archaic.

The alphabetic order, or *aicme* of four groups (three consonants and one vowel group) of five strokes or staves across the edge of a stemline, with a later group of five symbols for the diphthongs that were known as the extra letters, had not been forgotten. In the Middle Ages scholastic ogham was used on stones in Pictland, and in the fourteenth century *Book of Ballymote* there are two important texts showing numerous forms of oghams. There is no doubt of its continued use in the mediaeval bardic schools of Ireland, nor of its extensive modern scholarship in linguistics and epigraphy. Yet the interest in Ogham as a form of divination and even as the basis of early ethnic music relates back to its magical and incantational uses in the Irish literary tradition.

It is attributed to the divine Ogma – one of the gods of the Tuatha De Danann – who is said to have invented it as proof of his ingenuity, so that speech would belong with the learned. This would be to the exclusion of rustics and herdsmen! The first magical engraving on wood was the seven strokes cut on a birch rod. In the Beth-Luis-Nion tree-alphabet, the letter B for bethe (birch) is also the initial letter of the first set of five consonants, known as *Aicme Beithe*, and written in ogham as a straight cut to the right of the stem line. Seven such straight marks on one switch of birch would have had little resonance unless intelligible to the initiated with a knowledge of ancient magical practices. The hero Cuchulainn used a spancel or hoop to carve an ogham and his adversary Fergus could read it letter for letter – like you or I – yet he had to ask the druids to interpret its challenge. In another tale a druid found the hiding place of Etain by cutting four sides of a yew wand and making an ogham on each which were then known as the keys of divination. The translations of this form of Irish writing, known as word-oghams were related to early forms of poetry, particularly keening. That such magical and divinatory forms were intrinsically retained throughout its later use is apparent in the complete lack of verbs to be found on any of the monumental stones, and that in the mediaeval treatises known as the *Auraicept* or *Primer* and the *Ogam Tract* there is not even a simple sentence written in ogham. (O'Boyle, 1980)

The two symbols of the circle and cross carved almost next to each other are like time locks that may hold metaphysical keys to the Llywel stone. Both were exotics of their time with a simplicity that belies their universal significance as *memento mori*, remembering death and that you must die. It is possible that the Llywel stone with its cupmark originally came from a ritual interment. In fact according to one account, the stone was first noticed by the vicar of Llywel after it had been moved from a heap of stones of a nearby cairn. (Browne, 1917)

The Christian cross first appeared in Britain as the chi rho monogram, and by the sixth century variations of this form have been found stamped on imported glass and wine ware providing divine protection and a recognizable symbol of the holy sacrament. As an indication of the spread of the new religion here it has been found carved on stone slabs along the western hinterlands in Cornwall, Wales and Galloway in western Scotland. Based on the earlier Greek and Latin prototypes, that had come into general use after the Constantine edict in the fourth century, the simplified wheel-cross and the equal-armed cross were carved on large memorial stones, underlying the importance of Christianity to local leaders and their peoples across southern Wales. The former cross can be seen above the Latin and Ogham inscription to Votipor on the Castell Dwyran Stone. It is exceptional due to its close date range in the middle of the sixth century, at a time when Gildas denounced this Demetian king. He was designated on the stone in Latin as Protector, after the old Roman style. An example of the latter cross is on the Llywel stone between the two Latin names, significantly larger but still in proportion to the carved style of Roman lettering, perhaps even as an attempt to Christianize a pagan stone. The few such examples of carved crosses on inscribed stones that have survived from this early phase of Christianity are quite different from each other, but all exhibit a simplicity that is lacking in the more ornate styles on Welsh crosses of the following centuries.

A National Museum publication shows both sides of its cast with the carving right way up. The caption describes it as the enigmatic Trecastell Stone that once stood in the graveyard of the former Capel Ilid, Cwm Crai in Powys. It says that after it was reset, the plain face was inscribed with pictographs to be interpreted as Christian doctrines and scenes. It essentially repeats what Nash-Williams wrote in 1950, and neither explain why this pillar should have been placed upside-down in a graveyard in order to carve the other face. Nor does it explain who then reversed the stone and set it into its present plinth. (Rednapp, 1991)

The Pictographs

In a 1957 BBC radio tribute after the death of Nash-Williams, Mortimer Wheeler referred to his former student, colleague at the National Museum and fellow excavator at Caerleon as the author of a classified list of more than four hundred memorial stones in all parts of Wales and dated between the sixth and eleventh centuries. He also admitted that he himself enjoyed walking through the hills speculating on why the ancient stones were so situated, as some can still be found, although he does admit that he was the scoundrel who moved many to their final resting place in the Caerdydd museum. He then remarks that the other never took time off from his industrious task to dwell upon the niceties of their situation or environment. So I suppose it should be of no great surprise to read, that while admitting the distinctive style of decoration on the carving of the Trecastell stone was unique, the author of the standard work on the Early Christian monuments then indulges in a most convoluted wordy explanation to account for it. He finds its closest analogies are in the megalithic art of Ireland, on the monuments of Brittany and the Atlantic sea-board regions. However, this decoration somehow became intermixed with some figurative elements of Romano-Celtic popular art, that was then reintroduced into Wales twenty-odd centuries later in a Christian context. And by returning emigrants from Brittany! Furthermore this single unique monument may reflect a backwash of Breton and Gallo-Roman art into Wales, of what he terms 'unsophisticated incised decoration'. Hedging his bets, he even suggests that alternatively the art may have been introduced from Ireland, but that in either case the reuse of the stone followed at no great interval after its original erection. (Nash-Williams, 1950)

I am not conversant with the Gallo-Roman art he mentions, but in relation to the megalithic motifs from Ireland and a small group of tenth century cross-slabs done in the low art style that he refers to, it is hard to find similarities between the Llywel and other carvings that have survived. Nevertheless modern archaeologists generally accept it as from a late Christian period, based on the graffiti crosses that may be represented on the top two panels and the crosier in the lower one. Yet needless to say the cross is an ancient symbol with many meanings representing the sun, fire, and the four elements or four directions for many peoples, prior to it becoming the holy symbolic sign of the early Christian church. In fact the design next to the top figure enclosing a cross, dots and dots in circles can be duplicated on a stone in the Loughcrew megalithic cemetery in Ireland, and the crosier or hook are the dominant carved symbols inside the Gavrinis monument in Brittany.

Earlier historians of the prehistoric such as Samuel Ferguson, J.O. Westwood, John Rhys, Macalister and others have all grappled with the possible meanings of the pictographs. They attempted to present the seen – visible marks on the stone – in relation to the unknown meanings they surmised which were depicted by the carver. They each attempted different narratives in an attempt to fit the graphic details into a coherent single story. Their explanations were never finite and usually incorporated some previous readings, with a cognizance that their ideas might clarify or spark others after them to come closer to a passable rendition.

Westwood seems to have been the first to tackle some of the problems of interpretation. Indeed he, like others after him and myself above, thought the design was unlike anything he had seen on Anglo-Saxon, Celtic and Irish stones or monuments. He pinpointed a St Andrews Cross with circles beside a figure of a man or bird in the top right-hand corner, but that the other figures were partly defaced. He based this on the rubbings and drawings sent to him and to John Rhys by G.E. Robinson, who published the first (1878) account of it in *Archaeologia Cambrensis.* Rhys later visited the stone and by uncovering the lichen translated the Latin inscription.

Sir Samuel Ferguson in his lectures five years later noted that it had four panels and that the figure at the top had a shield with the St Andrew's Cross on it. The centre figure with a cross on either side appeared to be trampling on a serpent. He thought this compared with the one on the Chwitffordd free-standing cross, near Prestatyn. Maen Achwyfan, or the Stone of Lamentations has a large front panel with spiral loops surrounding an animal-headed figure that holds a spear in one hand and a writhing serpent in the other. Another small figure on one of the sides has what may be a rod behind it. In the lower panel Ferguson suggested the figure portrayed a bishop with a pastoral staff, but the crescents and other decorations around it seemed to have affinities with carvings on Irish megalithic monuments. More radically, he thought that the lunettes of the crescent device next to the bottom figure were three ogham vowels – O I U – representing the mystery of the Holy Trinity and the Divine Name of God. Also in the second panel he saw a tri-radial device – the bardic symbol of the Trinity – reminding him of the mystical ideas of Dafydd Nanmor, who was a fifteenth century Welsh bard who maintained that three divine rays symbolised the name and existence of God. Therefore the intermingling of survivals from pagan art with Christian symbolism suggested to Ferguson that the monument was carved at the very earliest age of Christianity in Britain.

Bishop Forest Browne in 1891 first took up the Ogham connection with the pictorial features on the stone but by 1916, in a popular lecture, he had reformed the basis of his exposition in terms of a warrior saint in ancient Wales. He thought that the small shield on the left was that of his youth, representing his life as a warrior. The grave with a mound of earth (the comb-like device) covered the bodies of pagans he had killed. He was then engaged in two battles and each time killed a large number of unburied pagans (two sets of seven oblique lines). Next he flings down six stones in order that he will win by spiritual means, hence his shield with the emblem of the Christian faith. Below this is a pagan temple with, from left to right – the ornamental temple posts, the tiled roof with ventilation (half-circle), a cat, and the folds of a curtain. Immediately below it the warrior is emerging from the entrance having rent the curtains (curvilinear lines) by the power of the cross. An idol lies at his feet. The bottom panel shows him as a missionary bishop carrying the crosier and the offertory bag on one of his journeys. The scenes in the three panels set out for Forest Browne the three important characteristics of the Welsh people – courage, high spirits and success!

Bird Allen published his comments of the Bishop's lecture in the same volume of *Archaeologica Cambrensis*. He accepted the division of the panels, with the figure on top as a warrior with two shields. However on the right, his hair has been cut as part of a Gnostic initiation ceremony, then drops to the ground as six dots. The oblique lines represent the altar. Below it is the temple with its network of ropes holding the roof, but the animal is a lizard rather than a cat, as it had some esoteric significance among the Gnostics. The warrior then leaves the sacred tabernacle. Before him is a serpent, that Bird Allen suggests was a symbol of a safe soul journey. In the bottom panel he is now a wandering fakir with a staff and a wallet or gourd bottle. He also saw significance in the crescent lunettes and curved lines that he added up to thirty, which was a mystical Gnostic number.

Both were new departures graphically using the idiomatic possibilities of the carving. Bishop Browne's is a bit thin without quite pulling it all together, and Bird Allen's mystical overtones are a caricature of Gnostic writings, especially since the Nag Hammadi hoard of sacred texts, discovered in 1945, have recently been translated and published. (Robinson, 1981).

Yet I like their approach, as the panels are carved in a linear narrative fashion and clearly tell a story. However, I would prefer to add some historical and local flavour in a slightly different context. It involves an early saint like Brynach, who was the soul-friend to Brychan the king of Brycheiniog, recounting in his old age the tale of his spiritual journey. He had married one of the king's daughters but decided on the holy life of the peregrinini rather than the court. On his long pilgrimage to the Holy Land he slayed a noxious beast near Rome. After his return to Brittany, he sat for three days on a stone by the sea-shore waiting for a boat to take him home. However the stone miraculously floated across the sea to Wales and landed at Aberdaugleddau (Haverfordwest). When he rebuffed the attentions of a woman, he was stabbed by a warrior who was in turn killed by a swarm of winged ants issuing from the wound. The spring that washed his blood henceforth turned red and was known by that name. Some of the folk narratives around the life of Brynach, with a stretch of the imagination, could be applicable to the triple set of pictograms carved on the Llywel stone.

A biblical exegesis of it was put forward by R.A.S. Macalister in his 1945 work on the inscriptions of Britain and Ireland. Below the man with his shield was a ship containing an animal which suggested Noah's Ark. In the centre, the man between the waves was perhaps a reference to Moses with the parting of the Red Sea and the snake to the earlier Miracle of the Serpent. The sheep at the bottom might be David's flock and the series of C's on his left could mean anything or nothing. At the completion of an address to the Cambrian Association, the President, having set out some of the explanations above, said that the theme of the carvings was the Christian doctrine of the Holy Trinity and that it could be dated to the ninth or tenth century when there was a revival of interest in Wales. (Jones-Davies, 1974)

For him the two inscribed circles in the upper panel were 'the greater and lesser lights' with the seven rays emanating from them. On the top right-hand corner was God the Father. The dots on his face and foot – eyes before and behind – were his omniscience and the phallus in his creative power. The divisions of the panel show the two aspects of creation – the fauna and creatures of the earth with the dome of heaven – rising above the waters of the Flood. God the Son who had come down from Heaven was the figure in the centre panel, with the cross that would redeem mankind and the serpent of evil crushed below his feet. At the bottom was God the Holy Spirit, calling and leading his flock. Seven lunettes – 'the Spirit blowing where it listeth' – and finally the two inverted combs, representing the outpourings of the Spirit (page 111).

On a simpler, more symbolic level the carvings could represent the wanderings of a soul/hero through the three realms of human consciousness, known in Welsh as abred, gwynedd and ceugant. Like the Triads whose concise formulations transcended ordinary speech, this stone could have been a visual transliteration of our life journey within the trinity of earth, water and air. It was a totality often represented as three concentric circles. The innermost circle of abred, seen here as the top panel, is a stage of evolution when life formed from annwn and in the lower half, is the struggle with cythrawl, which represented destruction and blackness. The second panel of gwynedd has life as pure force triumphant over evil. The final panel, as the outermost circle of divergent rays, shows a cosmic affirmation with the godhead. (Murray, 1988)

Trying to condense Iolo Morganwg's bardic cosmology, in terms of the Trinity of creation – 'through every form capable of life, in water, in earth, and in air' – brings up a strange and unwelcome thought. One that leads to a suggestion which certainly should not be put into words, namely that the poet himself may have carved this stone. It is certainly within the bounds of possibility, as Edward Wiliams (1747-1826) claimed to have learned to read from watching his father cutting inscriptions on gravestones. The poet lived at Trefflemin a small village near Y Bont-Faen in Morgannwg and supported himself as a journeyman stonemason while travelling through Wales in search of ancient manuscripts and even walking to London where he was known as The Bard. In his old age, when given a horse he declared that it was more dignified to walk with it rather than sit on top of the animal.

The stone appears to have been first noted by Rev. Lewis Price the vicar of Llywel at Pantycadno, as it was about to be set up as a gatepost to Pentrepoeth farm. He asked the farmer Thomas Price if he would accept an oak post in exchange as the stone should be placed in the church. It then seemed to have been moved to or even returned to its original site at Capel Ilid, less than a mile away, where it was noted as standing in the churchyard in 1870. Thomas Price however appears to have been what we might now term a stone freak and had many interesting stones, fine walls and culverts built on the land surrounding his house at Ty'r Capel. It was next to the old Capel Ilid site which by then was covered by turf, and most of the stones used for extending the house. Made aware of its possible value, his son, a medical student in London, probably arranged its sale. The British Museum recorded the purchase on the 11th February 1878 for ten pounds. Nothing more locally is known about the stone and if it had not been for the lively exchanges published in *Archaeologia Cambrensis*, it would probably have remained so.

Leaving aside its many varied interpretations, most scholars agreed that the actual carving and the figuration on the Llywel stone did not appear to have any common antecedents either in ancient or late mediaeval art. Unless there is an agreed visual or literary context, it is impossible to date concisely any carving on stone and this particular example could have been done at any period up to the late nineteenth century, when it was first noticed by Rev. Lewis Price, vicar of the nearby parish of Llywel. It would certainly be gesture of supreme irony if the writer who conceived, nourished and brought into being the Gorsedd y Beirdd Ynys Prydain – which is now the central ritual of the modern Eisteddfod – had carved a cartoon of his mystic philosophy on the back of an ancient inscribed stone. A work that has been standing upside down for over a century in the British Museum!

The Blaenawen figure

> How Dreadful is this Place . . . And he took the stone that had been his pillow and set it up as a monument and poured oil on top of it.
>
> Genesis

The immediate locality of the find-spot was by an ancient track through an area of wild flowers, old buildings and fields that sloped down to a stream. A shallow ford was a recent addition but the smooth stone sluices, and a rusted flywheel in the water indicated that the ruined farmhouse had sometime been a mill. The stream carried on through Trewyddel and into the sea at Ceibwr some miles away. A small rocky bay at the beginning of the coastal path is not far from the deep natural hollow of a collapsed cave known as Pwll y Wrach (the Witches Cauldron). This was perhaps alluded to in an episode from Culhwch and Olwen in which King Arthur's ship *Prydwen* landed here carrying the treasure of Ireland as 'in there is the measure of the cauldron'.

Not too far from the house, the track was a peaceful place to walk in the late afternoon, if there were no curious bullocks about. Regularly and at a particular spot midway along it I often had a feeling of presence, almost as if something ethereally interesting was about to happen. The area ahead looked picturesque with ruined farm buildings surrounded by trees. But as soon as I went further down the path towards the holdings, that had not been farmed for almost seventy years, the odd sensing would vanish. It had happened so often that I became convinced that there was something special hidden among the ruins. The largest one further upstream was roofless. Parts of its massive stone walls were lost amid overgrown laurel trunks. It may originally have been a manor house, but with rooms added, built in different ways at different times. A large ornate fireplace had its collapsed ingle-nook wide open to the sky. Rows of stone dog kennels and pigsties stood out amid the rubble. A carving of a small intersected or daisy circle had been made on an oak door lintel. These ritual or apotropaic marks, common from the sixteenth century onwards, were not decorative but intended for the spiritual protection of a house or building. In 1594 George Owen of Henllys had listed four messuage – occupied land with a dwelling house – at Llanawan, or Blaenawen, with yearly rents of 2s. 5d., 18d., 9d. and 8d, under the Manor of Trewyddel. From the entries in his rent-book, it is reasonable to suggest that this ruin was the larger rental and one of the smaller may have been the mill. Its secluded position, built on a raised terrace above the bend of a stream and with possibly a nearby church – indicated by the original prefix 'Llan' – is similar to that of the Iron-Age homestead at Castell Henllys, which is above a stream near Meline church and about eight miles away.

The old track was a popular walk on dry Sunday afternoons for local people. In fact I had mapped out a hard-packed ancient path around the small fields with occasional herring-bone patterned walls. It crossed the stream and went by the other bank up to the church at Eglwys Wythwr (Monington) where there is also the remains of an old mill. Regularly used in the pre-motor age, the path may even have been part of a earlier drove route from the well water at Têg y Pistyll with its three tall pine trees (one still stands) down the valley floor and up to the top of the hill to the next available water and grazing. This would have been a normal day's march for the drovers with their cattle, sheep, ducks, geese and dogs.

After one incredibly wet week in January, it was still raining heavy on the Sunday morning. Our house was so full of children and visitors downstairs at breakfast that I was reluctant to get out of bed. Eventually, in a kind of inner turmoil I quickly dressed, ignored everyone. I pulled on my wellies and went for a walk down the track without even bothering to put on a waterproof, sloshing through the mud to eventually reach the spot where I usually hesitated. The rain and sleet meant I could not go forward but as I turned away, pulling boots out of the mud, I saw what at first looked like a pair of wet eyes staring above the ground beyond the track. The front of a prone stone post had been washed away, revealing round carved markings. I was instantly aware that it must have been this that had beckoned me so many times when standing in line with it. After digging the mud away a little I saw that a round face was actually carved on it.

Moments like that make me aware that there is no good reason to limit awareness of time to a storybook simplicity, or to ignore odd occurrences that do not immediately fit neat rationalizations. To chat to gravestones and crosses is not so unusual if you spend a lot of time in churchyards. But that such stones can, and do talk back is harder to accept. It is as equally quaint and otherworldly to attempt to talk or listen to trees! It requires we enter differential time zones. A parallel universe that slows down our hectic blood-pace so that we may attend to the language a stone mumbles into its lichen. But to take such messages in good faith and even act upon them, is often termed mentally borderline in hospitalised situations.

Later that day, after the rain ceased and the sun began to shine, we trooped down the track to look at the stone. They were all mildly surprised that what I had earlier frantically described was actually in the ground. We dug away the mud from its front and the first photographs show the sequence of its emergence that day. In the progress of unearthing the carved pillar stone the face had been strange enough but the lower incised carvings suggesting a whole body was even more exciting especially with a small equal-sided cross carved at the neck.

During the next few weeks I was in a dilemma as to what I should do with such an extraordinary find. My first instinct was to leave the pillar in the mud where it lay. Yet to make its presence known to the archaeological world and perhaps have it end up in a museum of all places! Friends thought the latter notion unlikely and since it appeared as if I was chosen by the stone itself then others should be given an opportunity to see it. The owner, Mr Edwards was sympathetic when I explained that if I wrote a report of the finding, it was likely that others would visit and want to walk over his land. He told me to do what I thought was worthwhile, adding that his grandfather not only knew about the stone but had put it up as a gate post when he was a child. It had in all probability fallen over ages ago for its companion was still standing nearby. However he did not appear to realise the significance of the carving and I thought it best to write a note to him, confirming our conversation. I did not want any neighbourly disputes to arise in an area where everyone seemed to be related to each other. About a week later on St Non's Day I had a visit from Canon Cinnane of St Mary's Catholic church in Aberteifi. Waving my letter, he said that his parishioner had asked him to look at the find and he had brought along a tall man called Ken Murphy, who said he was an archaeologist. I was quite flabbergasted at this turn of events, but concerned that the priest's shoes would get too muddy. 'Nonsense' was his reply and with his black outfit flapping in the wind we followed him down the track. I had no idea who he was but realised there must be a Catholic enclave in this strong chapel area of northern Penfro. As we got over the gate, Murphy informed me that the one in front was a bit of an expert on the Norman buildings of Aberteifi. The three of us stood around the stone as in a meditation without saying much. In fact, all I can remember now was his comment that the stone probably lay at the bottom of a nearby pool. Its image would be clearer for people standing on it during baptism, which was the most important ritual of the early church. It was the first of many curious responses from people, young and old, on their reactions to the Blaenawen Stone.

The next time I saw the priest was during a field outing of the CBA Group 2 Wales, when archaeologists were visiting Aberteifi and late in the afternoon came to see the carved stone. In the meantime I had written a short report on the finding for *Archaeology in Wales*. A group of us had lifted the stone to ascertain if any other carving was present apart from on the broad flat surface, which was 90cm long x 34cm at its widest. No other decoration was found on it or on any of the many other stones in the neighbourhood. The 1.2m long wedge-shaped block of Preseli dolerite was carefully propped up in the shelter of an oak tree close to the findspot. Its growing roots had pushed it over where it once stood as a gate-post. I had begun a series of rubbings on paper that helped to unlock its layers of possible meanings. It also provided the impetus to check out the carvings on the many stone crosses locally. Ken Murphy, who also had made a rubbing of the stone, had suggested that it was similar to other *orans* or praying figures in Wales and Ireland. This is a form of arms raised above the head in an attitude of prayer, that was common form in the early Celtic church. However, when I looked into this I found that apart from a few matchstick type carvings, the Welsh corpus had no illustrations that remotely resembled the Blaenawen figure. (Nash-Williams, 1950)

I also spent time in exploring the area more thoroughly and cleared the brambles from a low-lying ruin on the other side of the track. I thought it may have been an early chapel, as it was similar in size and positioned by a well, similar to the ruined early 'llan' site at Cilsant in Sir Gaerfyrddin, that had a known saintly dedication and a holy well that flowed across the farmyard.

On the afternoon in question, with local historian Jack Arnell and photographer Micky Baines, who had given them a talk earlier on the use of stone gate-posts as marking possible sacred routes across the Preseli Hills, we waited for words of wisdom from the assembled archaeologists. No one said much about the carving. They stood about and a few commented on the state of the stone. As the non-professionals, we respectfully waited for their opinions. However, the priest stepped forward saying 'John tell us about the stone and what the carving means'. I was fairly dumbfounded. To tell experts from all parts of Wales what it meant, when I had been eagerly awaiting enlightenment from them! Not only of its meanings but how we should read it. I probably then spoke about finding the stone and even attempted to explain the relationships between its different parts and the possible contexts as to its age and provenance. Blaenawen is about five miles equidistant from two important ecclesiastical centres. These are Llandudoch Abbey, south of the Teifi estuary, and St Brynach's at Nanhyfer. Together, the church and St Dogmael house an interesting collection of Early Christian carved stones. Two in particular bear some resemblance to the motifs of the Blaenawen figure. They are the Marion Fawr stone with its heraldic quality, which then stood against the south wall of the Abbey refectory and the knotted-type stone cross that is thought to date from the ninth century and cemented into the sill of the chancel window of Nanhyfer church.

Afterwards we retired up to the house for tea. Perhaps it was the wine or a jocular reply, but one well known archaeologist when asked what he thought about the stone suggested that I had carved it. As far as he knew there was nothing resembling it in Wales and that the most likely explanation was that with friends, we had faked the carving. It was after the main party had left that his comments were repeated in the general chat about what we had learned from them. It was a salutary experience to realise that they probably knew as little about it as myself, and one that strengthened my resolve to follow through with the research that I had begun. Photographs, however good, can never reproduce all the cracks and blemishes on a stone's surface, that do appear on a cloth or paper rubbing. It provides an useful record in order to examine the totality and complexity of the actual outlines of a carving. Textures of a stone with any accompanying fragmentations, abrasions and weathering marks can be recorded directly in a manner that is almost impossible to appreciate in a photograph. So as well as the actual dimensions of the design relative to the overall slab, one can examine the style of carving, any minute changes occurring in design patterns and even perhaps even identify a local workshop where mediaeval carvings were made. (Sharkey, 1998)

This gave me the strength to carry on with the slow accumulative processes of insight that had begun when the stone beckoned me in the mud and rain. However negative the professional reaction was at that time, it made me value the thoughts and responses of those who came to visit the stone. Not only friends and local people who seemed to know and be proud of it but many artists, musicians and healers from elsewhere who divined the most extraordinary meanings from the figure. It was as if they related to the stone in their own special ways, and consequently they all had quite different interpretations. They also enjoyed the location, which was in many ways a natural garden with its wild orchids, and especially the benign atmosphere of the area that had not been worked over for more than a half-century. Since I was usually at hand to hear what they said about the stone, it seemed that during the early years since its emergence it had become an unique transcendent medium. One child appeared to be talking to someone invisible to the rest of us, but according to her there was a man behind the stone. Jack, who was a musician, seemed to have a special relationship with it. In one curious dream he walked down the track bathed in uncanny light towards a tall shining being who informed him he was the guardian of the stone. In fact his figure was in the actual carving, but he could not see it. This reminded me of the statement, that the world we see is not the world we see but a reflection of what we believe we see. Such stories helped to envelope the transpersonal reputation the stone was acquiring. My own sense of it was that somehow it was a healing stone. Whilst researching the old folklore connected with megalithic structures in the Outer Hebridian islands during the early 1980's, I had experienced a phenomena between a local healer and the particular standing stones that she could mysteriously contact to help people with all kinds of complaints. She explained that the healing was in the stone, which she could call upon only if asked. But the Blaenawen pillar was not just a cure-all for aches and pains, but in a significant manner made those who were aware of it whole again. It brought into focus that within each of us a dimension exists to help absolve our own acute pain and mental stress.

The Figure in the Stone

The upper part of the carving had a clear outline that was unfortunately lacking on the weathered lower end. The top seems to have been dished by a fraction of the centimetre prior to the chiselling of the face. This is a common method in classical art, in order to create an impression of height especially when a sculpture is destined to be placed above eye level. The bottom of the stone did not appear to have been broken off and so the carving on its broad surface seemed complete. Perhaps the wedge-shaped dolerite block may have been chosen especially for a niche, or in a corner of a building. The slight shift in the vertical axis of the figure, following a down curve on its flattish incised surface, indicates that the carver was also aware of the limitations of the chosen medium. Otherwise the figure would have appeared stiff and awkward in contrast to the elegance achieved. This is a pose that is more apparent on rubbings than from photographs, although this effect was best seen in situ when the stone was wet or catching the rays of the setting sun. Close examination revealed natural cracks that extended some of the original incised lines and that some had been utilized in a formal manner, incorporated into and shaping the figure. The small equal-armed Latin cross carved between the head and torso appears to have been boxed-in by such a natural fissure.

It is possible that the ornate grooves now distinguishing the face had widened over the course of time, the edges gradually flattening and becoming rounder to lose their once sharp quality. So what we now see as circular rings representing eyes and curving tendrils giving a dimensional aspect, may have been more stylized. There is a trace of ornamental scrollwork on the lower left side of the stone. Such ornament may have been extensive, even up to and perhaps inside the deeply incised oval line, making the head seem less stark than it does at present. As well as the obvious break at its topmost point, the large curve has at least four smaller protruding nicks. Such embellishment would certainly produce a different reading of the figure and perhaps a closer approximation in dating it.

It is the stark image of the head, the better preserved area of the carving, that instantly draws one towards considering the figure as representing a pagan god or even a Christianized deity. Its rounded eyes, tendril brows and the curving moustache in the Celtic manner over a long mouth, brings to mind some of the sculptured heads from the Le Tène period. Making allowances for the differences between cartoon and three-dimensional or relief art, it has a strong formal resemblance to a head from Mseake Zehrevine near Prague, dated to between third and second century BC. The wide staring eyes, nose and curving moustache were uniformly carved almost in relief on the broad smooth face, topped by short curls. The neck torc was a regular motif of continental Celtic art, indicative as a status of nobility as well as a symbol of divinity. Perhaps the carving of the small cross on the neck of the Welsh figure may equally indicate a divine and religious function, even as a comparable symbolic characteristic of early Christian society prior to the arrival of the Normans. In relation to this pronounced featuring of the head, as well as other shared aspects as in figurative emphasis and exaggeration, it has been suggested that the observer of such an image would be reminded that the potency of the god is linked to a specific part of the body, from which his power emanates. (Green, 1989)

The peculiar shaped marking at the top of the head, above the hollow in the brow may, as a Buddhist top-knot, emphasize godlike attributes.

Equally the large cut at the apex of the oval curve might have represented the phallus. Perhaps what we have here is a visible emblem of power, of virility and of divine protection.

The overall composition is divided almost in two equal parts by a horizontal incision across the mid-section of the figure. Below it is an x-rayed or outlined rectangular torso and its straight legs appear to rise from a cauldron, or stand in a boat. They are both represented by the double curve at the bottom with inverted terminals. Some terminals are still quite preserved and suggest zoomorphic ornament of a kind common to many forms of insular art, particular manuscript illustration. The use of such literary motifs on metalwork is usually indicative of a more plastic approach to the medium and subsequent stylization on stone consistent with a late, rather than an early date of Christian carving. (Young, 1990)

The terminal edges on the mid-horizontal line help to maintain an overall sense of symmetry by being fractionally wider than the broad oval curve at the top. It is only when one begins to actually measure the linear divisions with their clear outlines, and see a conceptual design in the carving that the figure can begin to be appreciated as a work of art. It is such exoteric considerations as well as the esoteric symbolism that can be read into the figure which makes it such an unique carving from pre-Norman Wales and perhaps even wider afield. A comparative pillarstone from the Scottish Borders, of a large incised figure with arms raised in a venerable attitude of prayer gives one some scope in this regard. The rather cartoon-like outline of the orans is equally evident in the eroded relief on a pillarcross at St Buryon's in Cornwall. Both are dated to later than the eight century AD. (Seaborne, 1989)

Within the rounded head of the Scottish figure, the eyes and nose have been formed into a square Tao-type cross that stands out in slight relief. A small cross above it may be a later addition as other graffiti is also present. There is another linear cross above what appears to be two small circles with centre dots, probably representing a loin-cloth tied on either side of the waist. The figure is considered to have commemorated a well-known hermit from Over Kirkhope in the Etterick Hills. If such a populist commemoration can be applied to the Blaenawen figure then perhaps it could have been Brynach Wyddel, the Irishman. He was portrayed in the eleventh century as the soul friend of Brychan, eponymous king of Brycheiniog. Sir Benfro folk traditions associated Brynach with many church and well dedications. The suggestion of the figure standing in a boat or rising from a cauldron can be related to miraculous events in his life. Even the wedge or boat-shaped stone itself may represent the one he crossed the sea on to land at Aberdaugleddau. The most well known topographical connection is the hill outside Trefdraeth known as Carn Ingli. The saint is said to have fasted on the summit and talked with celestial beings, so perhaps what we are dealing with here is an early saintly bishop in the Patrick tradition. The late Jeremy Knight of Cadw suggested, in a personal correspondence, that the figure may have represented a priestly bishop. Taking into account the weathering and ambiguity of the carving he thought a possible interpretation of the central part of the stone, was of a bishop clothed in vestments as an *orans* figure symbolically praying with burning fingertips.

The fiery tendrils curving up at each end of the mid-horizontal line may be visual references to this central episode in the story of Brynach. Angels told him to follow a white pregnant sow and wherever it gave birth to build his church. Nanhyfer eventually become the most important church in the mediaeval cantref of Cemaes. So perhaps it is not an exaggeration to view the carving of the Blaenawen stone as portraying a local saintly hero as an intermediate between the earthly and the celestial realms. It is a symbolic equilibrium of opposing forces and principles adhering to the older pagan oracular tradition and newer Christian religious observances. The small cross between head and body may have indicated the path of transcendence between the two. Its prominent inclusion in this figurative representation may have been associated with local tradition that has come down to us by way of Dewi Sant himself carrying the large decorated churchyard cross to Nevern. He was on his way to preach against Palaganism at the synod of Llanddewibrefi, so here again we have a meshing of both Irish and British popular hagiography.

The Hidden Face

voices in the wind
the saint in the lifeless stone
the face was his epitaph
look into the lifeless eyes
feel its curling overbrows
stroke its hard.facial hair
hanging mouth bloodless lips
the voices in the stone
travelled the known world

prayed at the Mount of Skulls
overcame a noxious beast
from Rome walked over Gaul
sailed on the wind to Cornwall
on a stone crossed Milfordhaven
beached on the Cleddau
voices clamouring in the heart
she was a chief's daughter
offering a love potion of wolfbane
the animal within repulsed her
maimed by a warrior's spear
who died in a winged ants swarm
water fell from the open wound
that coloured and named it well
fons rubeus ffynnon goch,
a healing miracle from the earth
a sign of the journey ahead
voices in the wind voices
in the silence of the stone
its memory etched in place-names
Llanboidy-church of the cowhouse
Cilmaenllwyd-cell of the greystone
Llanfrynach-enclosure by a spring
Pontfaen-flowing over howlings
Brynhellion-dismantled nightly
Carningli-heaven heard voices
wandering in the wilderness
calling the spirits of the mountain
a sign a stone a living wolf
from its sanctuary Buarth Brynach
follow the tracks of the white sow
a goddess by the crooked stream
laid his burden on an altar stone

(Dedicated to the memory of Numus, a healer, singer and storyteller who prophesied the end of the stone. He died in his African homeland, October 1994)

Mysteriously, the carving began to erode back into the stone, vanishing slowly from sight. Perhaps it had done the work it emerged to do. Of course the changes in the depth of the image were imperceptible at first. So it is hard to put a date to this occurrence except that I knew in my bones that once the world had intruded into this domain that its time had come. For almost five years the stone, standing at the base of a sessile oak had become like a shrine. Sometimes flowers, quartz pebbles, beads and other memorabilia could be found tucked in and around it. Of course winds and especially persistent driving rain would quickly alter the immediate terrain. Cows also caused ruts as they moved in and out of the nearby fields. So I had found my role as a guardian of the place. Visiting it on frequent walks down the old track, filling holes or moving pools of stagnant water from around it. Planting bulbs for the springtime and I suppose generally treating that corner of it as my private garden.

There is no doubt that I was obsessed and it is difficult now after more than a decade to imagine such a relationship. In the first few years the stone had become a kind of talisman. In moments of lucidity I knew it to be the central locus of my inner life. If feeling depressed or overcome with the housework from looking after three small children, the thought of a walk down the track later on would cheer me up. It could even work its magic with writer's blocks and the inevitable sticky patches with so much activity going on around me. Yet for long periods it was completely out of mind, as just another part of the local landscape. Only if I began to notice the lack of a certain something in my life or if passing by without noticing it, that I'd wonder how it was feeling and make a mental note to visit it. But often that thought too often went out of mind so I was always particularly glad when a friend called by to look at the stone. I could then walk a special journey. It seems crazy now to think like this when it was less than a half-a-mile from the house. My own obsession was private. It was part of the life the family lived, but at the same time we were tempered by it. Whereas for my friend Jack, his obsession was public. He lived miles away but when he talked about the stone it appeared that he only lived for it. Even recently, I met a painter for the first time, and he mentioned Jack and the stone in the same breath as he had heard what had long since become a local saga.

During a farewell party, Numus who was returning to Africa, entertained us for hours. He was a singer and a great storyteller, but he also had inherited the role of native witch-doctor and healer so Jack took him down to the stone. The telling of the encounter was somewhat unclear but he roughly stated that if you want anything, go three times to this stone with a good heart. But it could be that you had to do this for six weeks. I heard the story during the next few days and pondered on the ambiguity of it. In one way it seemed a fairly straight forward answer to my friend's question. It was up to him whether or not to actually do the suggested ritual at the stone. Yet the thought of within six weeks bothered me. But I never took it in a literal sense until almost to the day, coming home to see the broken trees on either side of the track as if a tornado had hit. It seemed impossible to put a sense to the destruction that had been wrought at that height. It looked as if an alien craft had hurtled down through the thick branches. I almost felt sure that this was what had happened, because I went through the gate into the meadow and looked over to see if the stone propped beneath the oak was still there. Nothing seemed changed and yet what had caused the devastation? There was a stillness, and it was apparent that something untoward had occurred. Then I saw a massive caravan parked in a corner by the ruined church-site. So this was what Numus had foreseen on the night of his farewell party!

The sudden entry of the young farmer and his family who had bought the surrounding land upended my corner of paradise. From being a common byway enjoyed by the world at large, it eventually became a farm with gates, sheds, dogs, tractors and machinery. Even the track was annexed. Telephone wires strung loose over the stone. The old ruins disappeared in a cluster of bright barns and the trees were cut back. It was a catastrophe and thereafter the carving began to fade. I still went down there occasionally and noted the changes. Some years later the stone itself was unceremoniously moved from its spot under the oak in a fit of rage and dumped on a sandy bank by the gate of the farm. It is still there but the carved figure has gone. It has receded back into the stone. Its visible contours lost to the naked eye, yet the inner form can still be revealed on a paper rubbing.

Coda

There was a deep sense of loss with the recession of the figure that called into being questions of personal identity. In a strange sense it had appeared at a time of inner confusion for me as an incomer in a rural community, and continued to sustain me socially and emotionally as a reality touchstone. It was certainly the nearest thing to a spiritual talisman that I had encountered. Unlike the death of a person whose sudden rush of remembrances can vividly recreate the past, the gradual fading of the stone's carved figure brought back the poverty of a world beyond the physical without that sweet sensing of otherness. Yet the hard material aspect of the rock obliterating the evidence of the actual incisions could not be ignored. Like a proverbial black hole, the stone itself was the only grounding for the former figure and the transience of the carved entity. We tend to take as metaphor what Plato wrote about the mind illuminating the inner cave walls, or Paul's vision of through a glass darkly. Yet to be confronted with the gradual disappearance of a deeply symbolic form, carved on a block of hard dolerite stone, is in a sense the reversal in time of its creative act. Becoming a fading outline of a figure so important to the stone-carver and so vital as to engage with and bring to life a haunting vision. It is an action closely aligned to both memory and lucid dreaming. We usually recognise in our night-time dreaming a confused tangle in somewhat strangely known landscapes. The representation of the figure as an early local saint or holyman known as Brynach Wyddel and his later mediaeval associations with Carn Ingli – itself beset by magnetic anomalies within its rocky core - created a rare dreamlike concordance that is hard to pinpoint. It was certainly a source of inspiration for the original artist and it became important for me – a millennium later – to follow through the various stages of interpretation of meanings within the figure from the initial revelation to its gradual fading from ordinary vision. A visiting sculptor had mentioned that the original block of hard stone had been smoothed off prior to the deep incision of the figure and the upper area had been slightly dished by the carver, in order to emphasize its rounded head. The resulting elegance would have been enhanced if seen above eye level and as we lay on the ground together squinting up at it, the stone appeared to confirm its figurative poise.

A different example of preparation on a flakier surface was evident in making the small diamonds and crosses at Tŷ Illtud. Here a small nail seemed to have been used to create a hole from which the rest of the outline was scraped out on the uneven inner walls of the stone chamber. Cupmarks may have been formed by rotating a hard stone to widen out what may have originally been a tiny natural cupola. Some of the portable stones have quite large hollows, including the single example of a cup and ring found in Wales that is edged with a deep cut around the double cupmark from Llangefni. Also in Ynys Môn, the curvilinear stone carvings at Barclodiad y Gawres appear to have been lightly incised on the inner smooth stones of the central chamber. But this may well have been caused by gradual erosion when the structure collapsed and had been exposed for centuries.

`The initial creative act was important. Seeking the residual of creativity in figures or symbols carved in stone at particular places, and within a time continuum of thousands of years is my contribution to the work of the unknown makers. Most of the fine visual examples throughout this book have faded to such an extent that even the most experienced searchers find difficulty in deciphering the original markings. One can compare drawings of a detail or from a carving by different people over hundreds of years, and marvel how differently each historian actually perceived and recorded their views. These perceptions can be slotted into particular time-frames reflecting social or cultural specifics. Even in relation to the time when such carvings were actually done the artists may have been recording concerns of a previous era. And in relation to the passage grave art perhaps a recreation of an even older mythic period attempting to visually meditate on important social or celestial events. This is a factor that many contemporary commentators of so-called abstract symbols tend to forget. They prefer to view such carvings in relation to current aesthetic concerns. They then lock them in prosaic descriptive detail when the very power of image and its symbolic weave of magic embellishment was once powerful enough to rout the reasoning mind. Memory too becomes a fickle flame. Not only personal remembrances but the written accounts by others are relied on for truth-telling. Many of the versions of the carvings that are gathered together here vary considerably in this regard.

Soon after midsummer's day I lay under a rock, the coverstone of a chambered tomb built many thousands of years ago. I had spent over an hour on the hot sunny afternoon vainly searching the fields for Tŷ Illtud. It was the second attempt in as many months on an equally hot day which now made me feel like a pilgrim searching for a lost shrine. When I returned to the farm where I had initially asked permission to cross the land, the farmer and his wife obviously took pity on my plight and drove me part way to the site. She had never been there and was curious as a popular television character had recently visited and talked about it on his show. We pushed through the shoulder-high bean plants and climbed over a fence onto the lower crest of a hill. The large round stone rested inconspicuously on its low chamber among tall grass and nettles. It took me a while to adjust to its actual presence, rather than the mental pictures and seemingly erroneous accounts of its position and situation that I had studied during the past year. It was also so much lower than expected and when I poked my head under the stone I could not make out any of the carvings that I had expected to see on the inside stones.

After belly-wriggling inside and adjusting to the uneven spread of the many rocks beneath me, the crude surface of the three uprights as well as the pitted stone over my head was devoid of anything that could be described as artificial markings. I was mortified, especially as I had already written a whole chapter based on the work of earlier observers that even included questions of who actually carved the designs. Lying there staring at the rocks in a kind of stupor, time slowed still.

Although the floor of the chamber was covered in small sharp rocks, I felt quite comfortable with a deep inner feeling in what could only be described as a stone womb. Outside it men were shouting and sheep bleating nearby as they moved up the hill. I wriggled my shoes, just to make sure that both feet were still out there protruding beyond the edge of the coverstone. Whether it was the hot afternoon or the effect of light coming through a large gap at the top end of the chamber, or it may have been the long interval needed for me to adjust to the physical situation, a sudden shift in perception occurred so that a few designs began to emerge as carved entities on the uneven rocky surfaces. There was a tiny lozenge with a cross inside and a similar motif shaped in the form of a long crossletted outline. It did occur to me that if I waited long enough perhaps the sixty carvings recorded by Leslie Grinsell twenty years previously might also magically appear. Even so it took me ages to accept that a seemingly rounded numinous outline in front of my face, was in fact the lyre he noted and photographed. It was only later when examining the rubbing with its small carving almost engraved on the paper, did I accept that the whole episode had not been a passing hallucination. It was almost as if lying horizontally enclosed within the stone chamber I had given up the body proper. I knew as I lay there – shifting slightly so as to avoid the nettle stingers while tracing the tiny incisions on the south facing and western stones – that I was unlikely to repeat such an experience once I wriggled out from under the large coverstone.

Yet when I stood up straight, stretched and looked around I marvelled at what I had been equally blind to previously. The sky now circled around the chamber in a 360 degree sweep – with the deep-sided walls of Bannau Brycheiniog to the west – culminating on the hillslope and a spreading tree up above me. The incongruity in trying to relate the prehistoric chamber to a ground-led geography of present-day undulating fields, slopes, hollows and endless clumps of trees now became apparent when the structure revealed itself as originally created. The central viewing area for a geocosmic drama.

W.O. Westwood on a days ramble in Powys is the only writer I know who remarked that the chamber had been built in the centre of an amphitheatre of high hills. He surmised that the scratches were much later but 'that the Druidical rites practised at Tŷ-Illtid', might be observed and telegraphed for a great extent of the country from the various stations on the summits of the elevated peaks. I realised that I was not alone in being affected by such a view. And perhaps equally inane, what it brought to mind, one hundred and fifty years later, was the memory of a very similar panoramic view a few miles north of the Callanish stone circle on Lewis in the Outer Hebrides. During the early 1980's I had an outrageous idea to build myself a small beehive drystone hut from which I could record the celestial journeys of sun and moon, as they rose and dipped among the many peaks to the west and the curving outline of hills to the south locally known as the Sleeping Beauty. The salient feature of my projected structure to be built of short slabs – that could be singularly removed depending on the visual frame needed – was to view the actual positions of the full moon at the Lunar Standstill (an 18.63 yearly cycle) as well as annual sunrises and sunsets of the solstices and equinoxes. By carving minitature symbols on the inner stones I could notate their positions vis a vis the contours of the hills outside.

Perhaps a similar method of observational astronomy was the key to the original carvings inside Tŷ Illtud. Certainly such an eminent authority on prehistoric art as Abbe' Breuil thought that some of the carvings were early and similar to those at Newgrange and other tumuli in Ireland. The recording in stone of such obviously celestial symbols was one popular explanation during the past century. According to Martin Brennan, who has written a number of important publications on the topic, the people of the Boyne Valley were concerned with the measurement of time and space, and with the cycles of the moon and conjunctions of the planets. It is interesting to note that the K52 kerbstone from Newgrange, confirming that its cupmarks were carved far back in time beyond the Bronze Age, was for him the initial confirmation of a grid for astronomical computations and on which he then superimposed the overall designs of other important monumental stones. He viewed K52 as a kind of plenisphere on which the designs described the movement of celestial spheres in space. It was essentially a time machine! Its complex geometry could only be understood if seen in motion and that an answer to the riddle of the stones is that they are time pieces, cosmic clocks. It was a transmission by the builders and master carvers of their knowledge and wisdom, that we can perhaps appreciate now by way of twenty-first century scientific and electronic technology (page 81).

Select Bibliography

S. Aldhouse-Green: *Palaeolithic & Mesolithic Wales* in F. Lynch, Prehistoric Wales, Stroud, 2000.

C. Barber: *More Mysterious Wales*, London, 1987.

C.T. Barber: *Chambered Tombs of SW Wales*, Oxford, 1992.

J. Barfoot: 'Nine Men's Morris', *Archaeology in Wales*, No.27, Gwynedd, 1987.

S. Beckensall: *British Prehistoric Art*, Stroud, 1999.

S. Bergh: *Landscape of the Monuments*, Stockholm, 1995.

W. Bird Allen: Correspondence, *Arch. Camb.*, 1917.

J. & C. Bord: *Mysterious Britain*, London, 1972.

G. Borrow: *Wild Wales*, 1865, (reprint) Llandysul, 1995.

R. Bradley: 'Stone Circles & Passage Graves' in A. Gibson & D. Simpson (eds.): *Prehistoric Ritual and Religion*, Stroud, 1999.

M. Brennan: *The Boyne Valley Vision*, Portlaoise, 1980.

T. Breverton: *The Book of Welsh Saints*, Bro Morgannwg, 1999.

F. Browne: The Llywel Stone, *Arch. Camb.*, 1917.

C. Burges: *The Age of Stonehenge*, London, 1980.

A. Burl: *The Stone Circles of the British Isles*, London, 1976.

J.L. Campbell: The Contribution of Edward Lhuyd to the Study of Scottish Gaelic, *Trans. Cymmrodorion*, London, 1962.

P.W. Carter: Edward Lhuyd the Scientist, *Trans. Cymmrodorion*, London, 1962.

H.S. Chapman & R.H. Roberts: An Unusual Cup and Ring stone from Anglesey, *Studia Celtica*, 1996.

B.G. Charles: *Place-names of Pembrokeshire*, Cardiff, 1992.

G. Children & G.H. Nash, *Prehistoric Sites of Breconshire*, Woonton Almeley, 2001.

G. Coffey: *New Grange and other Incised Tumuli in Ireland* (1912), (reprint) Poole, 1977.

G. Cooney: A Tale of Two Mounds, *Arch. Ireland*, Vol. 11 No 2 Issue 40, Dublin, 1997.

R. Cowell: *The Calderstones*, Merseyside Arch. Soc., (undated).

O.G.S. Crawford: *Long Barrows of the Cotswold*, London, 1925.

O.G.S. Crawford: *The Eye Goddess*, London, 1957.

G.E. Daniel: *The Prehistoric Chambered Tombs of England and Wales*, Cambridge, 1950.

G. Dimbleby: *Plants and Archaeology*, London, 1978.

T. Easton: *Ritual Marks on Historic Timbers*, 3rd Stone – No. 38, Devises, 2000.

R. Ellis: Journeys in Wales, *Trans. Cymmrodorion*, London, 1906/7.

G. Eogan: *Knowth and the Passage Tombs of Ireland*, London, 1986.

R. Fenton: *A Historical Tour Through Pembrokeshire*, London, 1903.

M. Gimbutas: *The Language of the Goddess*, London, 1989.

W.F. Grimes, *The Prehistory of Wales*, Cardiff, 1951.

L.V. Grinsell: The Later History of Tŷ Illtud, *Arch. Camb.* 131, 1981.

R.T. Gunther: Early Science in Oxford, *Life & Letters of E. Lhuyd*, Vol. X1V, Oxford, 1945.

E. Hadingham: *Secrets of the Ice Age,* London, 1980.
P. Harbison: *Pilgrimage in Ireland,* London, 1991.
R. Heath: *A Key to Stonehenge,* Dyfed, 1993.
W.J. Hemp: Bryn Celli Ddu, *Archaeologia,* Vol. LXXX, 1930.
W.J. Hemp: The Chambered Cairn of Bryn Celli Ddu, *Arch. Camb.,* 1931.
M. Herity, From Lhuyd to Coffey – information from unpublished descriptions of the Boyne Valley Tombs, *Studia Hibernica* 7, 1967.
M. Herity, *Irish Passage Grave Art,* Dublin, 1974.
H.L. Jones, Bryn Celli Ddu, *Arch. Camb.,* Vol. 2, 1847.
H.L. Jones, Tŷ Illtyd, *Arch. Camb.,* X111, 1867.
T. Jones: *History of Brecknockshire,* Vol. 11, 1809.
J. Jones-Davies: *The Kingdom of Brycheiniog in the Age of the Saints,* Brecon, 1956.
J. Jones-Davies: Presidential Address, *Arch. Camb.,* 1974.
J.M. Lewis: The Standing Stones of Pembrokeshire, *The Pembrokeshire Historian,* Vol. 2, 1966.
Edward Lhuyd, (Welsh section of) William Camden's *Brittania,* 3rd Edition, (ed.) E. Gibson, London, 1753.
F. Lynch: Barclodiad y Gawres, *Arch. Camb.,* 1967.
F. Lynch: *Prehistoric Man in Wales and the West,* Bath, 1972.
F. Lynch: Towards a Chronology of Megalithic Tombs in Wales, in (eds.) G.C. Boon & J.M. Lewis: *Welsh Antiquity,* Cardiff, 1976.
F. Lynch: The Later Neolithic & Early Bronze Age, in F.Lynch: *Prehistoric Wales,* Stroud, 2000.
G.T. Meaden: *The Goddess of the Stones,* London, 1991.
A.G. & P. Mein: Trostry Castle, *Archaeology in Wales,* No. 38, 1998.
D. Moore: Cambrian Antiquity, in G.C. Boon & J.M. Lewis (eds.): *Welsh Antiquity,* Cardiff .1976.
R.W.B. Morris: *The Prehistoric Rock Art of Argyll,* Poole, 1977.
L. & C. Murray: *The Celtic Tree Oracle,* London, 1988.
V.E. Nash-Williams: *Early Christian Monuments of Wales,* Cardiff, 1950.
S. O'Boyne: *Ogam – The Poet's Secret,* Dublin, 1970.
C. O'Kelly: Bryn Celli Ddu – A Reinterpretation, *Arch. Camb.,* 118, 1969.
C. O'Kelly: *Passage Grave Art in the Boyne Valley,* Dublin, 1978.
M. O'Kelly: *Newgrange,* London, 1982.
A. & W. O'Sullivan: Edward Lhuyd's Collection of Irish Manuscripts, *Trans. Cymmrodorion,* London, 1962.
M. O'Sullivan: Approaches to Passage Tomb Art, *J.R.S.A.I.,* Vol. 116, Dublin, 1986.
M. O'Sullivan, *Megalithic Art in Ireland,* Dublin, 1993.
G. Owen: The Extent of Cemais (1594), *Pembrokeshire Records Series* 111, 1977.
G. Owen: (ed. H. Owen) *The Description of Pembrokeshire,* 1892.
S. Piggott: *Neolithic Culture of the British Isles,* London, 1954.
T.G.E. Powell & G.E. Daniel: *Barclodiad y Gawres,* Liverpool, 1954.
RCAM(W), Taren Deusant – Pagan Cult Site, *Glamorgan,* Vol. 1, Part 3, Cardiff, 1976.

RCAM(W), Simondson Cairn – No. 344, *Glamorgan,* Vol. 1, Part 1, Cardiff, 1976.
RCAM(W), Stone with Spiral Ornament, *Llanbedr, Merioneth,* Cardiff, 1921.
RCAM(W), Neolithic Court Tomb (CT1-13; RCT1-11), *Brecknock,* Cardiff, 1997.
M. Redknap: *The Christian Celts,* Cardiff, 1991.
P. Rhind & D. Evans: *The Plant Life of Snowdonia,* Llandysul, 2001.
G. Melville Richards: Barclodiad y Gawres (Appendix E) in T.G.E. Powell & G.E. Daniel: *Barclodiad y Gawres,* Liverpool, 1954.
J. M. Robinson (ed.): *The Nag Hammadi Library,* N.Y., 1981.
A. Ross: *Folklore of Wales,* Stroud, 2001.
N.H. Savory: Prehistoric Brecknock, *Brycheiniog,* No. 1, Brecon, 1955.
A. Schnapp: *The Discovery of Archaeology,* London, 1993.
M. Seaborne: *Celtic Crosses of Britain,* Princess Risborough, 1989.
J. Sharkey: *Celtic Mysteries,* London, 1975.
J. Sharkey: Blaenawen Stone, *Archaeology in Wales,* No. 28, Gwynedd, 1988.
J. Sharkey: *Celtic High Crosses of Wales,* Llanrwst, 1998.
E. Shee-Twohig: *The Megalithic Art of Western Europe,* Oxford, 1981.
C. Thomas: *And Shall These Mute Stones Speak?,* Cardiff, 1994.
A. Watson & D. Keating: Architecture and Sound: an acoustic analysis of megalithic monuments in prehistoric Britain, *Antiquity,* Vol. 73, 1999.
H. Weaver, *Divining the Primary Sense,* London, 1978.
A. Weir: *Early Ireland – A Field Guide,* Belfast, 1980.
T.A. Westropp: *Folklore of Clare,* Ennis, 2000.
J.O. Westwood: *Lapidarium Walliae,* Oxford, 1876-9.
R.E.M. Wheeler: *Prehistoric and Roman Wales,* Cardiff, 1925.
R.E.M. Wheeler: *Roman Archaeology in Wales* (a tribute to Nash-Williams), BBC Cardiff, 1957.
J. Williams: *The Physicians of Myddfai* (reprint), Felinfach, 1993.
S. Wilson: *The Magical Universe,* London, 2000.
R. Worsley & P. Brinton: *Open Secrets,* Llandysul, 1987.
S. Young: *The Work of Angels – BM Catalogue,* London, 1989.

Index

Placenames
(Figures in bold refer to illustrations)

General

Images of Wales

Cover artwork by Eirian Llwyd

(Colograph of Barclodiad y Gawres, Môn)

'Most of my recent work has been inspired by Anglesey and the impact of moving to the island has had on me. The works, mostly worked in a variety of printmaking techniques, reflect a landscape that can be uncompromisingly bleak or amazingly beautiful, peaceful or magical. But I am not concerned just with the natural landscape but with what is in the landscape or created by people who have lived there.

It is the concentration, in such a defined space of nature, culture, history and spirituality that is so compelling. There is also a tension in the dichotomy of my relationship with the place. My Denbigh accent soon betrays that I am 'not from around here,' yet living in Anglesey and getting to know the place from the inside has reawakened an awareness of spirituality and my Welshness – two important themes to my work.

Printmaking has added an exiting dimension to the early emphasis on representational drawing and painting. It is a source of satisfaction to create the rich satiny black of an aquatinted copper plate or the mysterious marks of an etched plate. Other mediums such as lino, woodcuts and colograph add an abstract dimension to what is predominantly graphic work.'

Eirian Llwyd, Tŷ Newydd, Rhosmeirch, Llangefni, Môn, LL77 7RZ.
Contact at: eirianllwyd@rhosmeirch.fsbusiness.co.uk

Exhibitions include:

2003	Oriel Glyn y Weddw, Llanbedrog
	Oriel Myrddin, Caerfyrddin
	Canolfan Ucheldre, Caergybi
2002	Featured on Sioe Gelf, S4C
	Theatr Gwynedd
2001	Degree Show, Howard Gardens, Cardiff
	Oriel Canfas, Cardiff
	Eglwys Cyngar Sant, Llangefni

Leva livet med hund

BITTE LIND

Leva livet med hund

BILDA FÖRLAG
Naturia

Författare Bitte Lind
Redaktör Yvonne Envall
Formgivning Ulf Lindahl
Omslag Kerstin Granlund
Teckningar Ursula Wilby

Förlag Bilda Förlag F&D, Box 42053,
126 13 Stockholm
Telefon 08-709 05 00, telefax 08-709 05 31
e-post: info@bildaforlag.se
www.bildaforlag.se

Sättning och ombrytning Bilda Förlag F&D, ateljén
Tryck Sjuhäradsbygdens Tryckeri AB, Borås 1999

ISBN 91-604-0278-4

Innehåll

Hunden – ett flockdjur

Hunden är ett flockdjur, vilket innebär att den i vilt tillstånd är beroende av att ”samarbeta” med sina artfränder inom en grupp – flock – för att överleva. Och för att överleva inom flocken måste individen följa flockens ”regler och lagar”. Det är bl.a. detta som gör hunden till människans allra mest sociala, omtyckta och vanliga sällskapsdjur. Hundens instinktiva vilja att fungera i flocken/familjen gör att den, jämfört med de flesta andra djur, är betydligt lättare att lära beteenden som vi människor tycker är viktiga och trevliga.

Flocken uppfyller en mängd basbehov för individen/hunden. Flockgemenskapen ger den exempelvis föda, sällskap, trygghet mot faror, värme, kroppskontakt, lek och fysisk samt psykisk aktivitet. Hunden betraktar sin ägare och dess familj som sin flock. En hundägare måste alltså, precis som den vilda hundens flock, uppfylla hundens samtliga basbehov för att den ska må bra, såväl kroppsligt som mentalt.

En valp ska inte behöva vara ifrån sin flock annat än kortare stunder. Även en vuxen hund behöver få vara med sin flock större delen av dygnet. Den får inte sitt behov av sällskap tillfredsställt, och kan alltså inte må psykiskt bra, om den lämnas ensam mer än fyra timmar per dygn totalt. Kan du uppfylla detta och hundens övriga behov dygnet runt under ca 10 år framöver? I så fall har du en rolig och stimulerande men delvis också jobbig tid att se fram emot – som hundägare!

Välja rätt ras

Det finns drygt 200 olika raser i Sverige idag. Allt från små chihuahuor till stora irländska varghundar. En del raser är korthåriga medan andra knappt syns bakom all päls. Vissa raser är avlade för att användas inom ett väldigt specifikt och snävt område, medan andra är mer all-round-raser som kan tränas till att fungera inom flera områden. Det är ingen överdrift att påstå att vi idag har raser för varje behov och önskemål. Och alla raser har sina fördelar men också nackdelar och defekter.

För den som står i begrepp att bli hundägare finns alltså mängder av raser att välja mellan. Att bestämma vilken som ska bli din ras är kanske inte lätt. Men all den tid du lägger ned på att hitta den ras som passar just dig och din familj, har du igen under de kommande åren som hundägare.

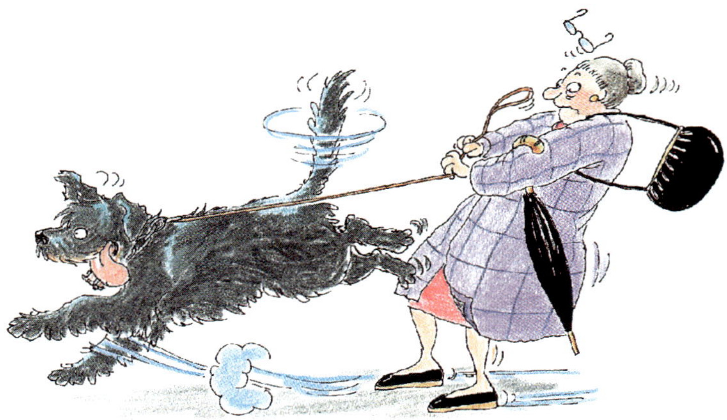

Det är inte alls givet att grannens rara hund passar din familj och ert sätt att leva. Vi har alla olika förutsättningar för vårt hundinnehav. Vi bor olika – på landet eller i stan, i villa eller lägenhet – och vi har olika mycket tid att ägna åt hunden. Och givetvis har vi olika stort intresse för att vara aktiva hundägare.

Och det är inte heller säkert att grannens hund är en bra representant för sin ras. Den kanske är ovanligt aktiv eller lugn för sin ras. Grannens hund är kanske inte ens utseendemässigt rastypisk.

Hur ska jag då komma underfund med vilken som ska bli "min ras"? Börja med att rannsaka dig själv tillsammans med familjen. Ställ frågor som; Hur motionskrävande hund klarar vi av? Hur många timmar per dag kan de vuxna i familjen avsätta till hundens behov? Är vi intresserade av att hålla på med krävande pälsvård? Vilka specialintressen har vi – jakt, bruks, lydnad m.m.? Hur stor hund klarar vi ekonomiskt och fysiskt?

Försök att ringa in typen av hund ni vill och kan ha. Exempelvis en brukshund, en dvärghund eller en jakthund. Nu först är det dags att titta i en hundbok över olika raser. Ta dock allt som står i raspresentationer i den här typen av "uppslagsböcker" med en rejäl nypa salt! Att välja ras huvudsakligen efter utseendet är förkastligt, för oavsett vilken ras den lilla valpen tillhör kommer du att älska den. Och en exteriört tilltalande ras kanske inte alls har den mentalitet som passar dig.

Mentaliteten viktigast

Visst är det viktigt att gilla utseendet på sin hund. Och kanske kommer ni att vara med på hundutställning ibland. Men den allra största delen av hundägandet är det vardagliga umgänget med hunden. En bra hund är en hund som är frisk och fungerar i det dagliga livet med flocken/familjen. Den är även sund i sitt umgänge med andra hundar och människor. En vacker hund som inte fungerar socialt är inte till glädje för någon!

Var väldigt noga med att bilda dig en realistisk uppfattning om en ras typiska mentalitet. Du måste dels träffa flera vuxna hundar av den rasen, dels prata med flera personer med erfarenhet av rasen. En bra början är att besöka en utställning. Där får du se många hundar och kan ställa frågor till uppfödare och hundägare om hur de raser är, som du funderar på. Var och när det ordnas utställningar kan du få reda på genom Svenska Kennelklubben (SKK). Fråga också hur mycket pälsvård som krävs och hur mycket av den du kan göra själv. För att klara vissa rasers päls bör man faktiskt vara både specialintresserad och kunnig.

Sjukdomar och defekter

På utställningen kan du även passa på att ta reda på vilka ärftliga fel och sjukdomar – defekter – rasen är drabbad av och i vilken utsträckning. Men nöj dig inte med de svar du får, hur vederhäftiga de än är. Ring SKKs informationsavdelning och fråga. Samtidigt ber du om telefonnummer till rasklubben och dess avelsråd. Genom dessa får du ytterligare kunskaper om rasens kynne och defekter samt tips på seriösa uppfödare.

En seriös uppfödare ska alltid och enbart använda hundar i avel som själva inte har några defekter eller sjukdomar. Inte ta för stora risker genom att avla för snävt d.v.s. para alltför närbesläktade individer med varandra. Inte para en tik vars syskon har vissa gemensamma defekter o.s.v.

Genetik är svårt och många defekter och ärftliga sjukdomar har en komplicerad eller okänd arvsgång. Vissa defekter och sjukdomar kan dyka upp, i till synes friska linjer, så långt som efter flera, flera generationer. Så fråga uppfödaren och avelsrådet om så mycket som möjligt, inte bara om föräldradjuren utan även bl.a. om de båda individernas tidigare kullar samt om deras syskon. Kom ihåg att **ingen** kan garantera att en veterinärbesiktigad frisk hund kommer att förbli frisk. Den kan senare visa sig vara behäftad med någon defekt eller sjukdom, som kanske märks först efter någon månad eller t.o.m. flera år.

Rätt uppfödare

Ja, det är en hel massa att tänka på, innan man ens bestämmer sig för vilken ras man ska satsa på. Och när väl det beslutet är taget gäller det att gå lika omsorgsfullt tillväga för att hitta en uppfödare som du kan få förtroende för och hjälp av.
Nu har du förhoppningsvis fått en rättvisande och heltäckande bild av det som kanske ska bli din ras. Kontakta därför

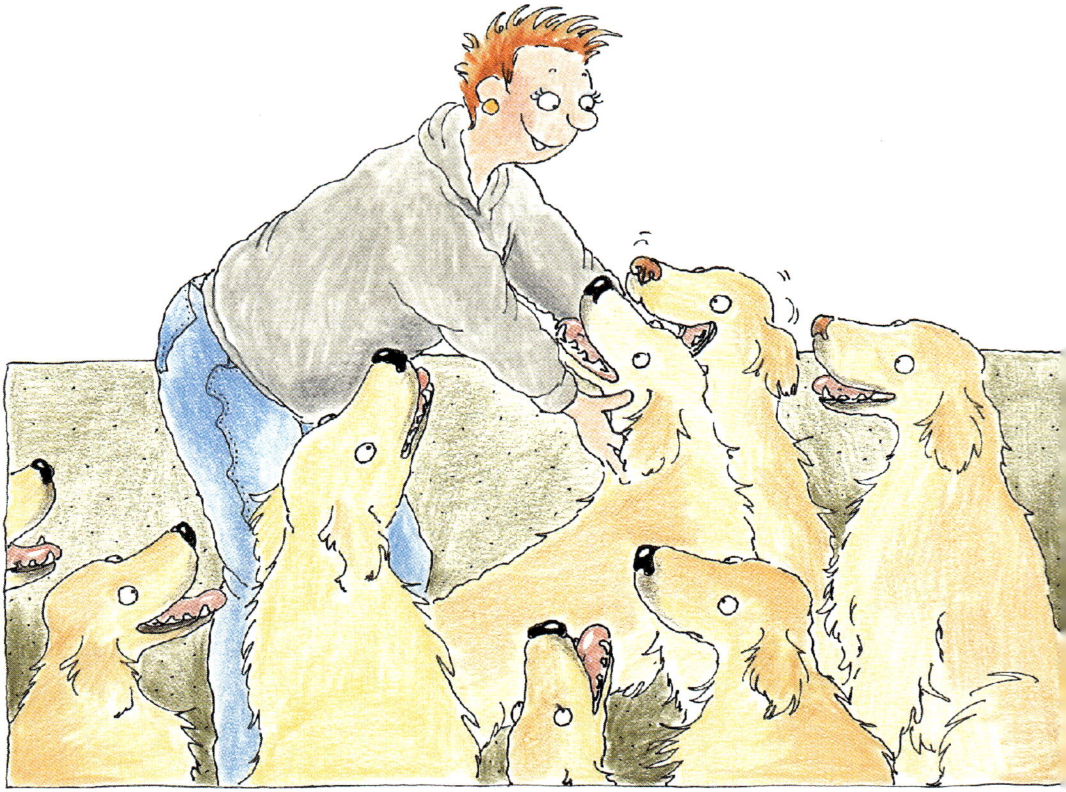

någon av de uppfödare du blivit tipsad om. Berätta att du vill veta mer om rasen och be att få komma och träffa hundarna i hemmiljö. Eftersom uppfödaren varje dag ska ut på promenad med sina hundar kan du fråga om du får följa med. Ta vara på besöket genom att studera hundarna. Försök att lära av och lära känna uppfödaren. Tycker du att hundarna är trevliga och att ni får bra kontakt, att uppfödaren är villig att dela med sig av sina hunderfarenheter och kunskaper, även i framtiden, så kanske du hittat rätt.

Förhoppningsvis planerar den här uppfödaren en valpkull vid en tidpunkt som passar dig. Om inte, och du fått förtroende för honom, be honom rekommendera en kollega han vet ska ha en kull. Oavsett var du till sist köper din valp ska du försöka träffa tiken och helst även hanhunden – han kan dock ofta bo i andra änden av landet – för att förvissa dig om att föräldrarna till din blivande valp är trevliga individer.

Ställ krav

Du måste ställa krav på din blivande uppfödare – han kommer att ställa krav på dig som valpköpare. Var inte rädd för att fråga om det du undrar över. Fråga om föräldrarna; meriter från utställningar och prov, eventuella defekter, ögonlysningsresultat, HD-status m.m. Du har också rätt att alltid kräva att följande följer med vid leverans av valpen: registreringsbevis från SKK, ID-märkningsintyg, veterinärbesiktningsintyg i original (får ej vara äldre än sju dagar), SKKs köpeavtal, matlista och skötselråd, SKKs informationsbroschyr – ”Välkommen valp”.

Det kan kännas jobbigt att vänta, kanske i flera månader, på att äntligen få hem sin valp. Men på många sätt är det en värdefull väntan inför det som komma skall. För när valpen väl är hämtad kommer inget att bli sig riktigt likt i tillvaron igen!

Vänta och lär

Utnyttja väntetiden till att förbereda dig så att du kan ta hand om din valp på bästa sätt. En tidig kontakt med uppfödaren har många fördelar. Och att vänta några månader på att få hem sin valp är också positivt. Då får du tid till att lära dig mer om hunden och dess beteenden. Ju mer du kan om hur en hund fungerar, desto större är förutsättningarna att din valp ska utvecklats till en trevlig individ, som du får glädje av i många år. Hur en hund blir mentalt styrs givetvis av arvsanlagen, men kanske ännu mer av miljön där den växer upp.

Innan tiken paras har den seriösa uppfödaren – ofta i samråd med rasens avelsråd – i god tid före löp omsorgsfullt valt en hane som bör vara lämplig för tiken. Han ska bl.a. passa henne linjemässigt (genetiskt), mentalt och exteriört. Inför parning, valpning och dräktighet måste tiken vara i bästa kondition samt avmaskad och omvaccinerad. Under dräktigheten måste hon få lagom mycket motion, en väl avvägd foderstat och hon måste få vistas i en bra miljö som hon är van vid för att fostren ska utvecklas optimalt.

Går parningen som den ska är det bara att hålla tummarna för att den ska resultera i en kull friska och vitala valpar. Numera finns det visserligen metoder för att ganska tidigt fastställa huruvida tiken är dräktig eller inte. Men den möjligheten finns ännu bara på vissa orter. Och även om det konstateras att hon väntar valpar är det omöjligt att veta vilken könsfördelningen kommer att bli eller hur många valpar det blir. Dessutom kan allt hända under dräktighet, valpning och den första tiden därefter. Det är ju faktiskt så i naturen att "svinnet" är ganska stort. Alla ägg som befruktas i tiken leder inte till en livskraftig och normalt utvecklad valp och en valpning är inte alltid komplikationsfri. Men för det mesta går allt som vi hoppats. Återigen har undret skett – nya liv föds och växer upp!

Föds blinda och döva

Tiken är dräktig i cirka nio veckor. Fostren utvecklas mycket långsamt i början men mycket snabbt under den sista tredjedelen av dräktigheten. Därför syns det knappast på henne under de första fem–sex veckorna efter parning om hon väntar valpar eller inte. Men under de sista tre veckorna ökar hon snabbt och mycket i omfång. Naturen ser på detta sätt till att tiken/den vilda hunden ska vara rörlig och kunna jaga så länge som möjligt.

Nyfödda valpar är tämligen outvecklade motoriskt. De föds blinda och döva. De reagerar huvudsakligen på värme/kyla och beröring. Deras luktsinne är dåligt medan smaksinnet är bra. Följaktligen är de helt beroende av tiken – inte bara för att få föda. En hundvalp kan t. ex. inte kissa och bajsa själv förrän den är runt tre veckor gammal. Tiken måste hjälpa den med detta genom ett intensivt slickande i valpens stjärt.

Vid ungefär två veckors ålder öppnar de ögonen och en knapp vecka senare börjar de höra. Nu har de också börjat gå upprätt på alla fyra tassarna, nästan som en vuxen hund. Men det dröjer länge än innan valparna behärskar sina rörelser. Det är först nu som de kan börja samverka med sin mor och sina syskon. Deras sociala utveckling, den s.k. socialiseringsperioden, har inletts. Och den perioden i valpens liv är synnerligen intressant för dig som valpköpare, eftersom den fortfarande pågår när du får hem valpen.

Mat och sömn och lek

Världen öppnas bokstavligen för valpen i och med att den börjar se och höra. Sakta men säkert börjar den upptäcka att det finns något bortom valplådan och mammas spenar. Den kräver mer och mer livsrum. Oftast får den i den här åldern flytta med sina syskon från valplådan till en större valphage och vid torrt och varmt väder vistas utomhus.

Nu introduceras också annan föda än mammas mjölk. Till en början får den små smakportioner som långsamt ökas efterhand samtidigt som den fortfarande får dia tiken. Övergången från tikmjölk till annan mat sker successivt för att vara fullbordad senast vid sju veckors ålder. Du bör ta reda på vilket foder valpen ska ha så du hinner köpa hem det innan den ska hämtas.

Valpen ska även avmaskas i flera omgångar hos uppfödaren. Högst sju dagar innan valpköparen hämtar den ska den genomgå veterinärbesiktning. Då bör den också vaccineras mot parvovirusinfektion och valpsjuka samt smittsam leverinflammation. Den ska ID-märkas också. Märkningen är en typ av tatuering som aldrig kan avlägsnas. På de flesta raser görs märkning med tång i vänster öra. Det ID-nummer som din valp får registreras hos Svenska Kennelklubben (SKK), tillsammans med uppgifter om ägaren. ID-registret finns även hos en del polisstationer. Genom ID-märkningen kan hundens ägare nås om den t.ex. skulle springa bort. Och möjligheten att någon fuskar på bl. a. tävlingar minskar.

Socialisering för livet

Socialiseringsfasen är oerhört viktig för valpens framtida samspel med både människor och djur. I åldern 3–12 veckor måste den lära sig umgås på rätt sätt med människor och hundar, annars riskerar den att bli en "värsting". En bra avelstik uppfostrar valpen så att den förstår andra hundars signaler och språk. Den bör även få umgås med andra sunda vuxna hundar under den här tiden. Det är alltså en fördel om din uppfödare har flera hundar i olika åldrar, som alla hjälps åt att uppfostra valparna.

En valp, vars möte med folk inskränker sig till att se någon som ställer ner matskålar 4–5 gånger per dag, kommer inte att anpassa sig till människor i tillräcklig utsträckning. En sådan valp kan bli rädd och svår att få kontakt med. Risken är stor att den kommer att ty sig till andra hundar i stället för människor. Följaktligen blir den svår att uppfostra och så småningom även onödigt jobbig att träna.

Uppfödaren måste se till att varje valp får mycket och positiv kontakt med människor från och med 4e–5e veckan. Det umgänget måste också ske individuellt, d.v.s. varje valp måste få vara ensam – utan sina kullsyskon – med människor en stund varje dag.

Här gäller det för dig som valpens nya matte eller husse att ta vid där tiken och uppfödaren slutade. I en familj där det inte redan finns en annan hund faller det sig naturligt att valpen får vara ensam med de tvåbenta. Men för den som exempelvis skaffar sig en andra hund är det viktigt att vara ensam med valpen ofta, så att den inte föredrar den första hundens sällskap framför mattes/husses.

Flytt efter åtta veckor

I takt med att valpen växer och ökar i vikt så utvecklas även hjärnan. Under de första levnadsveckorna kan den exempelvis inte lagra sina erfarenheter i minnet. Vid ungefär åtta veckors ålder är minnesfunktionen tillräckligt utvecklad för att valpen ska vara mottaglig för inlärning. I den här åldern är den nyfiken och som mest anpassningsbar. Först nu är den psykiskt rustad för att byta miljö och skiljas från uppfödare-mor-syskon och flytta till sitt nya hem. Därför ska du aldrig ta hem din valp innan den blivit minst åtta veckor gammal.

Det händer alltså en massa med valpen hemma hos uppfödaren. Och självklart vill alla blivande valpköpare komma och titta på valparna så snart de bara får. I vilken utsträckning uppfödare går med på besök under den här tiden är väldigt olika. Men de allra flesta är måttligt roade av extrabesök vars huvudsakliga syfte är att bara titta på valpar.

Alla uppfödare är rädda för att besökande ska föra med sig smittsamma infektioner som kan drabba valpar och tik. Späda valpar är känsliga för infektioner liksom en tik som just genomgått en valpning och ger di. Dessutom behöver tik och valpar lugn och ro. En stressad tik är inte någon bra mor. Oftast är chanserna större att få hälsa på om valpen kommer ur en sommarkull än en vinterkull. Under sommaren kan ju både valpar och besökande tas emot utomhus. Är kullen liten ökar möjligheterna ytterligare eftersom det är lättare att få tid över till ett fåtal besök. En kull på tio valpar innebär inte bara mer jobb för tik och uppfödare utan också fler som vill komma och titta på valpar.

En del uppfödare lägger in en särskild "valpköpefilt" eller liknande till valparna under de sista veckorna. Meningen är att den ska få samma lukt som tik och valpar. När det sedan är dags för valparna att åka iväg till sina nya hem klipps filten i bitar. Varje valp får med sig en bit hem. Det kan kännas tryggt för valpen att en lukt den känner igen återfinns i den nya miljön. Om din uppfödare inte brukar göra så här kan du i stället be att få skicka en egen liten filt som sedan följer din valp hem. Eller passa på och lämna den vid ett eventuellt titta-på-valp-besök.

Välja valp

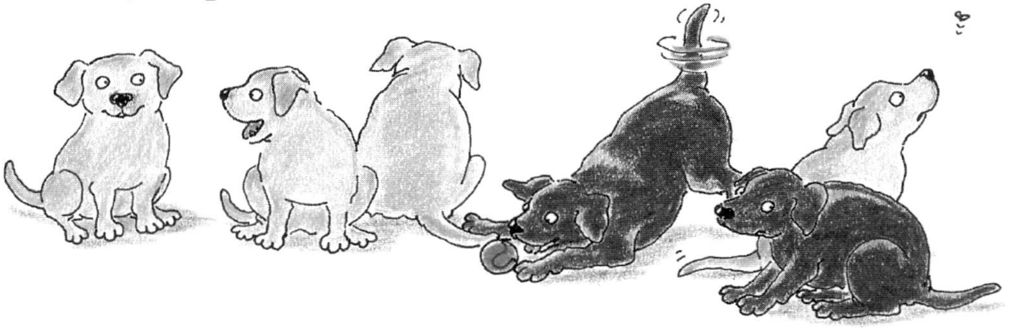

I varje kull kan man urskilja mentala särdrag mellan valparna. En del verkar tuffare än andra, någon kanske går för sig själv ofta, en annan verkar extra framåt och ytterligare en annan är lite blyg. Den som iakttar ett gäng valpar tycker sig alltid finna individuella särdrag. Men det är lätt att missta sig, och därmed dra förhastade slutsatser av det man ser under några timmar en viss dag.

Valpar har, precis som vi människor, mer eller mindre bra dagar. En valp som verkar lugn och lite tråkig just när du är där, kanske har varit i full gång timmarna innan du kom och är trött bara därför. Dessutom förändras valpar nästan från dag till dag. Det händer så mycket i deras utveckling de här veckorna och det händer fort. Den valp som är försiktig ena veckan kan vara tuffast veckan därpå. Och den som är minst vid fyra veckor kan mycket väl vara störst tre veckor senare.

Att välja valp är jättesvårt! En erfaren uppfödare har givetvis större chans än en vanlig valpköpare att välja den ”bästa” valpen i kullen, han har ju bl.a. umgåtts med dem dagligen i minst två månader. Men det är alltid något av ett lotteri för alla att välja valp. Och den som är den ”bästa” valpen för en person kanske inte alls är den ”bästa” för en annan. Det finns dock ingen som lärt känna valparna så bra som uppfödaren.

Val av valp bör ske så sent som möjligt. Det finns ju mer att ”ta på” hos en åttaveckors valp än hos en som bara är hälften så gammal. Alla valpköpare kan naturligtvis inte få välja själva bl.a. eftersom någon måste få sista valpen. Många uppfödare vill vara med och styra var de olika valparna ska hamna. Oftast vill han försöka undvika att exempelvis den tuffaste hanhunden hamnar hos en barnfamilj. Han försöker få rätt valp till rätt familj.

Även om du själv får bestämma vilken valp i kullen som ska bli din – lyssna noga på uppfödarens råd. Han känner ju valparna bättre än du. Är du dessutom utställningsintresserad ska du absolut be uppfödaren om hjälp att välja. Eller åtminstone att välja bort vissa individer så att du själv kanske bara får två–tre att välja bland.

Fråga om allt

Räkna inte med att du själv får välja valp eller att du kan träffa valparna mer än kanske någon gång före hämtning. I stället kan du hålla kontakt med uppfödaren per telefon. Har du utnyttjat din "väntetid" på ett bra sätt kommer du förmodligen att hitta fler och fler frågor som du vill ha svar på. Ju mer man lär sig om hundar desto mer undrar man nämligen över.

Skriv gärna ner dina frågor innan du ringer till uppfödaren. Har du ännu inte bestämt vilket kön du helst vill ha är det hög tid att göra det nu. Diskutera för- och nackdelar med tik respektive hanhund med uppfödaren. Inom en del raser är könsskillnaden stor, medan det hos andra raser mer är en smaksak om du väljer hane eller tik. En enkel och bra regel när man ska välja kön är att följa grannarna. Har du övervägande tikar i grannskapet kommer du sannolikt att få det jobbigt när dessa löper om du skaffar dig en hanhund. Är förhållandet det motsatta kommer antagligen en tik att dra till sig uppvaktande hanar, vilket kan vara nog så tröttande.

Låna eller köp hundböcker

Utnyttja uppfödarens raskunskaper och be honom rekommendera bra hundböcker. Det finns många utförliga böcker om hundar och deras beteenden och utveckling att köpa eller låna på biblioteket, som tar upp det mesta du behöver veta innan du tar hem valpen och täcker även grunderna för skötsel, utveckling och inlärning. Se dock upp med äldre litteratur som bl.a. kan lära ut förlegade dressyrmetoder. Du kan dessutom be uppfödaren att få SKKs broschyr "Välkommen valp" och rasklubbens eventuella valpbroschyr så att du hinner läsa dem i god tid innan du hämtar valpen.

På en del orter ordnar Svenska Brukshundklubben (SBK) eller Länsklubbarna kurser för blivande hundägare. Ring dit eller åk och hälsa på – telefonnummer och adress hittar du i lokala telefonkatalogen – och ta reda på vilka kurser de planerar. Vill du vara säker på att få plats i t.ex. en nybörjarkurs bör du vara ute i god tid – helst en termin i förväg. En del rasklubbar håller egna valp- och nybörjarkurser. Det bör din uppfödare kunna upplysa om.

Förhoppningsvis har du, under väntan på att få hem valpen, lärt dig en massa om hundar i allmänhet och din ras i synnerhet. Tänk på att alla i en familj bör förstå hur en hund fungerar och reagerar. En valp blir lätt osäker om olika medlemmar i familjen uppmuntrar olika beteenden. Klara regler för vad valpen får och inte får göra ger valpen trygghet. Skriv tillsammans en lista på regler för valpen. Och se till att den följs. Det är bättre med ett fåtal regler som hålls än en massa regler som ingen till slut orkar följa.

Bra basutrustning

Äntligen börjar så dagen då valpen ska hämtas att närma sig. Visst kan det kännas pirrigt och ytterligare frågor kanske dyker upp i sista stund. Har du förberett dig ordentligt, och har en juste uppfödare att luta dig emot, kommer det säkert att gå bra. Nu gäller det att ta vid där tiken och uppfödaren slutade. Försök hålla samma rutiner som valpen varit van vid och var som tiken; tålmodig och lugn, men bestämd när det verkligen behövs.

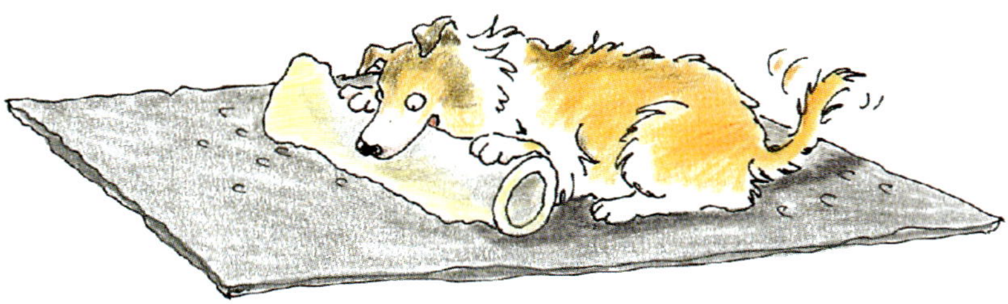

En viss basutrustning behöver du ha hemma när valpen kommer. Det finns en uppsjö av olika hundtillbehör på marknaden som gör det lätt att förköpa sig. Egentligen behöver din valp bara koppel, halsband, mat- och vattenskål, klotång, borste och kam, bädd eller fiberfäll och kanske något tuggben.

Lyssna med kritiska öron på alla goda råd från "hundexperter" och försäljare. Följ uppfödarens råd och använd ditt sunda förnuft. Gå framför allt inte på alla "förstå-sig-påares" idéer om extra vitaminer och mineraler. Det kan få ödesdigra konsekvenser för din hunds fysiska utveckling.

Även om en liten valp bör få gå lös så mycket som möjligt så måste den förstås ha ett koppel och ett halsband. Till att börja med ska den ha ett vanligt läderhalsband – absolut inte någon form av stryphalsband – och ett långt koppel. Hör med uppfödaren vilken längd du behöver på halsbandet. Det får inte sitta åt hårt men inte heller så löst att valpen kan ta sig ur det.

Plastskålar blir med tiden lätt repiga och därmed ohygieniska. Köp hellre en matskål i rostfritt. En vattenskål i rostfritt är lättast att hålla ren, medan en i keramik står betydligt stadigare på golvet och är inte så lätt för valpen att välta omkull.

Alla hundar kräver pälsvård. Vilken typ av borste och kam du ska ha beror helt på vilken ras du valt. Fråga därför uppfödaren vad du ska köpa. Till kloklippning finns särskilda klotänger. Använd inte samma som till dig själv, eftersom den inte rår på en hundklo utan trycker ihop klon och gör illa hunden.

Valpen ska ha sin egen liggplats där den får vara ifred. Till att börja med duger en enkel trälåda med dyna eller en fiberfäll. Vänta med att köpa en riktig hundsäng – finns i en mängd varianter – tills valpen ömsat tänder och lärt sig att endast gnaga på sina tuggleksaker. Rejäla märgben från nöt eller oxhudsben är de bästa tuggleksakerna. Leksaker i plast kan vara direkt livsfarliga. Valpen biter ofta sönder dem och kan därmed få plast i sig.

Åka bil med valp

Man bör vara två när valpen hämtas. En som kör och en som sitter i baksätet och håller i valpen. De flesta valpar har aldrig åkt bil förrän de ska till sitt nya hem. Ändå brukar premiärturen gå förvånansvärt bra, om den får sitta i knät och se vad som händer. En valp, oavsett ras, är för liten för att sitta ensam bak i bilen. Den skulle slängas fram och tillbaka i kurvor och vid inbromsningar. Och efter en sådan erfarenhet av biläkning skulle valpen sannolikt uppfatta bilen som något väldigt obehagligt. Låt valpen åka bil ofta i början! Då kommer den snabbt att lära sig att biläkning är en vardaglig självklarhet och inte ett dugg märkvärdigt.

Om din uppfödare bor i andra änden av landet blir kanske bilresan lite väl mastig för både dig själv och valpen. Då är flyg ett bättre alternativ än tåg eftersom flygresan går så mycket fortare än tågresan. På inrikesflyg får man ha en mindre hund/valp i knäet. Att, som var ganska vanligt förr, skicka en valp i bur med tåg eller flyg är helt förkastligt. Det är visserligen inte fråga om mer än ett par timmars vistelse i flyget, men bak i transportutrymmet kan ljudnivån vara näst intill outhärdlig för en hund.

Försedd med nedskrivna frågor till uppfödaren, hushållspapper, vattenskål, vattenflaska samt koppel och halsband – om valpen behöver rastas på hemvägen – åker du i väg för att hämta hem din lilla valp. Väl framme hos uppfödaren är det en hel del papper att gå igenom innan du kan styra kosan hemåt igen. Se till att du har god tid på dig, så att du tillsammans med uppfödaren kan gå igenom allt i lugn och ro.

Viktiga papper

Du ska få ett registreringsbevis (stamtavla) på din valp. Det ska vara utfärdat av Svenska Kennelklubben (SKK). Veterinärbesiktningsintyget är ett intyg på att valpen besiktigats av veterinär. Veterinärintyget kan självfallet inte säga något om valpens framtida hälsotillstånd. Det bestäms av hur du sköter den och av vilka anlag den bär på. Om veterinären upptäckt något onormalt för rasen eller tecken på sjukdom antecknas det på intyget. På veterinärintyget ska också stå när valpen avmaskats och vaccinerats. Din valps veterinärintyg får inte vara äldre än sju dagar. Även ett intyg på att valpen är ID-märkt (registreringsnumret tatuerat på insidan av en öronlapp eller i ljumsken) ska alltid medfölja.

Alla valpar måste vaccineras mot parvovirus, valpsjuka och smittsam leverinflammation (HCC). För att valpen ska få ett fullgott skydd krävs flera sprutor med ett visst intervall emellan. Var noga med att följa uppfödarens och veterinärens vaccinationsprogram ordentligt. Har valpen redan fått någon av sina första vaccinationssprutor medföljer ett skriftligt intyg från veterinären om detta. Där brukar veterinären också notera när nästa vaccinationsspruta ska ges.

Uppfödarens överlåtelse av valpen ska alltid ske skriftligt på SKKs förtryckta köpeavtal. Där fylls bl.a. data om valpen och dess föräldrar i. Avtalet fungerar även som kvitto på betalningen av hunden. När både du och uppfödaren undertecknat kontraktet behåller ni var sin del av det.

Rätt foderstat

Alla seriösa uppfödare lämnar med en skriftlig matlista, med detaljerade anvisningar om hur du ska utfodra din valp under uppväxten och som vuxen. Läs igenom anvisningarna grundligt och förvissa dig om att du förstått dem, innan du ger dig iväg med valpen. Hundar växer i en rasande fart. Vissa raser ska öka sin vikt från ett halvt kilo till upp emot 40–50 kilo på bara ett år! Därför är det synnerligen viktigt att den får i sig allt den behöver och i rätt proportioner. Annars kommer den inte att utvecklas optimalt.

Hunden har inget behov av omväxling i kosten. Därför finns det ingen anledning att ge hunden annat än det som uppfödaren rekommenderar. Byt inte foder så länge din hund mår bra av det den är van vid, d.v.s. är pigg, har god aptit, är bra i magen, blank i pälsen och växer i lagom takt. Gör inga avsteg från matlistan utan att först rådgöra med uppfödaren eller veterinären.

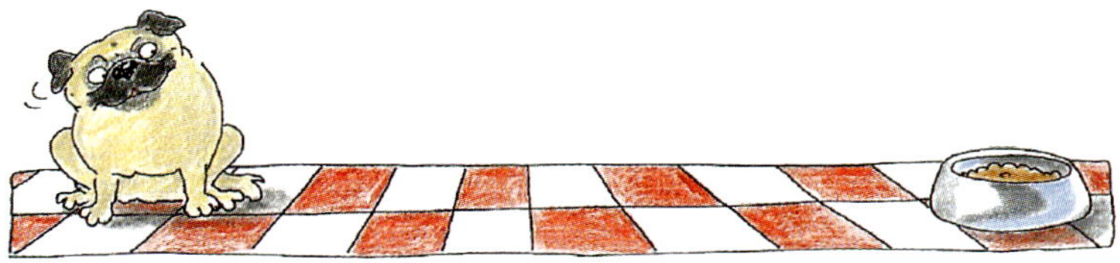

Efter all pappersexercis och alla goda råd är du förmodligen, liksom de flesta valpköpare, för trött i huvudet för att sortera ut alla nya frågor som dyker upp. Väl hemma kan du gå igenom alla papper i din egen takt. Då dyker säkert ännu fler frågor upp. Eftersom alla uppfödare uppskattar en första lägesrapport, redan de första dagarna efter hemkomsten, får du snart ett nytt tillfälle att få svar på dina frågor.

Svår omställning

De första månaderna efter att du fått hem din valp är en spännande men jobbig tid för både valpen och dig själv. Valpen ska dels anpassa sig till en helt ny miljö med nya flockmedlemmar, dels lära sig en mängd nya beteenden. Själv måste du anpassa dig till ett liv som hundägare. Låt den här omställningen ske i den takt som passar just dig och din valp. Det finns inga regler som säger att en hund t.ex. ska vara rumsren eller kunna ”ligg” vid en viss ålder. Liksom varje hundägare är en unik individ är varje hund det också.

Ingenting i det nya hemmet är på samma sätt som hos uppfödaren. Där finns ingen mamma, inga syskon, inte samma människor som den är van vid, den hittar inte i huset, den vet inte vad som är farligt eller vad som är tryggt. Och framför allt så låter och luktar det inte som den är van vid. Valpen ställs plötsligt inför helt nya levnadsbetingelser. Låt den därför få tid på sig att, i sin egen takt, komma underfund med vilka premisser den lever under.

Ett bra sätt att underlätta omställningen för valpen är att försöka följa de rutiner för mat, lek och sömn som fanns hos uppfödaren. Är den van att t. ex. få första målet klockan sju på morgonen och att lampan släcks för natten klockan nio på kvällen, så fortsätt med det, åtminstone till att börja med.

Man brukar säga att hunden är ett "vanedjur". Med det menar man oftast att den har lätt att lära sig det som upprepas på samma sätt många gånger. Och det som är sig likt från gång till gång ger trygghet. Därför är det snällt att följa samma rutiner och ställa samma krav varje dag. Då vet hunden vad som förväntas av den.

Hund "på foder"

Det finns också särskilda avtal som reglerar rättigheter och skyldigheter mellan säljare (överlåtare) och köpare (fodervärd) i de fall uppfödaren behåller ägande- och avelsrätten på valpen – helt eller delvis – på vissa villkor. Det kallas att "sätta ut hund på foder" och ska regleras i ett fodervärdsavtal.

Det finns olika varianter på fodervärdsavtal. Enkelt kan man säga att, i normalfallet, uppfödaren får ta en eller två valpkullar på "din" tik och "som tack för besväret" betalar du t.ex. bara hälften av normalpriset för valpen eller ingenting alls. Det finns även fodervärdsavtal för hanhundar. Då har uppfödaren rätt till ett visst antal parningar med din hanhund – gratis.

Det finns både för- och nackdelar med att vara fodervärd. Tänk dig för noggrant, förvissa dig om uppfödarens syfte med arrangemanget. Diskutera igenom villkoren i detalj med uppfödaren innan du bestämmer dig för att ta en hund på foder. Tänk över konsekvenserna hemma i lugn och ro innan du beslutar dig. Behöver du ytterligare information om vad det innebär att vara fodervärd kan du kontakta SKKs informationsavdelning. Skriv aldrig under något annat avtal än SKKs förtryckta fodervärdsavtal!

Köpa vuxen hund – omplacering

Det kan finnas många anledningar till att man väljer att köpa en vuxen hund i stället för en valp; börjar du själv bli till åren kan det bli väl jobbigt att ta hand om och uppfostra en liten valp, du kanske måste kunna ha med hunden på jobbet nästan från början och det är inte många arbetsgivare som ställer upp på en gnag- och kissbenägen ”anställd”. Du kanske får chansen att ta över en hund som du redan känner och tycker om från någon som inte kan ha den kvar eller du är specialintresserad av något, t.ex. utställning eller jakt, och får chansen att köpa en färdig topphund från en uppfödare.

För att hitta en bra vuxen hund använder du dig lämpligast av samma kanaler som när du letar valp. Besök prov och utställningar, prata med rasklubben och dess valpförmedling, ring SKKs informationsavdelning och kontakta olika uppfödare.

Oavsett anledningen ska man gå lika omsorgsfullt tillväga vid val och köp av en vuxen hund som vid ett valpköp. Men här finns dock en stor skillnad; du bör ha hunden ”på prov” en tid innan du bestämmer dig eller skriver på några papper. En vuxen hund har sina nackdelar och förtjänster befästa och är mycket mindre formbar än en åtta veckors valp.

För att det ska stå helt klart juridiskt vem som äger hunden under ”provveckorna” ska detta finnas reglerat skriftligen. Du ska alltså skriva under på att du endast har hunden till låns t.o.m. senast ett angivet datum och vilken försäkring den har och att denna gäller för den angivna tiden. Hunden kan ju t.ex. bli sjuk under ”provtiden” eller du upptäcker att hunden och du inte passar ihop så du vill lämna tillbaks den till ägaren, men denne hävdar att du redan lovat att köpa den.

Självklart ska den vuxna hunden också vara försäkrad, veterinärbesiktigad och ett köpekontrakt ska alltid skrivas under av köpare och säljare innan hunden är din.

Fråga alltid **varför** hunden ska omplaceras. Den vanligaste anledningen till att man placerar om en hund är allergi, ändringar av familje- och/eller arbetsförhållanden, men också att man inte "klarar av" hunden på olika sätt.

En hund som är stressad, full av olater och inte respekterar sina ägare är sällan lätt att ändra på till en lätthanterlig och trevlig hund. Tar man över en s.k. problemhund måste man vara beredd på att lägga ner otroligt mycket tid, arbete och pengar för proffshjälp för att få hunden att fungera normalt och ibland tyvärr utan att lyckas. Den som inte varit en aktiv hundägare tidigare bör absolut akta sig för att ta över en problemhund, hur fin och gullig den än må vara. De "knepiga" hundarna bör hanteras av erfarna och kunniga personer. För den oerfarne är det tillräckligt med jobb att lyckas med en "normal" hund!

Många tror att en vuxen omplaceringshund får man i stort sett gratis, men så är det oftast inte och bör heller inte vara. Man brukar säga att "varje valp är en blivande stjärna" d.v.s. att ingen kan säga hur den kommer att utvecklas; den kan bli jätteduktig att jaga men den kan lika väl bli en usel jakthund eller den kan bli en utställningsvinnare likväl som en exteriör medelmåtta. Att köpa valp är ju faktiskt till stor del en chansning.

En vuxen hund kan vi däremot syna i facit redan innan köpet. Har den meriter på jakt-, lydnads- och bruksprov och/eller utställning blir den kanske mer värd än en valp. Att den hittills varit frisk, är armbågs- och höftledsröntgad samt ögonlyst utan anmärkning gör den till ett säkrare kort än en valp och kan öka dess värde. En specialutbildad hund, som exempelvis en godkänd räddnings- eller mögelhund liksom en jaktprovschampion, betingar ett mycket högt pris.

Ett objektivt sätt att bedöma en vuxen hunds värde är att fråga försäkringsbolagen hur mycket de är villiga att livförsäkra hunden för. De bolag som specialiserat sig på hundförsäkringar har tabeller på vilka bruks- och utställningsmeriter samt veterinärundersökningar som ökar hundens värde och med hur mycket.

Försäkringar

Idag är det kostsamt att ta sin hund till veterinär. Några dygns vistelse på djursjukhus, samt efterföljande medicinering, kostar oftast flera tusen kronor. Har du inte din hund sjukförsäkrad får du givetvis stå för hela kostnaden själv. Så för både din och hundens skull ska du förstås se till att ha valpen försäkrad från den dag du hämtar den.

Du bör även livförsäkra valpen. Det vanligaste är att man tar en kombinationsförsäkring – liv- och veterinärvårdsförsäkring i ett. De flesta uppfödare hjälper sina valpköpare att teckna försäkringen. Dessutom finns en blankett för ansökan om hundförsäkring dels på hundägarbeviset, som följer med registreringsbeviset, dels i broschyren ”Välkommen valp”. Det finns en handfull bolag som tecknar försäkringar för hund. Villkoren är på ytan tämligen lika mellan de olika bolagen, men kan skilja sig väsentligt åt vid en djupare granskning. Lyssna med uppfödaren och jämför själv villkoren mellan bolagen innan du tecknar avtal med något försäkringsbolag.

Men du behöver ytterligare en försäkring. Din hund kan t.ex. orsaka skada på annans egendom eller på någon människa. Som ägare till hunden är du alltid skadeståndsskyldig för vad den ställer till med (se s. 106). Hör med ditt försäkringsbolag om hemförsäkringen räcker till för dig även sedan du blivit hundägare. Om inte – ta en tilläggsförsäkring.

Hitta ”hund-veterinär”

Räkna med att förr eller senare måste du gå till veterinär för att få hjälp när hunden råkat ut för en olycka eller blivit sjuk. Vilken veterinär ska du då gå till? Din uppfödare känner säkert till vilka veterinärer, i sin egen hemtrakt, som är intresserade och kunniga ”hund-veterinärer”. Bor du i en annan landsända än uppfödaren, kan du lyssna med mer erfarna hundägare på orten för att få tips om en bra ”hund-veterinär”. Eftersom du redan inom några veckor ska vaccinera valpen – ta kontakt med veterinären och beställ tid. Ta med vaccinationsintyget (oftast stämplat i registreringsbeviset) till veterinären.

Redan första veckan hemma kan du skapa rutiner för en daglig genomgång av hunden. Titta och känn igenom hunden från nos- till svanstipp. Syna päls, öron, ögon, tassar och mun extra noga.

Om du märker att allt inte står rätt till med din valp så tänk på att de flesta åkommor botas lättare och snabbare ju förr behandling sätts in. Dra dig inte för att kontakta veterinären om du misstänker att valpen blivit sjuk.

Den förebyggande hälsovården innebär att du håller ögon och öron rena, borstar och kammar pälsen, ger rätt foder i rätt mängd så att valpen alltid är i lagom hull, avmaskar den samt ger den motion. Allt detta avpassat efter valpens ras och ålder. Hur mycket och vilken typ av motion du kan ge den lilla valpen, unghunden samt den vuxna hunden ska du fråga uppfödare, rasspecialist och veterinär om. Generellt gäller att riktig motion ska de flesta raser inte ha förrän efter det första året, till dess räcker lek och korta promenader. För mycket motion under uppväxten kan belasta bl.a. ben och leder för hårt, vilket inte är bra eftersom valpen växer mycket och fort på kort tid.

Objudna gäster

Det finns en mängd olika anledningar till att en hund kliar sig onormalt mycket. Och det är ibland svårt att reda ut varför. Är du osäker på kli-orsaken måste du gå till en veterinär, helst en som är specialist på hud, för det finns allvarliga sjukdomar som ger upphov till bl.a. klåda.

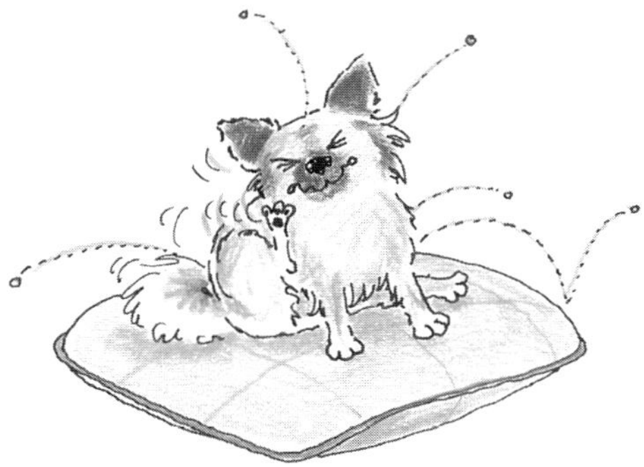

Hundlöss, rävskabb och fästingar är bara några av de vanligaste orsakerna till klåda. Loppor är mest vanligt i södra Sverige. Små, små objudna gäster i päls och hud då och då hör till hundägandet. De flesta småkryp som alla hundar riskerar att bli smittade av är dock ganska lätta att bli av med.

Själva lössen kan ses – små bruna djur – med blotta ögat i hudbotten, men ännu lättare är det ibland att hitta lusäggen, gnetterna, som ses som glänsande pyttesmå riskorn på pälsstråna. Löss "smittar" bara från hund till hund. Loppor kan även överföras från katt till hund. Det finns bra schampon och andra motmedel att köpa i djuraffärer och på apotek. Även hundens omgivning, framför allt liggplatser, måste rengöras noga.

Rävskabb ger ofta, men inte alltid, kraftig klåda, håravfall och sår. Misstänker man rävskabb på hunden måste den tas till veterinär för provtagning och behandling. Hunden smittas oftast utomhus när den vistas i samma områden som drabbade rävar. Även kontakt med andra hundars liggplatser m.m. kan leda till att skabbdjuren överförs från en hund till en annan.

När man råkat ut för ohyra på sin hund ska man vara noga med att informera alla sina hundkompisar så att även deras hundar behandlas. Om inte alla hundar i umgängeskretsen behandlas ungefär samtidigt blir det svårt att komma tillrätta med exempelvis ett lusangrepp. Det blir "rundgång" på lössen eftersom behandlade hundar smittas igen av kompisens obehandlade hund.

Fästingar kan överföra smittsamma och allvarliga sjukdomar, som borrelia, erlichia och hjärninflammation till hunden, därför gäller det att försöka förebygga fästingangrepp. Det finns ett flertal preparat, en del dock receptbelagda, på marknaden som hjälper till att hålla bort fästingar. Fråga din veterinär eller uppfödare om lämpligt preparat.

Akut erlichia kommer plötsligt och ger hög feber, trötthet och hunden vill varken äta eller dricka. **Kronisk** erlichia och borrelia ger diffusa symptom som trötthet, febertoppar, hälta, och symptom från nervsystemet som t. ex. beteendeförändringar. Erlichia kan tyvärr angripa vilket organ som helst i hunden och ge upphov till en mängd olika sjukdomssymptom.

Hur stor risk det är att få fästingar beror på årstiden, var i landet man bor, hur mycket och i vilken typ av natur hunden rör sig. Gå igenom pälsen noggrant varje dag på jakt efter fästingar och ta genast bort dem. Det är förstås svårare att hitta och ta bort en fästing som satt sig om pälsen är lång och åt det mörkare hållet. Ju förr fästingen avlägsnas desto mindre risk att den hunnit smitta din hund med någon allvarlig sjukdom!

Hund på semestern

Visst kan man ta med sin hund på semestern och det kan ju vara jätteskoj och ibland en nyttig miljöträning för den att t.ex. åka bil eller tåg och få bo i en stuga på landet, vandra i fjällen eller bada i havet. Men ibland är det nog bättre att lämna bort hunden under semesterveckorna. Ingen hund gillar eller mår bra av att kuska runt i en sommarvarm bil och du själv blir väldigt begränsad; många övernattningsställen tillåter inte hundar, på matserveringar och allmänna badplatser är hundar förbjudna, likaså på museer, nöjesfält och djurparker. En bil i sommarvärmen blir mycket snabbt överhettad, även i skugga, så det går inte att lämna hunden i bilen annat än någon minut.

Hundvakt

Då och då måste även de flesta hundägare resa bort. Och det är ju inte alla gånger man kan, vill eller får ta med sig hunden. Vad gör jag då av min hund? Vanligast är nog att man förlitar sig på bussiga vänner som ställer upp på att utöka den egna familjen med en fyrbent vän under en kortare tid. Men det är ju inte alltid den lösningen fungerar. I synnerhet inte i semestertider och vid storhelger då många av vännerna själva är hemifrån.

För att vara helt säker på att allt kommer att gå bra när du väl lämnat bort din hund till någon annan, är det vettigt att låta hundvakten låna hunden på prov någon dag eller två i god tid innan du reser bort. Då vet alla inblandade vad de ger sig in på och man slipper oroa sig på semestern för hur det ska gå.

En del uppfödare åtar sig att ta hand om andras hundar under kortare tid, oftast mot en skälig ersättning. Men det kan köra ihop sig; uppfödare har inte sällan egna hundar av båda kön. Vill du då ha hjälp med din hanhund och uppfödaren just då har en tik som löper kanske det inte fungerar. Och av samma skäl är de flesta uppfödare måttligt roade av att ta hand om andras löptikar. Den som har en valpkull vill heller inte gärna släppa in en utomstående hund i huset eftersom det då alltid finns risk för smitta.

Hundpensionat

Hundpensionat kan vara en god lösning och de finns lite varstans i landet dock med en viss koncentration utanför storstäderna. Om du inte känner till pensionatet personligen är det en del att ta reda på innan du lämnar dit din hund. För att driva hundpensionat kommersiellt måste anläggningen vara godkänd av SKK och kommunens miljö- och hälsoskyddskontor. Har du fått tips på ett pensionat är det bara att ringa dit och kontrollera att detta uppfyller kraven och är godkänt. SKK har en lista på godkända pensionat. Vill du veta mer är det nog förnuftigt att själv åka dit och se hur hundarna har det och bilda dig en egen uppfattning om den som ska ta hand om din hund. Du får betala en dygnskostnad och därmed kan du också ställa krav på hur din hund ska ha det när du är bortrest.

Oavsett var du lämnar din hund så ta med mat som räcker tills du kommer tillbaka. För en del hundar kan omställningen av miljö, rutiner och mat sammantaget annars bli lite för många nyheter på en gång och magen komma i olag. Ta också gärna med den bädd eller filt som hunden är van att ligga på så gör den sig lättare hemmastadd. Lämna, om möjligt, telefonnummer där du kan nås om något skulle hända eller om hundvakten behöver fråga om något väsentligt som rör din hund.

Åka utomlands med hund

Olika länder har olika regler för införsel av hund från annat land. Generellt kan man säga att Norge är det enda land du kan besöka med hund utan särskilda vaccinationer och intyg.

Till övriga EU och EFTA-länder, dock ej till England, Island och Irland, vilka kräver lång karantänsvistelse, krävs att hunden är vaccinerad mot rabies och leutospiros och att detta intygas på särskild blankett av Jordbruksverket. Rabiesvaccination ska göras två gånger med en månads intervall. Därefter ska ett blodprov tas för att bevisa att hunden verkligen har skydd mot rabies. Det måste gå minst två månader efter sista vaccinationen innan provet kan tas. Det här innebär alltså att den som vill ta med sin hund utomlands måste vara ute i mycket god tid, minst ett halvår innan resan! Har du otur och blodprovet inte visar att vaccinationen har "tagit" måste vaccination och blodprovsrutiner göras om!

Observera dock att dessa regler kan ändras med kort varsel och att vissa länder kan ha specialbestämmelser. Hör med Jordbruksverket och/eller respektive lands konsulat vad som gäller – i god tid – innan ni ska ge er iväg.

Uppfostran för trygghet

Även om du inte skaffat hund i syfte att exempelvis tävla lydnad eller bruks, så måste du uppfostra och träna valpen till att fungera bra i det dagliga livet. Den måste bl. a. lära sig att kissa och bajsa utomhus, gå i koppel utan att dra, inte tugga på mattor, vara ensam hemma ett par timmar utan att störa grannarna och komma när du ropar på den.

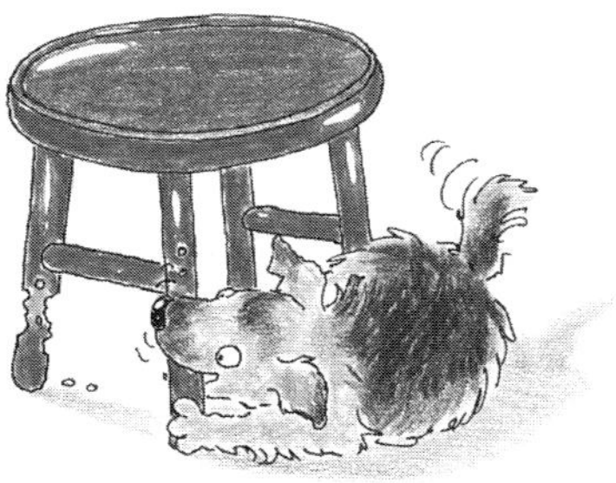

Många problem grundläggs redan i den tidiga valpåldern. Var därför konsekvent mot valpen ända från början. Då underlättar du tillvaron för hunden. Vad den får och inte får göra första dagen ska gälla även efter ett år. Man kan inte ha vissa regler när den är valp, andra när den är unghund och ytterligare andra då den är vuxen. Då bygger du in en osäkerhet i hunden och det är ju direkt elakt.

Det som är positivt för hunden kommer den att upprepa. Lär den sig att ta mat från bordet riskerar du att den gör det igen – det är ju gott/positivt med mat. Om du korrigerar valpen då den redan uppnått något lustfyllt kommer du inte långt i din uppfostran. När valpen väl är uppe på bordet och tuggar på en köttbit har den ju redan uppnått vad den ville. Om du däremot haffar den då den är på väg att göra något fel har det mycket större effekt. Ertappar du valpen på väg upp på bordet och då korrigerar den så har den inte hunnit uppnå vad den traktat efter.

Och kom ihåg att en korrigering **efter** att hunden redan gjort något otillåtet förstår den inte. Det enda du uppnår med det är en osäker hund som upplever sig utsatt för ett övergrepp. Ibland, eller snarare alltför ofta, hör man hundägare säga "titta nu skäms Fido, han vet att han inte fick göra så där". Hundar kan inte skämmas! Däremot kan den visa undergivenhet därför att ägaren visar med röst och kroppshållning att han är arg eller så har den lärt sig att förknippa mattes hemkomst med något obehagligt, men att det beror på att den t. ex. tuggat lite på mattan för en stund sedan kan den **aldrig** förstå. Även om vi tror att vi agerar normalt kan hunden läsa av vår sinnesstämning.

Hund och katt

Att man inte kan skaffa hund därför att man har en katt är oftast fel. Uttrycket "de är som hund och katt" betyder att de går inte ihop eller att de slåss huvudsakligen för att de har olika "språk" och därför missförstår varandra. I verkligheten är det sällan så att hundar och katter inte kan samsas under samma tak. Jo, visst finns det både katter och hundar som inte kan acceptera varandra, men de hör inte till vanligheten. En främmande katt flyende utomhus är en stor frestelse för många hundar att jaga. Men med husets egen katt som hunden lärt känna och respekterar är det annorlunda.

För att umgänget mellan valp och katt ska fungera är det viktigaste av allt att du låter dem lära känna varandra i sin egen takt. Försök aldrig att skynda på dem genom att exempelvis sätta ner katten på golvet till hunden eller liknande

”tvångsmöten”, då försätter du båda i en situation som de inte kan hantera. Risken är att ena parten känner sig så pressad och rädd att den går till anfall. Det kan ta många veckor innan de accepterar och respekterar varandra, men så småningom reder de ut sin relation alldeles på egen hand. Innan du är säker på att umgänget mellan katten och hunden fungerar ska de inte lämnas helt ensamma. Missförstånd kan lätt uppstå i början och då kan de ryka ihop... Men de lär sig så småningom att läsa varandras språk.

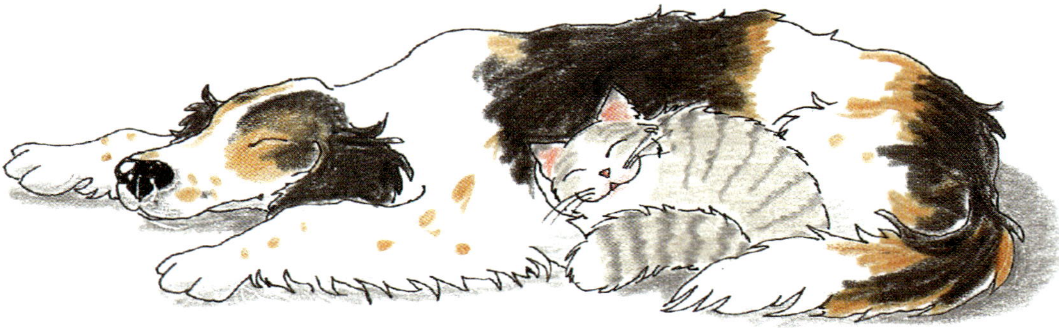

Det vanligaste är att valpen söker upp katten för att undersöka vad den är för konstig ”valp”. De flesta katter ”slår” då oftast till direkt mot valpen, så fort den kommer för nära, medan ett fåtal tar till flykten. Och att jaga något som flyr kan de flesta valpar inte motstå, men efter en kortare jakt stannar katten, vänder sig om och slår till valpen med tass/klor. Och därmed har valpen lärt sig att katten ”bits” och kan vara obehaglig. Om katten flyr upp på något, så valpen inte kan nå den, bör du sätta stopp för valpens försök att hoppa och klänga sig upp till katten annars riskerar du möblemanget. Dessutom ska du ju ändå lära valpen att det är förbjudet att hoppa och klättra på möbler. Att valpen är i full gång med kattjakt ändrar inte några regler!

Vara ensam

Alla valpar måste lära sig att vara ensamma, i bilen och kanske i rastgård men framför allt i hemmet, några timmar ibland. Det finns många tillfällen i alla hundägares liv då de inte kan eller vill ta med hunden. Då och då vill även hundägare t.ex. gå på bio, restaurang, fest och måste tyvärr ibland uppsöka läkare och sjukhus. Om valpen inte lär sig att vara ensam utan att störa grannar, tugga sönder inredning eller lösa prylar blir man väldigt låst i sitt sociala liv.

Eftersom hunden är ett flockdjur vill den inte vara ensam. Då protesterar den genom att gnälla och skälla eller blir så stressad att den inte kan vara inaktiv utan river ner saker och tuggar på allt möjligt. Hur pass lätt den lär sig att stå ut med ensamhet beror på ras, ålder och individ, men framför allt på vilka erfarenheter den har av att bli ”övergiven”. Därför är det viktigt att träna den redan som liten i att lägga sig och sova och vänta på att flocken kommer tillbaka.

Bor du i hyreshus kan du sätta upp en lapp vid porten och tala om att du skaffat valp och håller på att lära den att vara ensam. Be dina grannar ha överseende och genast meddela dig om hunden stör för mycket. Då får du förhoppningsvis även grannarna att känna sig delaktiga, samtidigt som du visat dem hänsyn.

Korta stunder

Börja med att lämna valpen ensam korta stunder vid tillfällen när den är trött och brukar vilja gå och lägga sig och sova; när den ätit, rastats och lekt. Se till att den har **ett** ben eller liknande att gnaga på, gör ingen affär av din sorti utan stäng dörren och bara gå. I början ska du bara lämna den några minuter eller tills den tystnat, kanske endast några sekunder. Ett annat bra sätt att börja lära hunden att vara ifrån flocken är att sätta upp en ”grind” mellan två rum. Hunden vistas på ena sidan och familjen på den andra. Samma princip används som när den är instängd bakom en dörr.

Om du öppnar dörren när valpen gnäller så kommer den bara att låta ännu mer nästa gång därför att det lönade sig att protestera – matte kom ju. I stället för att lära sig att gnäll och skäll är ett sätt att kalla in matte ska den lära sig att ”om jag ligger här och är tyst och väntar så kommer matte”. En del valpar protesterar hjärtskärande högljutt under lång tid medan andra snabbt lär sig att den inte lönar sig att föra ett himla liv.

Låt valpen vara ensam ofta, men under korta stunder, öka tiden pö om pö tills den klarar av ensamheten ett par timmar. Ta bort alla leksaker och lämna den helst i ett litet utrymme (prova dig fram – det finns enstaka hundar som reagerar tvärtom) t.ex. kök eller hall så dess rörlighet blir något begränsad. Då kan den inte vara lika aktiv. Eftersom aktivitet ger ökad stress minskar ett begränsat utrymme risken för att den far runt i huset och ”drar upp”/stressar sig själv.

Ett glatt ”Hej” räcker

Trots att du tränat och lärt hunden att vara ensam hemma innebär det inte att den därmed klarar det även i bilen och i rastgården. Den har ju lärt sig något i en viss miljö, så det är bara att börja om och träna på samma sätt på nya ställen.

Ditt agerande när du kommer tillbaka och släpper ut hunden kommer att ytterligare påverka dess upplevelse av att vara ensam. Vanligt är att hundägare tycker så synd om hunden att de ömkar, låter sig bli slickade och hoppade på och gör hälsningscermonien onödigt omständlig. Ja, helt enkelt gör alltför mycket affär av återförenandet så att hunden verkligen blir övertygad om att ”det var otäckt att vara ensam”. Det är bättre att göra som en annan hund skulle göra; en kort odramatisk hälsning, ett glatt ”hej” och sedan är det bra, om hunden ändå fortsätter ”misshandeln” (klänger och hoppar) så kommer ett bestämt morr/nej. Då ger du hunden uppfattningen att det här är naturligt och inget att hetsa upp sig över.

Vara uppkopplad

Lära hunden att vara uppkopplad bygger på samma princip som ensam-inlärning. Börja här med att binda hunden där det inte finns något som stör den, i skogen eller på tomten. Sätt dig en liten bit ifrån den och vänta tills hunden är lugn, gå tillbaka till den och säg lugnt med låg röst ”bra”. Koppla loss och var som vanligt. Låt den sitta en lite längre stund för varje gång, öka avståndet mellan dig och hunden och så småningom kan du själv befinna dig en bit bort och göra något; kratta gräsmattan, plocka blommor eller något annat naturligt. Nästa steg är att gå bort en bit så hunden inte ser dig; bakom ett träd, en sten eller runt husknuten.

Om hunden skäller, gnäller, slänger sig i kopplet så nonchalera den tills den lugnat ner sig. Går du i stället tillbaka till den så är ju risken stor att den lärt sig att detta lönar sig – husse kommer ju!

Problem växer inte bort

Var hellre lite ”tuff” mot den lilla valpen än att du försätter dig i en situation som du får svårt att klara ut när den är tio månader. Unghundar har så mycket mer vilja, självständighet och tuffhet än små valpar. Det är lättare att korrigera en valp.

Som flockledare måste du se till att det du sagt eller visat åtföljs. Du får inte ge dig förrän valpen gör som du vill. När valpen t.ex. vill sticka åt ett annat håll än det du visat att ni ska gå åt, ta tag i den, vänligt men bestämt, och säg ”nu går vi hitåt”. Gå bortåt och locka på valpen och visa din glädje över att den följde efter dig. När valpen är liten har du chansen att springa ifatt den. Ta den chansen, den återkommer aldrig sedan den blivit lite större. Likaså kommer du aldrig att utöva en så stark dragning på valpen som nu när den är liten – utnyttja det för att lära den inkallning.

Ingenting mognar och blir bättre av sig själv, utan du måste lära valpen hur du vill att den ska göra/inte göra. Barn kan, vid en viss ålder, förstå att något är fel om man förklarar för dem. Men hunden måste alltid upprepa en handling för att lära sig något. Hunden måste få försöka göra om det den just gjorde fel, t.ex. bita på ett bordsben, så att den inte bara uppfattar att du är sur utan också förstår varför du blev arg. Den måste få chansen att koppla ihop din ilska med att den gnager på bordsbenet. Först då har du möjlighet att berömma den.

Kan valpen tänka?

Visst tänker hunden, men inte på samma sätt som en människa. Den lär sig att vissa beteenden ger den tillfredsställelse och att andra inte gör det. Hunden anpassar sina handlingar efter vad som är positivt och vad som är negativt för den.

Lär dig så mycket som möjligt om hur en hund fungerar. Då får du möjlighet till en djupare relation med hunden. Och ju mer du lär dig om hunddjur desto intressantare och roligare blir ditt ”hundliv”! Du kommer då också att finna din hund mer och mer fascinerande. Vill du lyckas med valpuppfostran, träning, tävling, jakt och vardagsliv måste du lära dig se det som händer omkring er med hundens ögon.

Var positiv

Nu för tiden är kunniga och erfarna hundtränare överens om att inlärning ska bygga på hundens naturliga instinkter och att bästa, och säkraste, resultatet uppnås genom positiv träning. Den tid då man trodde att en hund kunde förstå och lära sig något genom skrik, hugg och slag är, tack och lov, historia. Råkar du trots allt på en sådan historisk kvarleva som vill hjälpa dig få ”fason” på din hund – vänd dig till någon annan kunnigare hundtränare!

Låter du en människa eller en annan hund göra illa din hund så sviker du ditt åtagande som flockledare. Du har då överlåtit ansvaret på hunden. Vill du vara en bra och pålitlig flockledare för din hund måste du också axla rollen som hundens beskyddare. Du måste alltså försvara din hund mot det som är farligt för den.

Som beskyddare måste matte eller husse ta första stöten i nya situationer. Om något verkligen är farligt skyddar du hunden. Blir den däremot rädd för något som egentligen inte är farligt, t.ex. en fladdrande presenning, får du aldrig ömka den. Då, om inte förr, blir den verkligt övertygad om att det faktiskt är farligt! I stället bör du glatt försöka övertyga hunden om att presenningar är jätteskojiga.

Rumsrenhet

Att lära hunden bli rumsren är oftast inga större problem. Men det tar tid och fordrar tålamod och påpasslighet. Små valpar kissar, liksom bebisar, många, många gånger om dagen. Att det blir pölar inomhus får du stå ut med. Det finns vissa tillfallen då valpen nästan alltid behöver kissa; efter att den har sovit, ätit och lekt. Om den ”misslyckas” inomhus, säg ingenting. I den tidiga valpåldern vet den ofta inte ens om att den har kissat och är heller inte fysiskt utvecklad för att kunna reglera sina behov. En hund vill inte förorena i sin egen ”lya”, så ha förtröstan – så småningom lär den sig att göra ifrån sig utomhus, bara du ger den chansen. Ta ut valpen till samma plats varje gång, gå inte långt, och beröm den direkt när den uträttat sina behov. Och se till att den verkligen uppfattar dina klappar och ditt beröm.

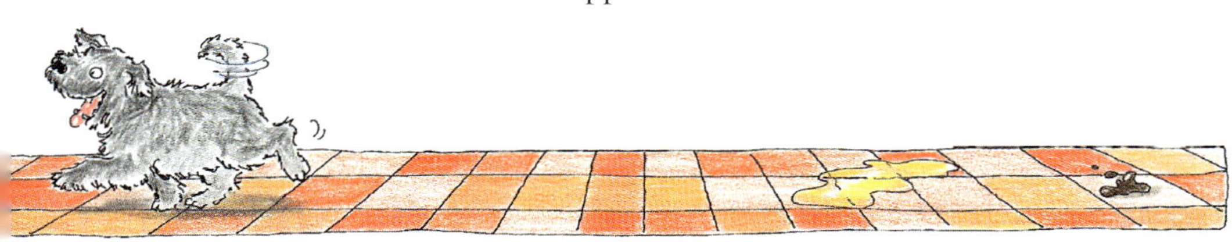

Belöning och korrigering

Allt som får valpen att se glad ut och vifta på svansen är belöning för den. Titta på valpen när du gett den beröm, är den inte glad så måste du belöna mer eller på annat sätt. Vem bestämmer vad som är en belöning? Jo, hunden förstås! En hund kanske tycker att en godbit är det bästa som finns medan en annan inte alls är matintresserad. Då är det dags att använda fantasin och komma underfund med vad just din hund uppskattar riktigt mycket. Pussa matte i ansiktet, busa med en trasa, rusa efter ett kastat föremål är bara ett fåtal tips, men självklart finns det mycket mer som en hund blir riktigt glad över. Det ska vara kvalitet på belöningen! Och du måste variera den, annars riskerar du att hunden "väger" det du har att erbjuda gentemot det som den själv vill. Nästan ingen hund upplever rejäla "dunkar"/klappar i sidan kombinerat med ett mullrande "duktig hund", som något trevligt...

Det finns dock tillfällen då du måste visa ditt ogillande för valpen. Ertappar du den gnagande på exempelvis en matta eller ett stolsben måste den få lära sig att det är förbjudet. Hur ska du då, utan att vara elak, få den att förstå vad som är förbjudet?

Var lugn hela tiden. Det finns ingen anledning att höja rösten, men väl att byta tonläge, när du säger till valpen att något är förbjudet. Börja med "nej" eller morra, se vad som händer. Slutar den inte med ofoget så räcker det oftast med att hålla i den med två fingrar under hakan, titta den i ögonen och säga nej/morra igen. Släpp hunden och se om den går tillbaka till det förbjudna. Gör den det så dit med två fingrar igen eller tryck bestämt, men ej hårt, till den över nosen (så gör tiken när hon uppfostrar sina valpar) och säg "nej".

Det gäller att vara envisare än hunden, men aldrig våldsam, och alltid följa upp en korrigering d.v.s. titta på hunden och se om den tagit åt sig eller ej. Och glöm aldrig att se till att ni blir kompisar efteråt, så valpen inte förlorar förtroendet för dig. Anpassa hela tiden korrigeringens intensitet efter just din hund, inte kompisens jycke som kanske är betydligt vekare eller tuffare än din.

Ha alltid i bakhuvudet att belöning eller utesluten belöning – ingen korrigering alls – ska vara den helt övervägande metoden vid all inlärning och träning!

Tala tyst

Hundens hörsel är otroligt mycket bättre än människans. Eftersom hundar inte talar med varandra med ord och meningar, så är deras tonläge desto mer betydelsefullt i kommunikationen med andra hundar, djur och människor. Enkelt kan man säga att en hund som är lite arg morrar nästan ohörbart, men om det inte respekteras höjer den rösten för att visa att den menar allvar – precis som vi själva. Den kan också modifiera sitt tonläge så att den i vissa situationer morrar tyst och dovt och i andra ljust och nästan gläfsigt. Hundens skall kan låta ”ljust” och glatt när den rusar för att möta mattes bil, men ”mörkt” och hotfullt när en främling kommer körande på uppfarten.

Du ska alltså aldrig skrika åt valpen eftersom den hör så väldigt bra, däremot bör du göra som hunden – ändra tonläge beroende på om du vill visa den ditt missnöje eller din glädje. Alla hundar är otroligt mycket mer lyhörda för våra rösters nyanser och tonlägen än vad vi själva är. Hunden uppfattar direkt om du är arg eller glad bara genom att lyssna till om tonen är mörk eller ljus. Det spelar mindre roll om volymen är högt eller lågt påskruvad.

Om du redan från början vinnlägger dig om att tala ”tyst” och lågt till valpen med ett normalt röstläge behöver du aldrig höja rösten mot den. När du är glad och berömmer hunden är det synnerligen viktigt att du övergår från normalläge till ett glatt diskantläge. Något som många hussar måste träna på då ett ljust tonläge inte ligger naturligt i mäns tonregister. Och när du är missbelåten och vill tala om för valpen att något är fel sänker du tonläget till en bister bas. En del, i synnerhet mattar, har svårt med basen. Det brukar lösa sig om matte morrar i stället eftersom det inte går att morra i falsett.

Ju tystare och mer viskande du talar till en hund desto mer uppmärksam blir den! Många hundar blir negativt upphetsade, stressade eller rädda och hör inte vad du säger om du skriker. Rösten är ett av dina absolut viktigaste verktyg för att "tala" med hunden och få den att förstå vad du vill, så missbruka den aldrig. Då riskerar du att få en hund som blundar med öronen och aldrig lyssnar, vare sig du är glad eller arg.

Tala med kroppen

Tillsammans med röstläget är kroppsspråket det viktigaste kommunikationsmedlet mellan hund och människa. Lika skickligt som hunden hör på ditt röstläge om du är hotfull eller trevlig, och de finaste nyanser där emellan, tolkar den även ditt kroppsspråk från minsta lilla rynka i pannan till en tydligt hotfull kroppshållning. Men här gäller det att se upp, för det är ofta som hunden talar, och därmed uppfattar, kroppens språk annorlunda och ibland till och med tvärtemot vad vi människor gör.

Tar du emot ett barn som kommer rusande och ska hoppa upp i din famn så böjer du dig förmodligen lite framåt, sträcker ut händerna och visar upp ett stort leende. Det tolkar barnet som att du är glad över att det kommer, och du välkomnar det med öppna famnen och böjer och sträcker dig fram för att tryggt kunna lyfta upp det.

Om du ropar på din valp och den glatt kommer springande till dig och du tar emot valpen på samma sätt som barnet är risken stor att den visar sig mindre frimodig ju närmare den kommer dig, i alla fall om den är av den lite blygare sorten. Är det en främmande person som lockar på valpen på det sättet är det t.o.m. möjligt att den inte kommer alls. Valpen uppfattar hela din hållning som hotfull. För den lilla valpen ser du ut som en jätte när du lutar dig framåt, med armar som kanske tänker hålla fast den. Och leendet som går från öra till öra kan ju inte innebära annat än att du tänker äta upp den. Ovanpå alltihop stirrar du den rakt i ögonen, vilket kan vara rena rama hotet för en liten valp.

Risk för missförstånd

Man kan lära sig mycket genom att studera hundarnas kroppsspråk när de "pratar" med varandra.

Risken för att du ska misstolka din hunds kroppsspråk är självklart lika stor som att hunden missförstår ditt. Du måste helt enkelt noggrant lära dig "läsa hund", d.v.s. lära dig tolka hundarnas signaler eller kroppsspråk som de talar med varandra. Skillnaden mellan exempelvis en glad och en hotfull svanshållning eller ett nyfiket eller aggressivt "öronspel", kan vara nog så knepigt att reda ut i lugn och ro när man tittar på en bild. När du umgås med din valp eller träffar på andra hundar blir det än mer svårt för den ovane – då står ju studieobjekten inte ens stilla...

Det finns många hundböcker som utförligt förklarar hundens kroppsspråk i text och bild. Läs och lär, annars finns stor risk att du och din hund misstolkar varandras kroppssignaler och därmed missförstår varandra – helt i onödan!

Du ska umgås väldigt mycket med valpen under den första tiden. Den måste få tid att komma underfund med vem du – och resten av familjen – är och hur ni reagerar. Valpen har ett stort behov av trygghet och närhet. Prata och kela mycket med den och låt den vara med i gemenskapen när den själv vill. Tvinga dig inte på den utan låt valpen ta kontakt. Vill den ligga för sig själv, respektera det och låt den vara ifred. Självklart ska den inte störas när den sover. En valp behöver mycket sömn och det är stressande för den att bli väckt.

Lär barnen att de ovillkorligen måste lämna valpen ifred när den sover!

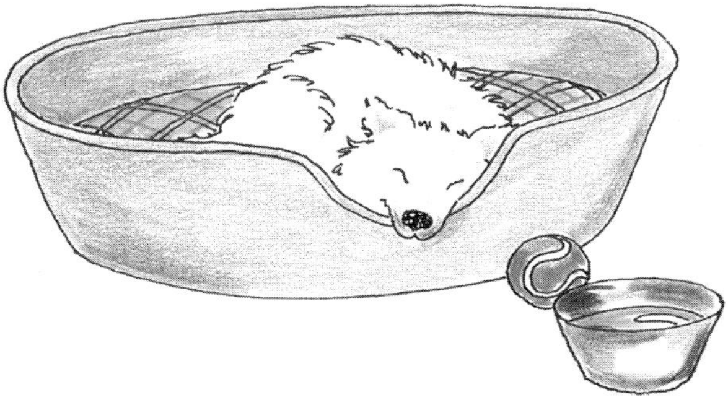

Träning på lek

När valpen var hos uppfödaren lekte den intensivt under relativt korta stunder med sina syskon. Alla valpar tycker det är kul att leka, så det måste din valp få göra ibland. Den behöver få tillfälle att leka med andra snälla hundar, likväl som med människor.

Det är faktiskt nödvändigt att den får leka med andra hundar som valp för att den ska fungera bra med hundar även som vuxen. Men, din valp behöver inte lära känna alla hundar i omgivningen. Låt den ha en handfull justa hundkompisar. Det finns ingenting som heter att t.ex. en främmande hund ska få ”tukta” din valp. Om en hund ni träffar på promenaden hela tiden försöker ”trycka ner” din hund så måste du försvara den. När däremot husets andra hundar eller nära hundkompisar tuktar finns det oftast en anledning till det – om umgänget gått konfliktfritt tidigare.

Lärorik lek

När valpen leker lär den sig! Den övar och förbereder sig för att klara sig i den hårda verkligheten, som den skulle ha levt i om den vore en vildhund. Under leken kan den t.ex. försöka brotta ned en valpkompis = fiende, eller att jaga sin lekkamrat = jaktbyte. Är lekkamraten äldre, starkare, snabbare och smidigare än valpen är det förmodligen oftast valpen som ”förlorar” lekarna. Ur valpens synvinkel är lek med människor samma ”träning” som lek med andra hundar. Därför är det viktigt att du tänker på vad du leker och hur du leker med valpen. Leken bör oftast, men inte alltid, syfta till något.

Du använder förstås leken till att grundlägga vissa beteenden hos valpen. Bra lekar är positivt för hunden, till skillnad från det mesta av vardagslydnaden som lätt kan bli negativ.

Det blir så mycket ”du får inte...” för en liten valp. Lär din valp att använda näsan och att ta kontakt med dig. När den gör det måste den belönas stort! Anpassa leken efter valpens intressen. Den ska ha kul hela tiden. Lek samma lek högst två gånger per dag och håll inte på mer än ungefär fem minuter varje gång eller sluta just innan den ledsnar eller blir alltför stressad. Leken ska ske på dina ”villkor” samtidigt som den aldrig får bli tråkig för valpen. Du bestämmer när ni ska leka och när ni ska sluta. Du bestämmer också vad ni ska leka. För hunden är skillnaden mellan lek och träning inte särskilt stor.

Apportlek

De flesta nyblivna hundägare har nog blivit varnade för vissa lekar, som att t.ex. kasta pinnar till sin hund. Någon framtida glädje av den aktiviteten lär man inte få. Tvärtom ger pinnkastning oftast negativa konsekvenser, såsom stressproblem. Att motionera en hund genom att stå och kasta något, t.ex. en boll, gång på gång är helt förkastligt, inte bara psykiskt utan även fysiskt. OK, då låter jag bli pinn- och bollkastning. Men vad ska jag då hitta på för lekar som hunden tycker är roliga och samtidigt är bra träning?

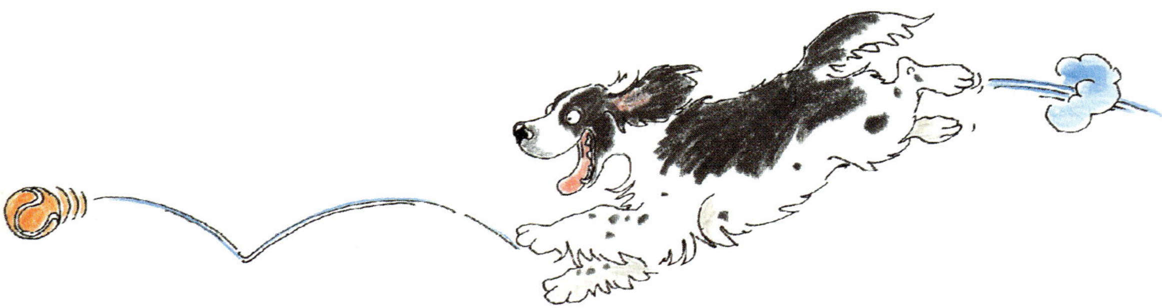

Jodå, visst kan man leka med bollar, men inte nöta. Det är en väldig skillnad på att stå och kasta en boll åt hunden upprepade gånger jämfört med att rulla en boll över köksgolvet två gånger. Rulla iväg bollen så valpen ser den och locka den till dig när den gripit bollen. Kommer den inte, så strunta i den. Börja i stället att själv leka med en annan boll eller något annat attraktivt föremål och nonchalera valpen. Då kommer den antagligen för att se vad du håller på med. Vare sig den kommer med boll eller utan så ta emot valpen – ta inte bollen direkt – med glädje. Om valpen visar tendenser till att inte vilja lämna ifrån sig bollen, prova med att lämna igen den till valpen efter att du fått den och låt den få behålla bollen en stund efter att leken är slut.

Söklek

I ”rulla-boll-leken” kommer valpen framför allt att använda sin jaktinstinkt. Den springer efter och fångar in ett ”byte” som den sett ”fly”. En mindre stressande och mer tröttande lek är att låta den söka rätt på bollen med hjälp av nosen i stället för med ögonen.

Att låta valpen leta efter föremål inomhus, t.ex. en boll, är en bra lek för en 9-veckors valp. Den tycker att det är kul att använda näsan. Om och när den hittar föremålet visar du den att du är överlycklig, springer bort från den och när den kommit ifatt, kela en kort stund och byt sedan bollen mot en godisbit. Om den inte hittar föremålet, så hjälper du den. Ni letar tillsammans helt enkelt. Syftet med den här leken är att lära valpen använda luktsinnet effektivt och dessutom att det är roligt att göra saker tillsammans med matte – att samarbeta.

En variant på söka-föremålsleken är att låta valpen söka efter hundgodisbitar inomhus. Du visar valpen att du har handen full med godisar ber någon hjälpa dig att hålla valpen medan du lägger ut bitarna på olika ställen i rummet. Lägg någon bit nära valpen och låt den leta upp och äta bitarna. I början får du kanske hjälpa den lite, men är den av den matglada sorten kommer den efter några gånger att ha fattat idén.

Om den tycker det är roligt och den lyckas hitta bitarna ökar du svårighetsgraden något för varje sök du lägger. Du kan t.ex. lägga en bit under en mattkant, på en stol, i en skål, i en sko/stövel. När hunden fattat galoppen och själv söker aktivt kan du uppmuntra den med ordet "sök", så lär den sig samtidigt att det ordet betyder att den ska leta upp något. Det kan du få glädje av i framtiden om ni ska jobba med olika sökuppgifter.

För den lite äldre valpen/unghunden kan det vara kul och nyttigt att flytta ut godissöket till tomten. Och varför inte låta hunden leta efter sin egen matskål ibland eller t.o.m. strö ut maten på tomten. Det brukar även stimulera hundar som inte är så matglada till att äta upp sin mat.

Kamp och brottning

När du en dag vill träna den lite äldre hunden mer på allvar är det bra att kunna använda boll och godis för att motivera och belöna hunden. Men en del använder sig också av kamp, alltså har dragkamp om ett föremål med hunden. Där måste det väl vara lätt att hamna i konflikt med hunden?

Ja, kamplekar ska alltid ske på dina villkor. Känns det det minsta jobbigt att kampa så ska man inte hålla på med det alls. Och kom ihåg att det är alltid du som vinner och bestämmer när leken ska sluta.

Lek gärna och ha brottningsmatch med valpen, men så fort den tar i så det gör ont på dig måste du visa den det genom att säga "aj". Om den reagerar på det kan du leka vidare. Om den inte förstår så "nyp tillbaka" lite försiktigt – ge igen – så är den van att umgås med sina syskon. Lek vidare, avbryt inte leken bara för att den tagit i lite för hårt. Då kan den ju dra felaktiga slutsatser...

Roligare än allt annat

Att få hunden att själv välja dig framför allt och alla är grunden till ett positivt och fungerande samarbete mellan er. Och detta är inget som kommer av sig själv och är heller inte enkelt. Nej, du måste på alla upptänkliga sätt övertyga hunden om att det lönar sig att förstå och göra som du vill. Hunden väljer det som ger den mest utbyte inom alla områden som den är i behov av, t.ex. lek/jakt, trygghet, värme, mat. Vi människor söker oss ju faktiskt också till den eller de vänner och intressen som vi får mest utbyte av på olika sätt.

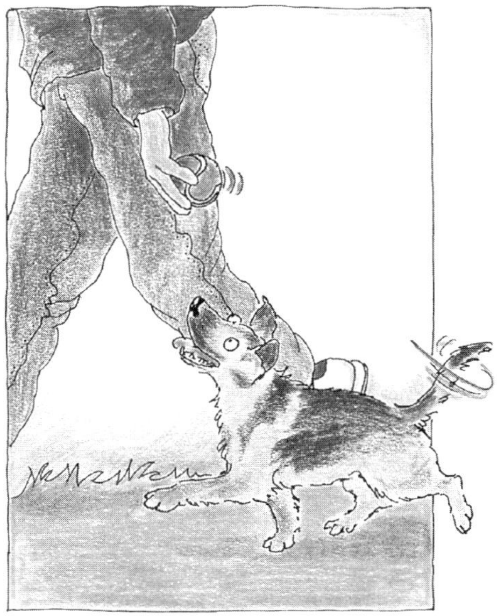

Försök få valpen att uppfatta dig som sin bästa lekkamrat! Är ni t.ex. ute och går, valpen är okopplad och ni får syn på en annan hund en bit längre fram, är det troligt att din valp kommer att rusa iväg för att hälsa på den andra hunden. I stället för att snabbt slänga dig över din valp och koppla den, påkalla valpens uppmärksamhet. Få valpen att titta på dig, locka på den samtidigt som du går i en annan riktning än mot den mötande och bort ifrån valpen. Om den stannar kvar, bryt vad den tänker göra (d.v.s. rusa iväg till den andra hunden) med ett bestämt "nej". Locka, låt intressant och få den att ta några steg efter dig. Nu plockar du blixtsnabbt fram något du vet att valpen tycker är jättekul – en boll, ett pipdjur – vad som helst som du vet att valpen älskar att leka med. Visa tydligt, bolla med föremålet samtidigt som du drar dig bort från valpen. Hänger den efter så beröm och låt den få leka med föremålet.

Är den inte road av leksaker så ta till något annat som din valp älskar, t.ex. en godisbit, eller spring fort iväg en kort bit och släng dig ner på marken och låt valpen kela eller busa med dig. Vad du gör spelar ingen roll, huvudsaken är ju att du är roligare än den andra hunden!

Står du bara still och gör ingenting så har din valp, inom en halv sekund, säkerligen börjat rusa iväg mot den mötande innan du ens fått chansen att konkurrera om dess uppmärksamhet. Nu är sannolikheten att du ska få stopp på valpen minimal. Väl iväg mot något spännande och roligt är valpens hela intresse vänt bort från dig och han är totalt koncentrerad på den andra hunden. Du har missat tillfället att få den att välja ditt sällskap/lek/godis/kel. Därmed kommer valpen nästa gång en liknande situation uppträder att ännu snabbare välja "det där andra spännande" i stället för dig, eftersom den inte förstått att det kan finnas ett bättre/roligare alternativ – du.

Om du däremot lyckas några gånger kommer valpen snart att "fråga" dig i liknande valsituationer om du har något bättre att erbjuda och så småningom ta det för självklart att du är bäst/roligast såvida du inte talar om för den att; OK, stick iväg och lek, för just nu har jag inte tänkt att vi ska göra något tillsammans.

Valpen ska följa dig

En vanlig orsak till inkallnings- och kontaktproblem är att man låtit valpen leka, leka och leka med andra hundar, i stället för att lära den att koncentrera sig och leka eller arbeta med husse och matte – även när andra hundar är i närheten. Som hundägare vill du ju att hunden ska bry sig om dig mer än om omgivningen. Att den ska vilja ha kontakt med just dig och inte följa med bara för att du t. ex. håller i kopplet.

Ju mer sällan du har din valp kopplad desto bättre kontakt och lydnad får du. En valp som får möjlighet att röra sig fritt utan koppel, lär sig att följa efter och hålla reda på sin förare i betydligt större utsträckning än den som oftast går i koppel. Det är ju valpen som ska hålla reda på dig och inte tvärtom! Utnyttja den lilla valpens osäkerhet och behov av dig som trygg flockledare så ofta du kan, genom att helt sonika gå ifrån den om den inte följer med dig av sig själv. En liten valp blir nästan alltid skraj om den blir övergiven och inte vet var matte är och lär sig därför snart att hela tiden följa efter flocken.

Om du inte bor på landet utan i tätbebyggt område, kan du passa på under promenader där det inte finns trafik att då och då gömma dig för valpen. Den kommer då att ta till alla sina sinnen för att leta reda på dig. Den blir nämligen rädd när den lämnas ensam på ett främmande ställe och lär sig att hela tiden ha åtminstone ett halvt öra och öga öppet som håller koll på var du är. Här gäller det att ha is i magen och förstås inte gå långt bort, i början räcker det kanske att gömma sig bakom närmaste sten eller träd och vänta tills valpen helt på egen hand finner dig. Återföreningen ska vara fylld av glädje från din sida. Intensiteten av valpens glädjeyttringar ger dig en vägledning om hur stark dess rädsla varit. Du bör gömma dig så bra att valpen får jobba några minuter innan den finner dig och verkligen visar sin glädje när ni träffas. Beroende på hur benägen valpen är att tappa kontakten med dig kan du gömma dig ofta eller någon gång ibland, svårt eller lätt. Är din valp självständig och inte verkar bry sig så mycket om du försvinner kan du öka valpens känsla av att det varit läskigt att bli "övergiven" genom att ömka den när ni ses igen – "oj, oj stackars lilla Fido, var det så otäckt", säjer du med en röst som verkligen menar det och klappar tröstande.

Här lägger du samtidigt grunden till en bra inkallning. Om valpen inte kommer genast du ropar så försvinner du och gömmer dig. Nästa gång du ropar skyndar sig nog valpen att komma, annars kan ju matte försvinna...

Gå fint i koppel

Bästa sättet att lära en hund att gå "fint" i koppel är att träna utan koppel! Nej det är inget tryckfel. Det är nämligen så att vi människor har förbaskat svårt att låta bli att använda kopplet som ratt, broms och dragkrok. Har du koppel på din hund så använder du det, ibland utan att ens vara medveten om det. Och kopplet är avsett som "livlina" inte som styr- och draglina!

Målsättningen med koppelträning är alltså att inte behöva använda det annat än i en nödsituation. Hunden måste lära sig att vara lös och ändå hålla sig alldeles runt omkring sin förare och inte rusa iväg utan att ha fått tillåtelse till det.

Du kan visa hunden med kroppen och rösten att "nu går vi åt ett annat håll" eller så kan du rycka i kopplet och därmed i halsen, vilket innebär mer eller mindre smärta för hunden, och på det sättet tvinga den att gå dit du vill. Rycker du bara i kopplet är du inte juste mot hunden. Den får inte ens chans att göra rätt och du ger den obehag för att den ska följa dig. Då är det heller inte konstigt att hunden inte vill komma till, eller vara nära, sin matte på promenaderna!

När hunden vill dra i kopplet, gå fortare än du, så stanna och vänta, gör ingenting förrän hunden vänder sig om och tar ögonkontakt. Om väntan blir för lång – böj dig blixsnabbt och nyp till den i baken, då vänder den sig om och du få chansen att påverka den igen. Nu backar du bort från hunden, lockar den till din sida och visar den att här lönar det sig att vara genom att du belönar den, men inte förrän den är bredvid dig igen. Upprepa varje gång den drar så kommer den så småningom underfund med att det är hos dig det är trevligt att vara på koppelpromenader. Varje gång du byter riktning på promenaden gör du likadant.

Gör snabba och/eller oväntade ändringar av din färdriktning och aldrig åt det hållet hunden befinner sig. Om ni går på en stig och valpen är en bit framför dig så kliv plötsligt rakt in i skogen (90 graders vinkel från stigen), gå vidare som om ingenting hänt. Förr eller senare kastar valpen en blick bakåt – "ingen matte, jag är ensam, hjälp!" – och vänder för att leta reda på sin "flock". När valpen hittat dig tar du emot den med glädje och belöning. Om du "lurar" valpen så här ofta, så lär den sig att det alltid är säkrast att hålla ett öga/öra på dig!

Om du lär hunden att det lönar sig att vara nära dig och att komma när du lockar på den får du i stället en hund som **vill** vara i din närhet – "matten kan ju ropa på mig och det brukar alltid löna sig att komma och jag vill inte missa nå´t; kul, kel eller godis" – eftersom det är trevligt/lönsamt där. När hunden går vid din sida, vare sig du lockat den dit eller den bara råkar gå där, säger du "fot"/"sidan"/"bredvid" eller något liknande och belönar den. Efter upprepade gånger kommer den att förknippa det ordet med att gå vid mattes sida och att det är trevligt. Slutligen kommer alltså hunden att uppsöka "rätt" plats bredvid föraren när denne säger exempelvis "fot".

Att lära en hund gå perfekt fot, så som krävs på lydnadstävlingar bygger på samma princip men med betydligt mer "finlir" så att belöningen kommer i **exakt** rätt ögonblick d.v.s. precis bara när hunden rör sig på rätt sätt och är på exakt rätt plats bredvid föraren och samtidigt söker ögonkontakt med denne.

Det finns ytterligare en fördel med att ha sin valp okopplad så ofta det går; du tvingas hela tiden jobba med ditt ledarskap, såsom bestämmande lekledare. Det går inte att slappna av och inte hålla ordning på vad valpen gör eller bara dra iväg med den i kopplet, utan du måste jobba med kontakt och följsamhet hela tiden. Alldeles för många hundar får jämt gå i koppel för att ägaren inte ansträngt sig tillräckligt att lära sig och hunden att hålla ihop genom ett osynligt koppel – kontakten mellan hund och lek- och flockledaren. En sådan hund ges inte mycket frihet precis under sitt korta hundliv.

Kopplet bör alltså fungera som en säkerhet för att den inte ska bli överkörd eller frestas att störa eller jaga vilt, men inte för att tala om för den exempelvis vart ni ska gå eller inte gå – då använder du händerna och rösten för att visa vad du vill. Och belönar förstås när hunden gör rätt.

Lär valpen fråga

Kontakt, det är när hunden tittar dig i ögonen och frågar vad ni ska göra. Det tränar du med den lilla valpen vid varje måltid. Du håller matskålen och väntar tills valpen tittar dig i ögonen och "frågar" om den kan få maten. I samma ögonblick som den hittar din blick ställer du ned skålen. Likadant gör du innan ni går ut genom dörren; valpen får inte gå ut förrän den sett dig i ögonen/bett om lov att få gå. När den tagit ögonkontakt ger du ett kommando som antingen betyder "var så god – gå ut" eller visar med exempelvis handen om det är OK att göra det den vill.

Försök att göra valpens namn till något positivt. Säg namnet, vänta tills den tar ögonkontakt, beröm när hunden tittar dig i ögonen, vare sig du bett om det eller inte.

"Godisspott"

"Godisspott" är ett ypperligt sätt att få valpen att titta dig i ögonen d.v.s. fråga "vad vill du?". Skär upp, i små godisbitar, en bit ost, korv, eller något annat som du själv tycker är OK att ha i munnen. Stoppa in några av gottisarna i munnen. När hunden tittar dig i ögonen, men **endast** just precis då, spottar du ut en bit till hunden. Du ska alltså lära den att ögonkontakt med husse/matte är positivt och att det lönar sig.

Säg hundens namn och om, men bara om, den vänder upp huvudet och ser dig i ögonen så spottar du direkt ut godis till hunden. Då lär du den att lyssna, reagera och söka ögonkontakt när den hör sitt namn.

Vartefter träningen fortskrider ökar du långsamt tiden mellan ögonkontakt och belöning. När hunden befinner sig 10–15 meter bort är det få som klarar att spotta ut godis ända fram till hunden! Belöna då på olika sätt, t.ex. genom att kasta en boll eller något annat kul till hunden på längre och längre avstånd ifrån dig. Men kom ihåg: tar inte hunden ögonkontakt så får den absolut ingen belöning men givetvis inget klander heller! Som vid all hundträning så är det bara att gå tillbaka några steg, göra övningen lättare, och inse att hunden inte förstått leken. Ropa inte namnet mer än **en** gång, annars avbetingar du namnet i stället för att jobba fram ett positivt kontakttagande.

När hunden lärt sig ”fråga”, alltså ta ögonkontakt, kan du börja ”svara” den med andra kommandon. Hunden hör sitt namn – tittar på dig – får höra ett glatt ”hit” – och belönas när den kommit ända fram.

Lär hunden ett eget ord för att den ska få springa iväg på egen hand. Då säger du hundens namn, väntar på ögonkontakt, sen säger du t. ex. ”hopp och lek”. Har man bara en hund är det lätt att undvika att använda namnet vid korrigeringar, d.v.s. på ett negativt sätt. Det är betydligt svårare i en flock med flera hundar.

Respekt i alla situationer

Titta på tävlingslydnadshundars uppförande när de lämnat tävlingsplanen. Då saknas inte sällan lydnaden. Det beror bl.a. på att lydnad som bara lärs in på samma ställe eller i mycket likartade miljöer – lydnadsplanen – inte finns för hunden på andra platser. Lydnaden har blivit **situationsbunden**. Detta kan vi alla se hos våra hundar, fast på olika sätt och mindre tydligt. Vare sig vi är medvetna om det eller ej har vi faktiskt olika regler, på olika ställen och vid olika tillfällen, för våra hundar. I husses bil t.ex. får hunden ligga i sätet medan matte endast tillåter den att sitta på golvet.

Situationsbunden inlärning finns förstås även i hundens respekt för förbud. Håller du inte på ditt ledarskap och dina förbud i alla situationer och miljöer så får du förstås en hund som struntar i dig om den är på "fel" plats.

Som oftast lyckas du bäst om du tänker och agerar redan när den är liten valp. Hemma är många kanske inte så noga med att se till att "nej" verkligen åtföljs, men när de är på besök hos någon annan eller i en rörig situation med andra hundar kräver de plötsligt denna respekt.

Vill du få hundens respekt överallt i alla situationer ska du vända på steken. Håll på respekten extra noga hemma till vardags! Där är allt välkänt, tryggt och lugnt, inga andra okända hundar eller ovanliga störningar för hunden. Just därför har du där som lättast att lyckas med dina korrigeringar, att få hundens uppmärksamhet och därmed stora chanser att belöna med kvalitet i rätt ögonblick. Svårigheterna för hunden – längre avstånd från dig, ny miljö, andra människor och hundar samt nya situationer – ökar du, bit för bit, under en lång tid.

Respektövningar

Har du lärt valpen att ”fråga”, ta ögonkontakt – spontant och när du säger dess namn – att respektera ditt ”nej”, så blir inlärningen desto lättare: när du ser exempelvis en katt en bit bort, säger du ”nej” precis innan/i samma ögonblick som den får syn på katten. Vad händer? Jo hunden stannar upp och tittar på dig och då får du chansen att tala om för den att ”nej, du får inte jaga katten utan ska gå här vid min sida” alternativt; ”titta här vad jag har att erbjuda i stället”.

Kom ihåg att det alltid måste löna sig för hunden att göra rätt. Och att det alltid bara finns **ett** ”nej” och respekteras inte det så ska det kosta för hunden. Om du säger ”nej” och hunden nonchalerar ditt förbud ska den uppleva situationen så att den säger ”oj, oj det här var det inte värt – det aktar jag mig för att göra om”. Har du t.ex. sagt ”nej” inför katten och hunden ändå sticker dit, så måste du rusa efter den, ta tag i den i halsskinnet och exempelvis stirra den i ögonen, morra och släpa tillbaka den till utgångspunkten igen. Hur hårt ska jag då ta i? Ja det beror givetvis på hur mjuk – hård din hund är. Rent generellt gäller att du ska vara så otrevlig som behövs för att hunden inte ska tycka att det är värt att göra om det.

Ibland måste man provocera fram situationer som ställer hundens vilja i konflikt med mattes för att verkligen lära den att det alltid lönar sig att respektera ”nej”.

Föremåls-intresserad hund: lägg eller kasta en boll/annat kul föremål en bit ifrån dig och hunden. Gå snett mot bollen, säg ”nej” så fort den tittar mot bollen, (skulle den sticka iväg för att ta bollen, så gäller det att vara mycket snabb och springa ifatt hunden och tydligt visa missnöje och börja om igen) passera bollen (givetvis utan att använda vare sig koppel eller godis), belöna med godis och hämta den själv eller använd bollen som belöning d.v.s. vänd dig om , peka på bollen och säg "varsågod". När hunden lyder ditt "nej" och därmed förstått att det är lönsamt att respektera matte är det dags att försvåra övningen. Kasta flera bollar och gå sicksack mellan dem.

Matglad hund: Visa hunden att du lägger ut godisbitar – eller varför inte ställa ut en frestande matskål med smaskigt hundgodis – gör likadant som i ovanstående boll-övning. När godiset är passerat kan du ibland belöna genom att säga "varsågod" och ibland sätta hunden och själv hämta godiset och ge hunden (då tränar du också "sitt-stanna kvar").

Lägg ut köttbullar eller annat godis, med några meters avstånd sinsemellan, till höger och vänster om en stig. Gå med hunden utefter stigen och säg "nej" respektive "varsågod" när hunden precis är på väg att upptäcka nästa köttbulle. Du bestämmer vilken som får tas och inte tas.

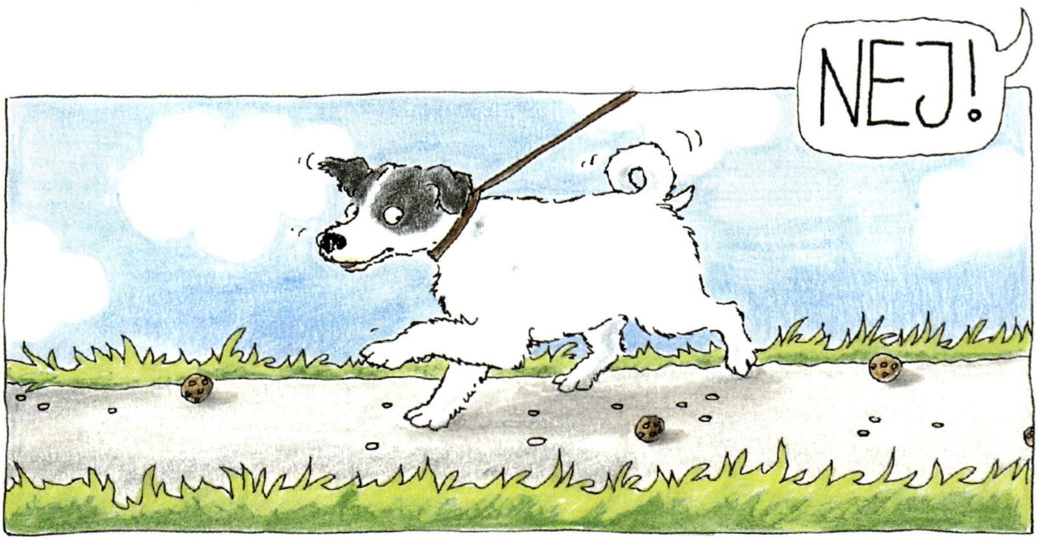

Ta ett, för hunden, attraktivt föremål i handen exempelvis en smörgås eller en godis, gå odramatiskt och dingla med det. Om hunden skulle försöka ta föremålet, så ryck inte undan handen – hunden måste hela tiden ha chansen att ta det för att förstå – säg ett bestämt nej och fortsätt gå vidare med föremålet i handen. Om den inte respekterar ditt "nej" så gör som en äldre hund skulle göra; morra, gör utfall och "nyp till" den. Ur hundsynpunkt är detta aldrig fel eftersom en ranghög hund aldrig skulle tillåta någon i lägre rang att sno något för den. Respekterar inte den ranglåga ett morr så "smäller det". Hundägare/flockledare ska inte behöva "gömma", hålla undan något för sin hund för att få ha det ifred. Alla vill vi väl kunna passera vår hund med exempelvis en matbricka utan att behöva parera en hoppande hund som riskerar att välta brickan...

Använd fantasin och arrangera liknande övningar och utnyttja vardagliga situationer till att lära hunden "nej". Kräv t.ex. att hunden väntar med att gå ut genom ytterdörren tills du ger den tillåtelse, att den sitter kvar i bilen tills den fått lov att hoppa ut. Provocera med att kasta roliga föremål/mat utanför bilen efter det att dörren öppnats. Det är otroligt viktigt att din hund inte slänger sig ut ur bilen så fort det finns en dörrspringa öppen – ofta parkerar vi ju där det finns annan trafik... Ta själv upp föremålet/godiset, ge det till hunden och säg därefter "varsågod, hoppa ut".

Lägg en frestande godbit på bordskanten, titta inte på hunden, vänta, om den närmar sig och försöker ta den, då kommer ditt oväntade och bestämda "nej". Lär den att låta bli kattens mat på golvet, kattlådan m.m. på samma sätt – det är förbjudet. När den respekterar ditt "nej" – ge den ett roligare alternativ som exempelvis lek eller godis från dig.

Inlärningsmetoder

”Sitt” och ”ligg”

Du kan gå tillväga på flera sätt för att lära hunden ”sitt”, ”ligg” eller nästan vad du vill... Här är bara några av de vanligaste metoderna. Och oftast använder sig förare av en ”mix” av flera olika metoder.

Varje gång du ser att valpen är på väg att sätta sig, så säger du ett glatt ”sitt” precis i det ögonblick den slår ned baken och sätter sig. Du uppmanar den alltså inte att sitta utan passar bara på när den sätter sig på eget initiativ. Och du behöver den inte heller. Efter en tid så förknippar hunden sin handling – att sätta sig – med ordet ”sitt”. När det ”känns rätt” så prova att säga ”sitt” när ni har ögonkontakt. Om inlärningen/kopplingen är befäst kommer den att sätta sig. Om den inte gör det så backa tillbaka i ”träningen” och börja om från början igen. Rätt som det är bara funkar det. Du säger ett positivt ”sitt” och hunden ”lyder” d.v.s. sätter sig – då får den en belöning! Samma sätt kan du använda för att lära den exempelvis ”ligg”.

Se till att du har ögonkontakt med valpen och visa den en godisbit. Håll godisen i handen och för den framåt, uppåt ovanför valpens huvud. (Vid ”ligg” så för du handen nedåt och håller den kvar på marken tills hunden ligger ned med båda armbågarna i backen.) Vänta tills den sätter sig och exakt då säger du ”sitt” och ger den godisbiten. Här styr du hunden att göra något, utan att tvinga den, och när den utför det du vill så får den en vinst – mat – av sitt ”rätta” beteende. Om den inte sätter sig så stoppar du tillbaka godisen i fickan och nonchalerar den för att efter en liten stund prova igen. Klandra aldrig hunden om den inte förstår vad du vill! Om den fattar vad du försöker få den till så kommer den att göra det. Hunden vill ju ha matbiten och hundar gör ju det som lönar sig för dem. I sinom tid kommer den att göra rätt, förutsatt att du är tydlig och den gillar mat förstås. Om den inte traktar efter mat, så gör ändå på samma sätt men med exempelvis en kul leksak i stället. De här sätten att lära hunden något kallas för **klassisk betingning**.

Du kan också gå tillväga på följande vis: ta en godisbit i handen, gör ingenting utan låt hunden själv pröva sig fram till hur den ska göra för att få godisen. Du är själv helt passiv, i lugn miljö utan något som stör den, och låter valpen testa sig fram och när den plötsligt sätter sig så får den godisen eller föremålet. Att helt låta hunden själv komma på vad som lönar sig för den att göra kallas **operant inlärning**.

Shaping är en inlärningsmetod som hittills mest använts vid delfinträning. Intresset för shaping på hundar har emellertid ökat under 90-talets andra hälft. Principen är att varje gång hunden gör rätt, vare sig den är ombedd att göra det eller inte, använder man sig av en visselsignal eller en ”klicker” – ett litet metallföremål man har i handen som ger ifrån sig ett ”klick-klick”-ljud varje gång du trycker på den. Signalen eller klickern används i exakt det ögonblick hunden utför rätt handling. Man börjar med att klicka och belöna länge och ofta. Till slut blir själva ljudet hundens belöning. Ljudet har blivit så väldigt positivt för den så att när den hör det kopplar den ihop ljudet med något positivt som exempelvis leder till mat.

”Stanna”

All inlärning ska, i möjligaste mån, bygga på det hunden redan kan. Exempelvis som här: Hunden kan, har lärt sig, ”sitt” och att ta ögonkontakt när du säger dess namn. Då använder du dessa färdigheter i inlärningen av något nytt t.ex. ”stanna” (och bli kvar där tills jag säger något annat). Säg ”Fido” – han tar ögonkontakt, säg ”sitt” och sätt upp handen som ett ”stopptecken” för hunden, säg ”stanna” och backa något steg från hunden, behåll ögonkontakt och stopptecken hela tiden, stanna till någon sekund, gå till hunden och när du är intill den: belöning och sedan ”hopp och lek”.

Öka avståndet och ”väntetiden” allt eftersom ni lyckas. Om hunden inte sitter kvar så för tillbaka den till utgångsplatsen och börja om och förenkla övningen. Nästa steg blir att lägga på fler och fler störningar tills du når dit du vill. Använd samma metod för att lära in annat nytt, som exempelvis ” ligg-stanna”. Använd fantasin och du kommer att finna på en mängd saker att lära hunden där du kan bygga på något välkänt för hunden.

Variera träningen

Upprepa inte exakt samma övning på precis samma ställe mer än ett par gånger per tillfälle. Annars kan hunden bli osäker på vad du egentligen förväntar dig av den. Efter ett par lyckade gånger finner hunden inte längre uppgiften lika spännande och rolig – den tappar koncentrationen.

Hunden kan även börja ”slarva” om den upplever en övning som alltför lätt och ointressant. Den blir också mer självsäker, så den ger sig tid att tramsa, nosa lite i backen, innan den slutför handlingen eller lyssnar på dig. Risken är stor att du parallellt med det önskvärda utförandet bygger in felbeteenden samt minskar hundens lyhördhet, koncentration och motivation. Alltså: se upp för att bli stereotyp i träningen och akta dig för att fastna i ett enda sätt att träna! När något fungerat bra en tid så gå vidare med att försvåra, förändra och ge hunden och dig själv nya utmaningar.

Om du provat en variant några gånger och det inte fungerar, så hitta på ytterligare en variant. Det är meningslöst att fortsätta i samma banor om det inte ger avsett resultat. Prova en ny träningsidé ett par gånger, utan att på något sätt bli besviken på hunden för ett eventuellt misslyckande. Fungerar det inte; analysera ur hundens synvinkel och förändra och testa på nytt.

Fysisk könsmognad

När valpen blivit runt halvåret fungerar den oftast bra i familjeflocken och är tillfreds med sig själv och omgivningen. Vardagslivet har blivit rutin och du och din valp känner varandra väl. Och förhoppningsvis vet valpen vad den får och inte får göra, den kommer glatt på inkallning och alla familjemedlemmar är självklara ledare för den.

Men plötsligt fungerar inte allt lika friktionsfritt som tidigare. Valpen kanske blundar med öronen när du ropar på den, blir rädd för sådant den redan känner till eller morrar hotfullt när du ska ta saker ifrån den. Under den här perioden blir det lätt en viss turbulens mellan unghunden och resten av flocken samt i relationen med hundkompisarna. Plötsligt börjar andra hundar bli mycket tuffare, mindre toleranta och kanske till och med aggressiva mot unghunden. De vill gärna dominera den lilla och t.ex. ”rida” på den. De sätter hårdare gränser, oftast med all rätt. Och unghunden själv testar, mer eller mindre intensivt, sin rang gentemot andra. Då är det bara att konstatera att valpen håller på att bli fysiskt könsmogen, d.v.s. komma upp i tonåren.

Beroende på ras och individ börjar valpen normalt bli könsmogen ungefär någon gång mellan 6 och 12 månader. En del är dock ännu yngre eller äldre. Hos en del hundar passerar könsmognaden utan några direkt synliga tecken mer än att tiken börjar löpa och hanhunden börjar lyfta på benet när han kissar. Hos andra individer kan puberteten ställa till en hel del problem, för både unghunden och omgivningen, lång tid både före och efter de fysiska tecknen på könsmognad. Oavsett intensiteten av tonårsfasonerna så är detta en jobbig period för valpen, då den påverkas såväl fysiskt som psykiskt av hormonförändringar. Låt därför unghunden få ta sig igenom tonårstiden i lugn och ro och bli psykiskt stabil igen innan du kör igång med ny inlärning och nya krav – men håll på de gamla.

Löpning

Normalt löper de flesta tikar två gånger per år i tre veckor. Men stora variationer förekommer beroende på ras och individ. Hur vet jag då att hon löper? Hanhundar visar ofta intresse av tiken innan själva löpet startar. Tikar doftar "gott", tycker hanarna, någon eller några veckor innan själva löpet. En del tikar börjar att kissa fler gånger än vanligt på promenader. Hon signalerar därmed för traktens hanhundar att "håll er beredda – snart är det dags"!

Säkraste tecknet på att hon verkligen löper är att hon blöder eller åtminstone har en rosafärgat flytning. Är du osäker; ta en tuss bomull eller toalettpapper och tryck in mot könsöppningen (vulvan) en stund. Om pappret är minsta rosafärgat löper tiken. Precis som på människor varierar mängden blod väldigt mycket från tik till tik. En del lämnar små pölar efter sig medan andra blöder så lite att det knappt märks. Enstaka tikar kan ha s.k. "torrlöp" d.v.s. hon löper utan att blöda alls.

Hur väl tikar sköter "hygienen" där bak är mycket olika, somliga är minutiöst noga medan andra inte ens bryr sig om att slicka sig ren eller slicka upp på golvet efter sig. Inomhus är det vettigt att använda ett s.k. tikskydd, en slags "byxa" som finns att köpa i djuraffärer. Inuti tikskyddet lägger man en binda/trosskydd som byts flera gånger per dag. Glöm inte att ta av tikskyddet när ni går ut…!

Oönskad parning

Tikskyddet är alltså till för att bl.a. skydda mattor och soffor mot blodfläckar. Det ger däremot inget som helst skydd mot parningsvilliga hanhundar! Nej, enda sättet att slippa "tjuvparningar" är att ha tiken i koppel **hela** löptiden. En parning kan ske på några sekunder. Det finns faktiskt tikägare som fått sin tik parad, i koppel, när de vänt ryggen till vid ett hanhundsmöte. När väl hanen kommit in i tiken är det helt försent att göra det ogjort. Hanens penis sväller direkt i tiken och då sitter de fast i varandra s.k. hängning. Precis i början av parningen är hanen uppe på tiken, som när de "rider" på varandra. Efter en kort stund tar oftast hanen sig ner och de står sedan bak mot bak mot varandra under resten av hängningen. Det går **inte** att dra isär dem. Ett sådant agerande är omöjligt och orsakar båda hundarna smärta och skada. Är sparningen väl påbörjad är det bara att vänta tills hängningen är över, de åker isär själva, och sedan direkt ringa veterinär för att få hjälp och råd. En normallång hängning håller på ungefär fem minuter upp till en timme.

Skendräktighet

Oavsett om tiken är parad eller ej så förändras hennes hormoner mer eller mindre efter löpet. Hormonförändringen är densamma vare sig tiken är dräktig eller inte. För vissa tikar kan detta bli besvärligt om hon blir skendräktig, vilket märks allt tydligare ju närmre "skenvalpningen" (ca. två månader efter mitten av löpet) hon kommer. Förutom att ändra beteende går hon upp i vikt och får mjölk i juvren.

Bästa sättet att vända hormonerna tillbaka till det normala igen är att behandla tiken på motsatt sätt som en dräktig tik. Hon ska ges mycket mer fysisk och psykisk aktivitet och mindre mat än vanligt! Hjälper inte detta och hon har rik mjölkproduktion är besök hos veterinär den enda lösningen. Ibland kan skendräktigheten behöva vändas med hjälp av medicin. Mycket mjölk i juvren kan nämligen leda till mjölkstockning och juverinflammation, vilket är väldigt smärtsamt och farligt för tiken. Hos en del tikar blir skendräktighet ett så stort problem att kastration (bortoperering av livmodern) är enda utvägen.

Svårt med tonåring

Fortsätt gärna träna sådant som hunden redan har lärt sig ordentligt. Men bli inte förvånad om den inte fungerar som tidigare. Valpen strävar nu efter att få veta var den står gentemot omgivningen. Den testar olika förhållningssätt på resten av flocken för att bl.a. ta reda på exakt var på rangskalan den befinner sig.

Valpen provocerar dig för att få tydliga bevis på sin egen betydelse och därmed få veta sin plats i flocken. Låt dig absolut inte provoceras till att ta upp kamp med hunden. Nonchalera hunden och gå lugnt ifrån den, visa att du t.ex. inte vill leka mer. Avled intresset från apporten, om valpen inte vill komma med den, genom att t.ex. börja leka med något annat. Om den här typen av ”samarbetslekar” inte går bra längre, lägg dem helt sonika på hyllan en tid tills hunden kommit ur tonåren.

Försök i stället att inte försätta dig i situationer som leder till kamp mellan dig och valpen. Ge alltså inte hunden tillfälle att ”vinna” över dig, vare sig det gäller att strunta i att komma tillbaka med en gömd leksak eller att morra över ett ben.

Om valpen morrar när du vill ta något ifrån den, kan du antingen nonchalera den eller resolut ta grejen. Väljer du att ta den ifrån valpen får du absolut inte visa någon tvekan eller rycka tillbaka handen, för då har hunden ”vunnit” eller 1-0 till Fido. Ta lugnt och bestämt ifrån hunden föremålet och ge den något annat i stället. Om du redan från början lekt byteshandel med valpen litar den förmodligen på dig även i puberteten. Då blir det inte så dramatiskt för valpen att bli fråntagen saker nu heller.

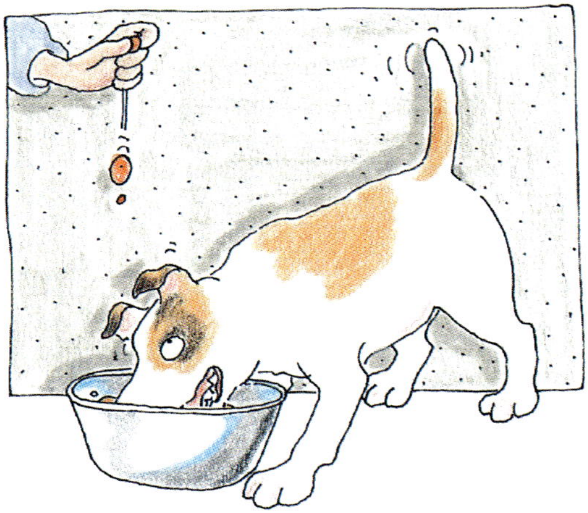

Lär barnen att aldrig störa hunden när den äter och låt hunden äta ifred på en avskild plats. Alla djur vill ha matro! Låt dock barnen, i förebyggande syfte, släppa ned extra "godis" i eller vid valpens matskål någon gång ibland. Att träna valpen att inte morra över matskålen genom att ta skålen ifrån hunden när den äter, stressar förmodligen hunden mer än det vänjer den vid att bli fråntagen sin mat.

Lösa problem

Träna sådant som din valp redan kan och aktivera den ofta med övningar där den själv måste lösa problem för att lyckas. Kom då ihåg att om du hjälper den så får den ingen egentlig "hjärnaktivitet", så låt den lösa problemen själv. Att låta hunden tänka själv gör den avstressad. Du kan exempelvis låta den söka efter godis/mat inne eller ute, "öppna-godispaket", gå balansgång på breda ofarliga plankor/stockar, putta eller rulla en boll framför sig, ta sig upp på en stor sten efter godis m.m. Använd fantasin och se till att leken fortfarande sker på dina villkor. Lek mestadels inomhus eftersom hunden under tonåren ofta har svårt att koncentrera sig och är extra känslig för störningar från omgivningen.

Låt även barnen aktivera valpen, men visa först hur de ska göra. Var själv åskådare och kontrollera att det går juste till – barn är ju "valpar" de också. Aktiveringsövningarna hjälper barnen att bli en ledare i hundens ögon.

Konfliktfritt spår

Spårövningar är speciellt lämplig problemlösning för tonårshunden. Den får arbeta med både huvud, kropp och nos. Under spårarbetet arbetar hunden helt självständigt och måste lita till sin egen näsa. Att självständigt klara ett spår ger förstås också hunden ett ökat självförtroende, varför spårning är extra bra aktivitet för en lite vek hund. Föraren intar en passiv roll under spårning, på sin höjd talar hon lite uppmuntrande eller dämpande till hunden. Vid spårträning finns mycket litet utrymme för konfliktsituationer mellan hund och förare, eftersom spårning inte bygger på samarbete i samma utsträckning som exempelvis apportering.

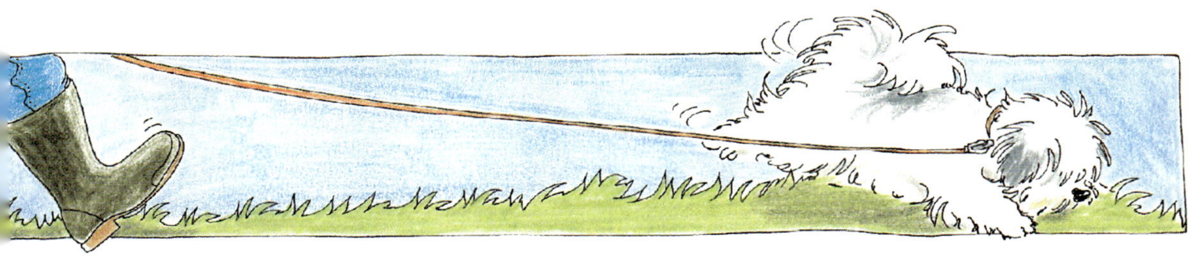

Du kan antingen börja med personspår eller viltspår. Vilket du väljer beror mycket på dina intressen och vilken ras du har. Personspår går ut på att hunden ska kunna leta upp människor som försvunnit eller gömt sig. Viltspårsträning lär hunden att spåra upp skadskjutet vilt, men du behöver absolut inte vara jägare för att hålla på med viltspår. Vältränade och dokumenterat duktiga viltspårshundar efterfrågas alltmer av jaktlag utan egen eftersökshund, samt av polisen för att spåra upp trafikskadat vilt. Har du ingen erfaren bekant eller en uppfödare som kan visa dig hur du ska göra spårövningar så finns det bra böcker i ämnet att låna eller köpa. Kurser i personspår ordnas av SBK (Svenska Brukshundklubben), och viltspårskurser av special- och rasklubbar samt av Jägareförbundet.

”Spökåldern”

”Min hund var plötsligt livrädd för grannens soptunna. Hon morrade och skällde på den och ville inte gå fram och nosa på den förrän jag uppmuntrade henne och följde med och tittade på ”soptunnemonstret”. Och så har det fortsatt nu i flera veckor; ena dagen är stubbar hundätande varelser och nästa dag vågar hon inte gå förbi en bil, fast motorn inte ens är i gång. Tidigare var hon inte rädd för någonting utan gick nyfiket fram till vad som helst. Nu verkar hon dessutom lite mörkrädd. Hon lämnar inte gärna min sida när vi är ute i skymning eller mörker. Har min frimodiga valp gått och blivit en rädd hund? Vad ska jag göra?”

Ja, det här är en vanlig fråga från hundägare som haft hund i ungefär ett halvår. Valpen är inne i könsmognadsperioden och överdriven rädsla är ett vanligt tecken på detta. Genom att själv gå fram till ”monstret” och visa dig orädd samtidigt som du uppmuntrar hunden med lugn och säker röst att hänga med, hjälper du hunden att komma över rädslan. Och belöna inte en hund som tvekar. Vanligt är att föraren plussar på fel beteende när hunden inte vill/vågar: ” Bra, duktig hund, här får du en godis”, får hunden höra när den exempelvis inte vågar gå uppför en ”farlig” trappa. Då belönas ju tveksamheten! I stället bör hunden få höra ”ja, ja, gå på, kom igen, larva dig inte” och få lite draghjälp uppåt genom att du själv går först och kanske milt drar med den i kopplet. När den sedan äntligen tar sig upp ett steg; då kommer beröm/belöning. Titta inte på hunden utan på det läskiga annars förstärker du rädslan – ”kanske matte söker stöd hos mig”. Lägg godis högre upp i trappen och fortsätt ”peppa” hunden.

Ömka eller tvinga aldrig en hund som är rädd. Då förstärker du bara hundens övertygelse om att ”monstret”/stubben verkligen äter hundar. Utsätt heller inte en hund som visar sig mycket rädd för allt möjligt under den här perioden i hopp om att den då ska komma över sin rädsla. Det kan få motsatt effekt. Om hunden är av den mjukare sorten kan det bli för mycket, då klarar den kanske inte av att ta sig igenom alla ”farligheter” och komma över dem. Den kan fortsätta att vara rädd även efter det att den stabiliserats psykiskt igen. Hur mycket man ska uppmuntra en osäker hund är mycket individuellt beroende på situationen och hundens mentalitet.

Lek med ”snälla” kompisar

Under könsmognadsperioden testar valpen, inte bara var den står inom familjeflocken utan ibland även gentemot främmande människor och framför allt provar den sin ”styrka” gentemot andra hundar. Nu är det extra viktigt att hunden får många tillfällen till umgänge med signalsäkra, sunda och ”snälla” hundar. Kompiserfarenheterna under tonåren kommer i hög grad att prägla din hunds sätt mot andra hundar framgent.

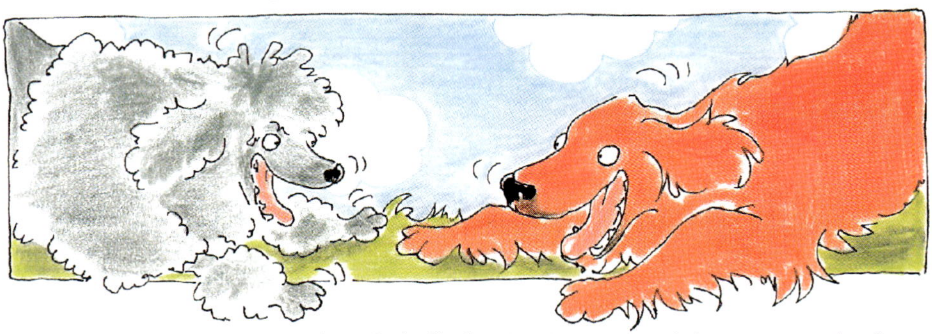

Om din hund skulle börja visa aggressivitet mot andra hundar är det viktigt att du själv uppför dig lugnt och sansat. Hetsar du upp dig, skriker och sliter i kopplet eller i hunden, stegras hundens aggressivitet. Bästa läromästarna i hund-umgänge är oftast de lite äldre mogna hundarna, av båda könen, som får fungera som snälla men hårda uppfostrare åt en kaxig tonårsvalp.

"Hälsa-träning"

Blir eller är hunden vänlig, glädjeskäller, hoppar, slickar, vill rusa fram hälsa och klättra på alla den träffar, får du tänka lite annorlunda. Påkalla dess uppmärksamhet: namn, ögonkontakt eller "nej" exakt när du (bäst chans att lyckas då) eller hunden upptäcker någon hund eller människa. Genast lockar du på hunden, tar fram något som hunden gillar att leka med och går direkt åt motsatt håll och gör något som hunden tycker är jättekul. Så småningom, när ovanstående alltid går bra, så har du fått en hund som vänder sig till dig och undrar: "vad ska hända för kul nu?". Nu kan du börja sätta hunden vid möten – "sitt" + "stanna" – och själv ta några steg mot den intressanta, ropa hej och direkt gå tillbaka till hunden och sedan göra en kul lek åt andra hållet.

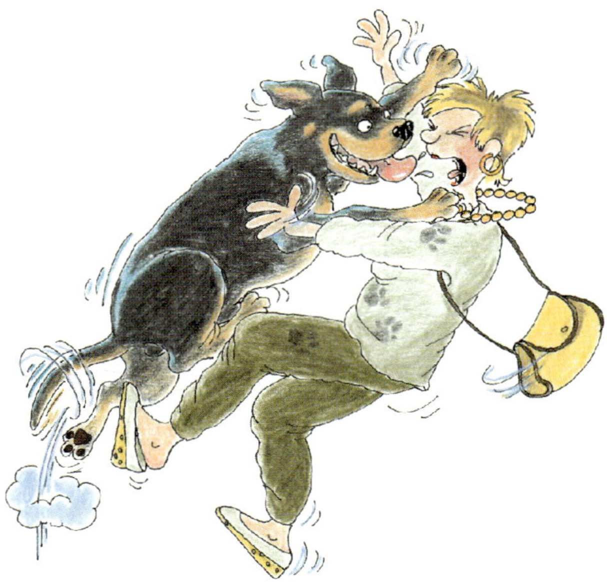

Efter en tids övning, där du ökat svårigheterna steg för steg, så går du till slut ända fram till den mötande, hälsar, växlar några ord medan hunden sitter en bra bit bort och väntar. Vad har hunden lärt sig nu? Jo, att sätta sig vid möten, vänta på att du kollar att den andra inte är farlig (”du skyddar mig”), rikta all koncentration mot dig (”husse tar ju roliga initiativ”). Du har alltså fått en hund som uppför sig sansat och lydigt vid möten samtidigt som hunden upplever dig som en bättre ledare!

Vakta och skälla

Varför skäller hunden t.ex. på brevbäraren? Försök se det ur hundens synvinkel: brevbäraren dyker upp snabbt, kommer farande rakt mot hund och hus (= hot) , stannar till vid tomtgränsen eller dörren, rör något som är flockens – brevlådan, då skäller hunden och direkt ”flyr” brevbäraren. ”Jippi, han blev rädd och jag lyckades få bort honom.” Vilken seger för hunden! Hunden har tillåtits ta en framträdande roll och rang i flocken – dags att tänka på ledarskapet igen.

Vad gör jag åt det här då? Ja, har du en samarbetsvillig brevbärare så häng en påse godis vid brevlådan. Likadant kan du göra om hunden är avvaktande, rädd, för dina besökande. Be dem att varje gång de kommer vara bussiga att ge hunden godis. Då lär den sig att de inte är farliga/ett hot. Med köttbullar m.m. ger brevbäraren och gäster hunden positiva signaler. Till slut lär den sig att gilla besöken, att inte vara rädd och att sluta skälla aggressivt. Däremot kanske den kommer skällande, glatt viftande på svansen, rusande i glädje mot brevlådan eller ytterdörren efter en tid…

Utställningsdebut

Ofta infaller utställningsdebuten med hundens tonårsperiod. Om valpen är inne i puberteten och visar sig mycket rädd och osäker i nya miljöer, är det nog bättre att vänta tills den blivit lite mer säker på sig själv igen. Utställningar bjuder nämligen på en ganska rörig miljö med mycket ljud, massor av folk, ofta hala golv och sist men inte minst en mängd hundar.

En ganska tuff miljö för en blyg tonårsvalp att ge sig in i, kan man tycka. Men de allra flesta hundar klarar utställningsmiljön förvånansvärt bra och många hundar stortrivs, både i ringen och vid ring-side. För husse och matte kan det vara roligt att få en bedömning av hunden, träffa andra hundägare och helt enkelt titta på den härliga show som en välordnad hundutställning är.

Om valpen redan varit iväg på några valputställningar har den givetvis lite lättare att acceptera utställningsmiljön även i den här lite oroliga åldern.

Träna och förbered hemma

För att få en så bra och rättvis bedömning av hunden som möjligt, och för att underlätta för hunden, bör du träna utställning hemma, helst tillsammans med hundkompisar. Vänj valpen vid att främmande människor får titta på bettet, d.v.s. lugnt särar på läpparna och tittar på tänderna, inte bänder upp käften och tittar in i munnen. Valpen måste också vara van vid att främmande tar i den och klämmer på den samt stryker och trycker den lätt över ryggen och benen. Det gör nämligen domaren.

Träna även att ställa upp valpen snyggt framför dig. Och att springa vid din sida i en stor cirkel, i en trekant och fram och tillbaka. Exakt hur din ras ska visas måste du fråga uppfödaren eller nån annan raskunnig person. Ett nyttigt sätt att lära sig "visa hund" är att låta någon utställningsvan bekant leka domare åt dig och din hund. Och självklart kan du lära dig massor genom att gå på utställning och bara studera hur rutinerade utställare visar sina hundar. Väl i utställningsringen har du bara några minuter på dig att visa upp din hund för domaren och då lyckas ni alltid bättre om ni kommer väl förberedda, både du och hunden.

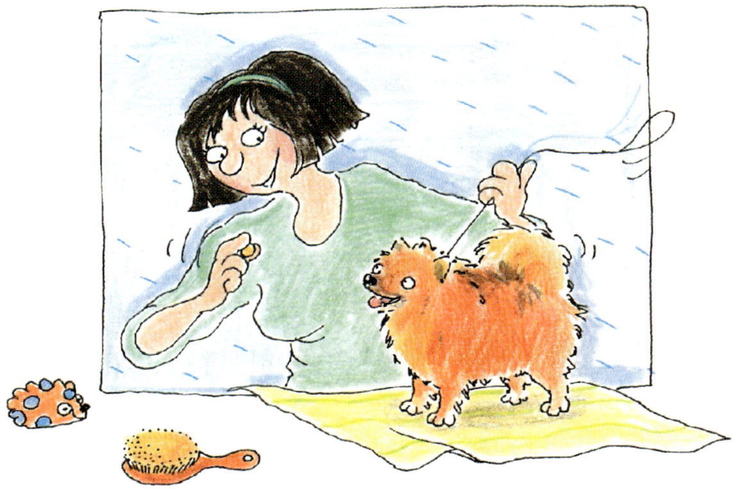

Till förberedelserna räknas förstås också att se till att hunden är i rätt hull och kondition samt pälsvård; att hunden är ren, kammad, borstad, klippt, trimmad, fönad o.s.v. beroende på ras. Prata med uppfödaren eller annan raskunnig person i god tid, på vissa raser måste pälsen klippas eller trimmas flera veckor före utställningen. Ta reda på, genom uppfödaren eller rasklubben, var du kan få hjälp med pälsen inför en utställning. Akta dig för att själv försöka klippa och trimma din hund om du inte innan lärt dig av en erfaren utställare. Felaktig användning av saxen kan ödelägga din hunds päls för många månader framöver.

Hur hitta utställningar?

Utställningar annonseras i Hundsport (Kennelklubbens tidning) och i ras- och specialklubbarnas tidningar. Börja gärna med att delta på någon utställning som hålls utomhus eftersom dessa erbjuder en mer ”lättsmält” miljö, framför allt för hunden, än de som hålls inomhus. Anmälningsblankett beställer du genom SKKs kansli eller via arrangerande klubb. Vanligtvis ska anmälningsavgift samt anmälningsblankett vara insända till arrangören ungefär en månad före utställningsdagen. Vilken klass din hund ska anmälas till beror på hur gammal den kommer att vara när utställningen går av stapeln. Be uppfödaren om hjälp vid anmälningen eller fråga arrangören till råds om vilken klass din hund ska gå i.

Skriftlig kritik

För den oinvigde kan det i början te sig rent omöjligt att hänga med i bedömningsgången och de olika klasserna. Men oroa dig inte, undrar du över något finns, förutom en massa medutställare, även funktionärer, bl.a. utställningssekreterare, på plats som kan hjälpa dig tillrätta och svara på frågor. Från SKK kan du beställa utförligare information om utställningsregler och bedömningsgång. Det finns även böcker som ingående tar upp allt som rör utställningar. Som alltid är det bra att vara påläst och efter några utställningar har du lärt dig det viktigaste.

Cirka en vecka före utställningen får du en bekräftelse på din anmälan med bl.a. vägbeskrivning, tider för veterinärbesiktning och bedömning samt nummerlapp och i vilken ring du ska vara. Om du inte har eller kan få låna ett utställningskoppel hinner du oftast köpa det på morgonen på utställningen. Det bör du nämligen använda för att din hund ska se så snygg ut som möjligt. Fråga gärna uppfödaren om vilken typ av utställningskoppel du bör köpa, så att du verkligen får ett som gör din hund rättvisa.

När turen kommit till din hund att gå in i ringen så försök att inte bry dig om allt som händer runt omkring er, utan ha all din uppmärksamhet på hunden. Nu gäller det att få den att visa sig så snyggt som det bara går under en kort stund. Efteråt får du alltid en skriftlig kritik på din hund från domaren. Ta inte kritiken för något ”faktablad” om hur din hund ser ut. Varje domare dömer efter ”eget skön” och föredrar sin ”typ” av rasen, dessutom är din hund mitt uppe i att växa och förändras. Hur det än har gått för din hund så vet du ju själv att just din hund är världens vackraste och finaste jycke!

Efter puberteten

När hunden blivit könsmogen stabiliseras den så småningom mentalt igen och kommer oftast in i en lugn period fram till ungefär två års ålder. Då ska den igenom den psykiska könsmognaden. Under tiden mellan könsmognadsperioderna är unghunden mottaglig för nyinlärning och träning. I den här åldern får vilda hundar och vargar lära sig, av övriga i flocken, hur de ska agera och samarbeta för att nå bl.a. ett lyckat jaktresultat. Nu bör du därför ägna mycket tid till att vidareutveckla det hunden kan och lära in nya moment, som helst bygger på det hunden redan lärt sig.

Ni kan träna en eller flera gånger om dagen, men alltid i korta pass så att hunden inte ledsnar. Du kan visserligen nå resultat även om du bara tränar en gång per vecka, men det går betydligt långsammare och hunden går miste om värdefull stimulans och aktivitet. Genom att bli hundägare har du ju förbundit dig att tillfredsställa hundens behov varje dag för att den ska må bra. Och alla hundar behöver få använda muskler, nos och huvud dagligen för att verkligen må bra både fysiskt och psykiskt.

Liksom tidigare är det förstås flockledaren som tar initiativet till gemensam aktivitet, gör träningen/leken lustfylld och intressant samt bestämmer när träningen ska sluta. Eftersom varje hund är en individ som formas av arv och miljö så finns givetvis en stor spridning på beteenden och reaktioner hos våra hundar. För att kunna styra din hunds beteenden måste du förstå dem. Du måste känna din hund och kunna läsa dess signaler/kroppsspråk, så du förstår vad den gör och varför.

Kontakt och stimulans

Du bör vid det här laget också ha klart för dig hurdan din hund är. Då kan du anpassa och stegra svårighetsgraden i träningen efter just din hunds förutsättningar och mognad. Ställ lagom höga krav både fysiskt och psykiskt på din unghund. Var t.ex. försiktig med vissa höga hinderhopp när du tränar lydnad, bruks och agility. Vänta med mer avancerad hoppträning tills hunden vuxit färdigt.

Du måste också rannsaka dig själv genom att fråga dig hur du är och agerar som hundförare. Bra kontakt med hunden är grunden till all lyckad träning. Umgås mycket med hunden, låt den få vara med dig så mycket som möjligt samt belöna och gör all trevlig kropps- och ögonkontakt positiv.

Under uppväxten bör du förstärka respektive dämpa hundens medfödda lust till att utföra vissa handlingar. Det gör du genom att göra dem mer eller mindre lustbetonade. Du höjer respektive sänker hundens motivation till att vilja göra vissa saker. Belöna, uppmuntra och öva ofta sådant som du vill att hunden ska göra. Undvik sådant som du inte vill att den ska göra. Lär hunden att det lönar sig för den att utföra vissa handlingar och låta bli andra. Vill du så småningom t.ex. lära din hund att söka efter försvunna människor under svåra miljö- och vittringsförhållanden, bör du stimulera och uppmuntra hundens sökintresse. Och dessutom tidigt lära den att det är positivt att träffa på nya människor.

Tonåring – igen!

Under en lugn period efter den fysiska könsmognaden har hunden varit ganska mentalt stabil och kunnat koncentrera sig. Den här tiden har ni förhoppningsvis tillsammans provat på olika aktiviteter och lärt er en massa nytt. Nu är det dags för en ny tonårsperiod.

Runt två års ålder kan en del hundar vara ganska stökiga och överdrivet stöddiga eller rädda en tid. Under den här perioden, som brukar benämnas psykisk könsmognad, genomgår hunden en hormoniell och mental mognadsprocess. Först därefter kan den betraktas som psykiskt mogen att klara de krav en vuxen hund ställs inför.

Hunden kanske börjar bli kaxig mot andra hundar, överdrivet intresserad av tikar eller/och visar dålig samarbetsvilja. Många hundar testar återigen sin plats i flockhierarkin. Det kan yttra sig på olika sätt eller inte alls, bl.a. beroende på hundens tidigare erfarenheter. Har man flera hundar i huset är det ofta när någon är i tvåårsåldern som det uppstår tvister mellan hundarna inom flocken.

Det är väldigt ofta just i samband med den psykiska könsmognaden som många jobbiga beteenden accentueras och blir till ett problem för såväl ägare som hund. Oftast ligger en stark könsdrift, dåligt ledarskap samt för lite psykisk aktivitet till grund för de flesta problem. Visst finns det hanar som är alltför hanhundsaggressiva och "översexuella" för att fungera i vår hundtäta miljö. Har du provat allt och tagit hjälp av hundproffs utan att bli av med problemet, så kan du diskutera med veterinär och eventuellt låta kastrera din hane.

Vargens pubertet styr

När en varghane blivit könsmogen brukar han lämna flocken för att söka sig en tik att bilda en egen, ny flock med. Och eftersom vargen blir fysiskt könsmogen först vid två års ålder, så kommer frigörelseprocessen hos våra hundar först då och inte samtidigt med den fysiska könsmognaden.

Vargen har olika hierarkier i sin flock; mellan valpar och ungdjur är rangordningen mixad mellan könen, d.v.s. en hane kan mycket väl stå högre i rang än en ungtik som i sin tur är ranghög gentemot en annan unghane. De vuxna vargarna har däremot en könsbunden hierarki. Det är en anledning till att hunden vid två års ålder plötsligt kan visa aggressivitet mot individer av det egna könet. Hunden har först nu "förstått" att det är hundar av sitt eget kön som den ska mäta sig mot.

Om en tik ska paras och få valpar får det inte ske förrän den här fasen är avklarad. Hon är helt enkelt inte mogen psykiskt och socialt tidigare. Det är ju inte heller en ung tonårsflicka, trots att hon rent biologiskt kan bli mor. Innan hunden – gäller lika mycket för hanen som tiken – är färdig socialt och psykiskt kan man ju inte säkert bedöma hur den verkligen är mentalt. Hanhundens uppförande gentemot andra hanar kan exempelvis förändras ganska rejält i och med att han blir riktigt vuxen. Och en aggressiv hanhund ska inte få möjlighet att eventuellt nedärva sitt asociala beteende – oavsett hans kanske exteriöra fördelar och fina meriter.

Håll på ledarskapet

I och med att hanhunden började lyfta på benet och markera upptäckte både han och du att han är hane. Nu kan han försöka ta över allting – bli general! Nu gäller det att se upp och inte låta honom klättra för högt på rangskalan. Låt honom på sin höjd avancera till sergeant, eftersom viljan att vara till lags inte finns hos "chefstyper". Därför får du en mer lätthanterlig hund om du låter honom förstå att han aldrig ska axla den manteln efter dig. Om du parerat problemen tydligt redan vid de första trotsperioderna kommer det att gå så mycket lättare nu. Då har du redan gjort det mesta av jobbet. Om inte – var desto klarare och mer konsekvent i din ledarroll nu.

Det är nu (senast!) du ska förebygga beteenden så att din hund inte ska gå genom livet och vänta på en chans att ta generalsgraden ifrån dig eller alltid försöka få andra hundar att bli dess underställda.

Vi tillåter inte våra hundar att bli vuxna inom ett flertal områden, som exempelvis jakt. Vi behöver inte heller låta hunden bli helt vuxen sexuellt. En varg leker exempelvis inte med bollar som vuxen. Men det gör våra hundar eftersom vi låter dem vara valpar och leka hela livet. Du underlättar för både dig själv och din hund om du ser till att hunden får hålla sig på valpstadiet gentemot det andra könet.

Dämpa hanhundens lustar

Du kan faktiskt påverka hur hög nivå av könshormon, som styr bl.a. aggressivitet och sexualitet, din hund har. Under hela uppväxten bör du vakta på din hund och inte tillåta överdrivet nosande och uppvaktande av tikar eller utsätta honom för spända situationer med andra hundar. När han hälsat och nosat igenom en tik så är det tillräckligt. Ytterligare uppvaktning är förbjudet. Är det någon som får uppvakta och i förlängningen para så är det du som flockledare som bestämmer vem.

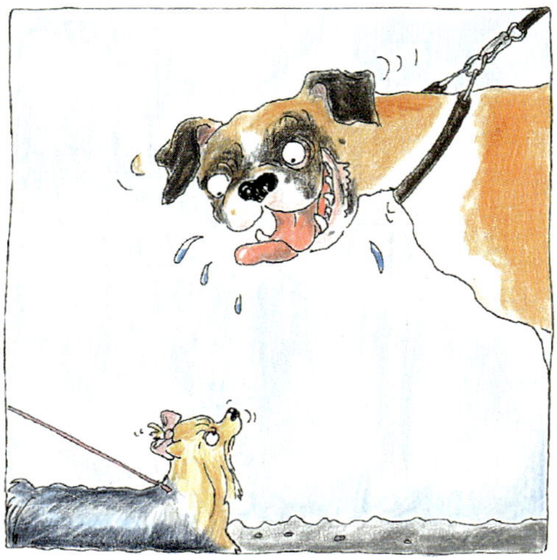

Om du står högt i rang i förhållande till din hund och om hundens nivå av manligt hormon är lågt, leder det till att hunden har litet behov av att klättra i rang. Du underlättar alltså hundens tillvaro och förstärker ditt ledarskap genom att dämpa hans nivå av manligt hormon. Det finns många beteenden och situationer, som vi oftast inte tänker på, som verkar höjande på hundens hormonnivå.

Oavsett om en hund – tik eller hane – rider på andra hundar för att dominera eller "para" så leder det till en hormonhöjning. Om din hund rider på någon i familjen så gör ingen affär av det första gången, ta bort honom med ett bestämt "nej". Det brukar räcka. Om hunden däremot visar sig påstridig och försöker rida ofta, så säg ifrån på skarpen och intressera den för någon vettig lek i stället. Glöm inte att ridning på andra hundar också påverkar hormonerna. Dessutom leder det ibland också till slagsmål mellan dem.

Förebygg slagsmål

Slagsmål är nästan alltid en strid om rang. Det är vanligare att hanhundar testar sin rangställning mot andra hanar än att tikar gör det mot varandra. Självfallet ska ett slagsmål mellan två tikar lösas på samma sätt som för hanhundar.

Det är som bekant lättare att stämma i bäcken än i ån. Därför är det viktigt att styra hundens umgänge med andra hundar direkt då hunden börjar testa. Har man väl fått en "fighter" har man ett problem som är mycket svårt att reda upp själv. Sök då hjälp av en erkänt kunnig specialist. För varje slagsmål hunden är med om ökar risken att han råkar in i ett nytt.

Din hund får inte slåss eftersom du är flockledare. Och då tar du också på dig det ansvaret – du måste ta alla stötar åt din hund. Du ska vara flockledare i alla lägen – även då det är otrevligt och obekvämt för dig. Får hunden för sig att hussar och mattar passivt accepterar slagsmål och inte visar sitt ledarskap i spända och trängda lägen, så upplever den att det är OK och positivt att slåss – och gör om det.

Tänk på hur du uppför dig när ni träffar andra hundar. Hundens uppträdande påverkas starkt av hur du beter dig. Självklart ska främmande hundar få hälsa på varandra utan koppel. Det är rent praktiskt enklare, och hunden kan uppleva kopplet som ett alltför kraftigt stöd av flockledaren. Ett spänt koppel eller ännu värre – ett ryck i halsen – hetsar bara hunden och ökar aggressiviteten. Samma effekt ger höjt röstläge eller skrik och gap. Du och den mötande hundens matte bör hela tiden hålla er i rörelse, som om ni promenerade tillsammans. Står ni och ser avvaktande ut och passivt betraktar hundarna finns ju risken att hundarna missuppfattar situationen och tror att ni spänner mot varandra...

Det är synnerligen viktigt att vara noga med att låta sin hund bara umgås med andra hundar som är "snälla". Hundvännerna ska, även under den här tonårstiden, vara bussiga och överseende mot din hund, men också sätta gränser på ett juste sätt. En äldre hund bör inte trycka ner en yngre i onödan, men heller inte låta den få övertaget.

Om din hund och hans kompisar umgåtts bra hittills kan det nu komma till en punkt då de äldre säger ifrån. Är det då gamla polarn som läxar upp sin ungkompis är det oftast befogat. Konstatera då att, eftersom de lekt så bra ihop tidigare, nu testar din hund sin plats gentemot kompisen. I det här fallet kan man oftast låta hundarna få försöka göra upp rangstriden själva.

Lugna hanhundsmöten

Stöter ni på en helt främmande hund så försök förvissa dig om att den andra hunden är sund och snäll – innan du låter din hund hälsa. Om din hund är stöddig mot den andra så ta tag i honom och läs lusen av honom (du måste vara otäckare än den andra hunden), så att han skärper sig och lugnar ner sig. Uppträd alltid mycket lugnt och höj inte rösten i spända lägen mellan två hundar. Släpp lös dem igen, promenera en bit tillsammans. Släpper inte spänningen mellan hundarna eller om de börjar slåss, så koppla upp dem. Undvik den andra hunden i fortsättningen.

Om det däremot gäller kompisens eller grannens hund, d.v.s. hundar som ni absolut skulle vilja kunna umgås med, så låt det gå en tid innan ni försöker igen. Under mellantiden bör din hund få träffa äldre snälla hundar. Stäm träff på en plats som är neutral för båda hundarna, var i rörelse hela tiden och framför allt; försök att själv uppträda så avslappnat och naturligt som möjligt.

Vid ett slagsmål som inte är över på ett ögonblick bör man alltså axla sitt flockledarskap och sära på kombattanterna – lugnt men tveklöst. Låt sedan hundarna lugna ner sig en stund. Ta därefter en lugnande promenad – stå inte stilla – då hundarna får mötas efter en stund igen förutsatt att de lugnat ner sig helt.

Mötas på nytt

Efter ett slagsmål ska man försöka låta hundarna träffas igen – så snart de blivit kontaktbara och fått sansa sig en stund. Men det finns undantag då det är bättre att låta dem förbli åtskilda. Vissa raser, som t.ex. en del terriers, kan det emellertid vara bättre att inte släppa ihop igen därför att de har svårt med underkastelsesignaler. En terrier som avlats fram för jakt i gryt är ju ämnad för jakt och inte för ett flockliv som sällskapshund. Och i ett grävlingsgryt slutar det kanske inte så bra för en grythund som underkastar sig grävlingen...

Om din hund kaxar mot en annan hund, trots att den andre visar underkastelse – ta bort din hund. Blir det däremot ett jämnt och spänt dödläge vid kontakt med en annan hund – gå bort ifrån hundarna. Blir det slagsmål – sära på dem. Se till att nästa hundkontakt blir desto trevligare. Sök upp en stabil, snäll och gärna lite äldre hund.

En riktigt dominant hund har en så stark självkänsla att den mycket sällan eller aldrig behöver slåss. De flesta stöddiga hundar är egentligen osäkra. Och lyckas de då skrämma någon annan genom ett anfall lär de sig snabbt att anfall är bästa försvar, och tenderar att göra om det nästa gång de träffar en hund som de egentligen är lite skraja för.

Den här åldern kan uppenbarligen innebära en massa negativt för hunden – mycket är nej och förbjudet. Glöm därför inte att vara en rolig lekkamrat, som avleder och hittar på skojiga aktiviteter.

Gå på kurs

För att få hunden att lära sig vissa beteenden på kommandon krävs att föraren vet hur hunden ska tränas och att hunden har klart för sig vem som är ledare – i alla situationer. Och båda ska ha klart för sig att träning bygger på samarbete och inte tvekamp. När hunden inte lyder, betyder det nästan alltid att den inte förstår vad du vill eller att den inte finner uppgiften tillräckligt lustfylld. Då måste du bli enklare, tydligare och öka belöningen för hunden. Planera varje träningspass, bestäm vad du ska träna och varför o.s.v. Analysera noga såväl framgångar som motgångar i träningen och fråga dig alltid efter ett träningspass varför det gått bra eller dåligt.

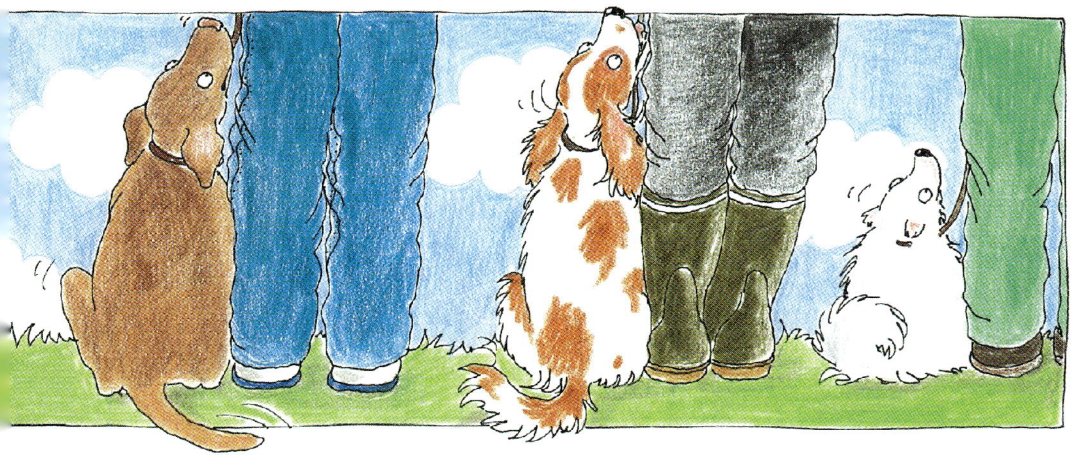

De allra flesta hundägare behöver hjälp av någon mer erfaren och hundkunnig person för att undvika de vanligaste nybörjarfelen. Innan du anmäler dig till en kurs, vare sig det är en valpkurs eller avancerad lydnadskurs, förvissa dig om att den leds av kunniga och erfarna instruktörer. Fråga om kursledarens utbildning och egen erfarenhet, lyssna eventuellt med tidigare kursdeltagare. Du ska ställa krav på bra utbildning, den är nämligen inte gratis.

Att gå på kurs betyder inte att du och din hund måste ha målsättningen att tävla. Utbildningen kan syfta till att lära sig olika sätt att aktivera och stimulera sin hund på och få en bra vardagslydnad. Det är dock bra att sätta upp individuella mål för sig själv så att man har syftet med sin träning helt klar.

På kurser träffar du andra hundägare. Du får tillfälle att fråga och diskutera träning och övriga "hundangelägenheter" med andra. Ju mer du lär dig om hundar och hundträning, desto roligare kommer du och din hund att få tillsammans.

Anmäl dig alltid i god tid! Det är ofta köer till de vanligaste och grundläggande kurserna och att komma med på en valpkurs när hunden börjar bli runt året blir fel, då har du ju missat hjälpen när den behövdes som allra mest.

Lydnad

Alla hundar, stora som små, bör bibringas en hel del lydnad för att de själva och omgivningen ska må bra. Att hunden t.ex. kommer på inkallning, kan gå fint i koppel, kan sitt och ligg, och dessutom utför det med glädje, är ett rimligt baskrav. Svenska Brukshundklubben, SBK, ordnar olika kurser över hela landet för alla hundraser och hundar i alla åldrar oavsett förkunskaper. Grundkurserna innehåller grundläggande vardagsdressyr. Många har en väldigt bra tävlingslydnad, men sämre vardagslydnad. Vardagslydnad ska fungera även utanför lydnadsplanen. Steget från bra vardagslydnad till tävlingslydnad är inte stort, dock kräver tävlingsmomenten högre precision och snabbhet i utförandet än vad som behövs till vardags.

Efter genomgången unghunds- eller grundkurs är man oftast klar att börja tävla i lydnadsklass I. Efter ett första pris där flyttas hunden upp till klass II, därefter lydnadsklass III och slutligen elitklass. Och vartefter hunden flyttas upp i klasserna ökas svårighetsgraden. Tre förstapris i elitklass leder, tillsammans med vissa andra meriter, till lydnadschampionat.

Bruks

De flesta klubbarna ordnar också kurser i bruksgrenarna spår, sök och rapport. Lägsta klassen kallas appellklass. I nästa klass – lägre klass – tillkommer även skyddsgrenen. Bruksgrenarna innehåller dels specialmoment, dels en lydnadsdel.

Målet med **spårträningen** är att hunden ska söka upp ett människospår i ett bestämt område, följa det åt rätt håll. I spåret ska hunden hitta ett antal apporter – träpinnar – under vägen. En vältränad och duktig spårhund ska i alla lägen hålla sig till just det anvisade spåret, oavsett störningar som t.ex. ett korsande spår av vilt.

Sökträningen går även den ut på att hitta en försvunnen person, inte genom att spåra utan söka igenom ett område och där markera personer, antingen genom skallmarkering eller markering med s.k. sökrulle. Detta är också grunden för utbildning av räddningshundar.

Rapporthunden användes från början av militären för att skicka meddelanden mellan olika förband. Meddelandet bars i en hylsa runt hundens hals. I dag används också en hylsa, men nu med hundens tidlapp i. Här gäller för hunden att ta sig från en station/förare till en annan så fort som möjligt. En rapporthund ska inte bara vara snabb, utan också tyst för att inte avslöja ”lägret”, dessutom måste den kunna ta sig förbi olika störningar på egen hand utan förarens stöd.

Skyddsträningen går ut på att skydda föraren mot överfall, stoppa flyende personer samt att bevaka gripna personer. Detta anses allmänt som den svåraste grenen inom bruks. Därför krävs en mycket erfaren tränares hjälp och en mycket stabil hund för skyddsutbildning.

SBK, försvaret och Räddningsverket samarbetar vid utbildningen av tjänstehundar; räddnings- och bevakningshundar.

Godkända tjänstehundar är befriade från hundskatt eftersom de används i samhällets tjänst. För att bli antagen till utbildningen krävs bl.a. godkänt Bevaknings- och karaktärsprov och godkänt anlagsprov.

Räddningshunden är specialiserad på att söka rätt på människor som försvunnit, exempelvis under rasmassor efter en jordbävning eller under snömassor efter en lavinolycka. Allt fler hundägare utbildar sina hundar till räddnings- eller "katastrofhundar". Under träning får hunden jobba med kroppen, huvudet och nosen. En viktig och meningsfull aktivitet för både hund och förare. Men det ställs höga krav på att hunden är så stabil att den klarar av att söka effektivt, utan att låta sig störas av något, i en kaotisk katastrofmiljö. Även föraren måste kunna klara miljön på en olycksplats.

Bevakningshunden ska, precis som det låter, påvisa "fiender" genom att tyst markera obehöriga inom ett bevakningsområdet. Föraren måste kunna lita på sin hunds signaler och kunna läsa dess kroppsspråk för att veta när hunden markerar. Bevakningshundar används inom det civila och militära försvaret.

Även Hundskolan i Sollefteå utbildar räddnings- och bevakningshundar. Där utbildas också andra tjänstehundar, bl a ledar-, narkotika- och vakthundar.

Agility

Agility är en relativt ung och mycket populär hundsport i Sverige. Hunden ska ta sig igenom en uppgjord bana med olika hinder, såsom tunnel, stege, slalompinnar och hopphinder på så kort tid som möjligt. Föraren springer bredvid och styr hunden med olika kommandon så att hindren tas på rätt sätt och i rätt ordning. På tävlingar deltar man i lag eller individuellt och hundens mankhöjd bestämmer vilken klass den startar i.

Alla kan vara med och ha kul tillsammans med sin hund på

agilitybanan, men en hel del lydnad bör fungera innan själva banträningen börjar. Den idealiska agilityhunden är snabb, smidig, lyhörd och lydig samt har bra kondition.

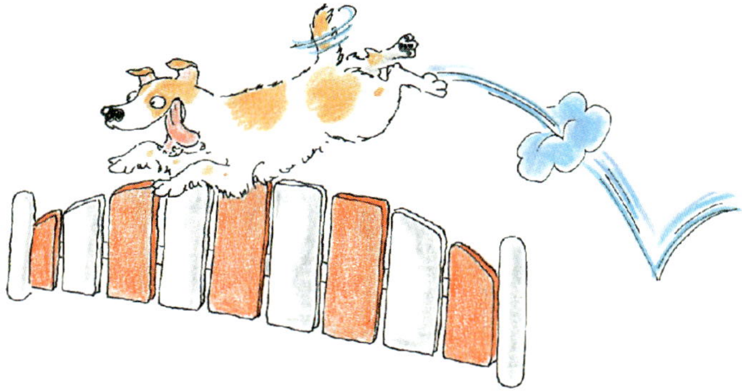

Svensk Hundungdom har hand om agilityverksamheten. På många brukshundklubbar finns agilitybanor och där ordnas ofta kurser.

Jakt

De flesta jakthundsägare har eller borde ha klart för sig vad deras hund är avlad och avsedd för. Att ha en utpräglad jakthund till enbart ”sällskap” är en otjänst mot både hund och ägare. Alla jakthundsraser är mer eller mindre specialiserade på vissa typer av jakt. Genom medveten avel har en del egenskaper ”förstärkts”, så är exempelvis taxen en tuff grythund och retrieverraserna suveräna apportörer. Oavsett specialisering är flertalet jakthundar också bra ämnen till eftersök på skadat vilt.

För att få en duglig och bra jakthund krävs, som vid all hundträning, god kontakt mellan förare och hund, kunskap, erfarenhet, bra grundlydnad och ”goda jaktanlag”. Special- och rasklubbarna håller i utbildningen för jakthundar. Kurser i lydnad och jaktträning ordnas på många håll, för olika raser eller rasgrupper, även av lokala jaktvårdskretsar.

Kantarellhund

Trots att människans tekniska kunnande ständigt förbättras och förnyas så finns ingen "apparat" som överträffar hundens nästan ofattbara luktsinne. Genom att ta hundens näsa i tjänst för att finna specifika ämnen har en mängd olika "sökspecialister", utanför de mer traditionella sökområdena, utbildats bland våra hundar. Idag finns mögel- och granrötehundar, till nytta för både hälsa, miljö och ekonomi. Det finns även s.k. miljöhundar som t.ex. kan påvisa läckor av gas. Nya användningsområden för hundens näsa upptäcks och prövas kontinuerligt.

Att lära sin hund att söka efter kantareller eller murklor är en spännande, lönande och skojig aktivitet för den "vanlige" hundägaren som vill förena nytta med nöje för både sig själv och hunden. Genom annonser i hundtidningar kan du hitta kurser – oftast i privat regi – för kortare specialutbildningar, som svampletning. I ras- och specialklubbarnas tidningar finner du kurser och tävlingar skräddarsydda för rasen, t.ex. vallhundsprov för vallhundar eller livräddningskurser för New Foundlandshundar.

För den som vill är det bara att ta för sig av det stora kunnande och kursutbud som finns. Är du en intresserad hundägare kommer du säkert att hitta någon aktivitet som är vettig och rolig för just dig och din hund.

Flera hundar

Förr eller senare kommer du som hundägare att fundera på att skaffa ytterligare en hund eller att överväga köp av en ny hund. Även om du kan mer nu ska du självfallet gå lika omsorgsfullt tillväga vid val av ras, föräldradjur och uppfödare som när du köpte den förra hunden.

Köpa ny hund

För alla hundägare kommer en dag det oundvikliga – en sjuk, skadad eller gammal hund måste avlivas. Vi är skyldiga hunden att inte låta den behöva lida i onödan. Ett tungt beslut och en smärtsam sorg är priset vi får betala för den fina tid vi fått tillsammans med vår hundkompis.

Bara tanken på att hunden en dag inte finns mer, leder ofta till planer på att så småningom skaffa ytterligare en hund. Och visst slipper du tystnaden och saknaden av mycket som ett ”hundliv” för med sig om du har ytterligare en hund när den ena dör. Men sorgen kommer du aldrig undan och en ny hund kan aldrig ersätta den förra. Rusa inte åstad och köp en valp, så lik din förra hund som möjligt, i hopp om att få en ”ersättare”. Nej, planera, med hjälp av dina nya erfarenheter som hundägare, även nästa hundköp noga.

Skaffa en hund till

Det finns många skäl till att hundägare väljer att köpa en hund till. En vanlig anledning är nog att hundintresset har ökat hos en eller flera i familjen. En hund kanske inte längre räcker till för alla att träna och tävla på lydnadsplan eller i utställningsringen med. Eller den första hunden kanske inte fungerar till det den var avsedd för; om exempelvis en älghund inte ställer älg, så har den ändock blivit en kär familjemedlem och får därför sällskap av en ny hund som förhoppningsvis ligger mer åt "älg-hållet" till.

Om du tänker köpa en hund till, så vänta tills den första hunden åtminstone kommit över den psykiska könsmognaden. Hund nummer ett bör fungera utan problem till vardags, och ha en befäst grundlydnad, innan hund nummer två kommer in i flocken. Vänta dock inte alltför länge; den äldre hunden ska orka umgås med en aktiv unghund på heltid och tycka det är trevligt.

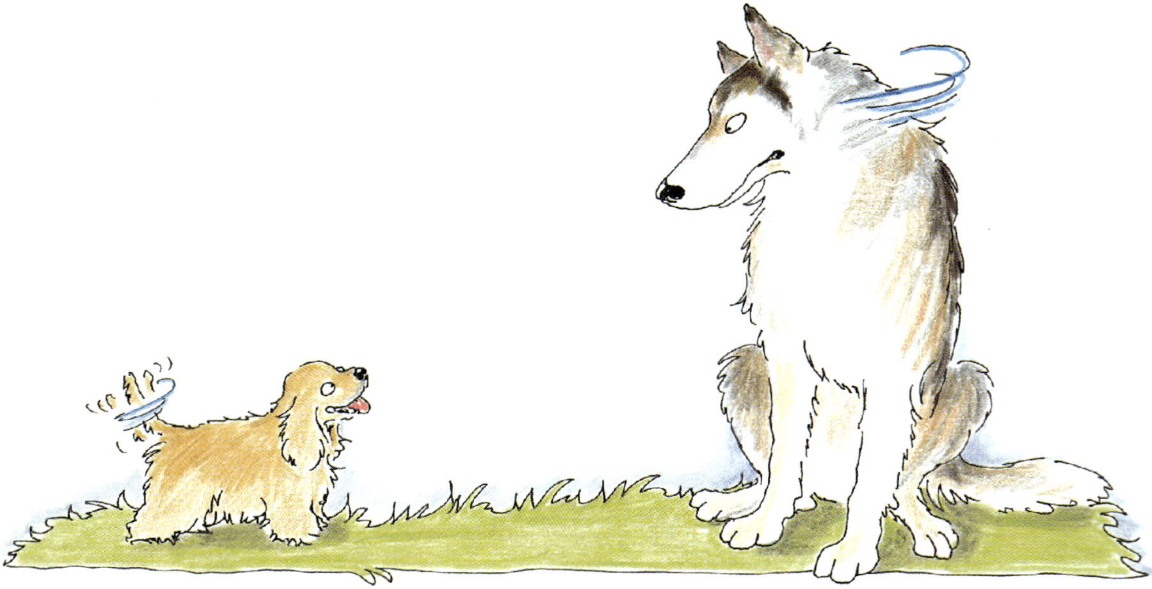

Nästan alla normala hundar tycker att det är roligt att få en kompis att dela livet i "hundperspektiv" med. En hund kan ju inte helt ersätta människans behov av mänskligt socialt umgänge. Lika lite kan människan helt ersätta hundens behov av lek och samvaro med andra hundar. För hunden är det alltså kul och stimulerande att få in en annan hund i flocken. Det är det för resten av familjen också – om förutsättningarna finns;

tid, intresse och pengar. Att ha två hundar är inte riktigt dubbelt så jobbigt som att bara ha en hund. Du behöver ju t.ex. inte gå ut på två kvällspromenader, men räkna med att träningstid och kostnader fördubblas. Om du behöver hundvakt när du ska åka bort blir det knepigare ju fler hundar du måste få hjälp med.

Samma kön eller...?

Visst finns det hundar som inte alls skulle uppskatta en ny hund, men de är få. En hund som i vanliga fall inte kan umgås med andra hundar kommer kanske inte heller att acceptera, eller till och med attackera, en ny liten valp. Om du har en alltför aggressiv eller konkurrensmedveten hund bör du nog avstå från ännu en hund. Eventuellt kan du överväga att köpa en valp av motsatt kön, vilket man annars bör avråda ifrån.

Generellt är det mest praktiskt att alla hundar i flocken är av samma kön. Har du en hanhund och skaffar en tik måste du vara inställd på att kunna lämna bort en av hundarna när tiken löper. Utgå inte ifrån att det "ordnar sig alltid" när den dagen kommer. Förvissa dig, före köpet, om att du t.ex. kan lånbyta hund med någon annan under sammanlagt sex veckor om året då tiken löper.

Försiktig presentation

För valpens, uppfödarens, den äldre hundens och för den framtida hundrelationens skull, lämna hund nummer ett hemma när du hämtar valpen. Även om din hund brukar vara snäll och trevlig med andra hundar och valpar så var extra uppmärksam på hundarna den första tiden. Var säker på att "gammelhunden" accepterat valpen till fullo, vilket kan ta veckor, innan du lämnar dem utan uppsikt.

Det allra första mötet mellan valpen och den vuxna hunden bör ske på helt neutral mark – alltså inte inom den äldres revir – på ett lugnt och odramatiskt sätt. Gör som alltid då ni träffar en ny hund; låt hundarna hälsa utan koppel, samtidigt som förarna pratar lågmält med varandra och går sakta tillsammans bort från hundarna. Gå en liten sväng så hundarna får bekanta sig. Gör sällskap hem och gå in tillsammans. Hemma ska hundarna få umgås utan nämnvärd inblandning av hussar och mattar, som dock bör hålla dem under total uppsikt de första dagarna. Försök aldrig forcera fram en kontakt och vänskap mellan hundarna. De måste få vänja sig vid varandra i sin egen takt.

Äldre hunden – en förebild

Så snart den lilla valpen inlemmats i flocken kommer den att bli en mer eller mindre lydig elev till den äldre hunden, läraren. Det är detta som oftast komplicerar tillvaron för flerhundsägaren. Den unga hunden härmar den äldre och lär sig lätt olater av sin lärare. Jo, visst lär sig den lilla eleven ett och annat vettigt också, men tyvärr inte lika fort och inte lika ofta som den lär sig "dumheter". Har du exempelvis en hund som skäller i tid och otid är risken stor att valpen också blir skällig. Den "hjälper till" när den äldre skäller och, om du inte löser problemet snarast, lär valpen sig och befäster ett icke önskvärt beteende.

Det här elev-lärarförhållandet kan leda till allvarliga tråkigheter om man inte ser upp och förebygger problemen.

En ung hund påverkas i högre grad av andra hundars reaktioner än av människors sätt att reagera. Visar sig den första hunden rädd vid skott då unghunden är med, kommer troligen unghunden att göra det också, trots att husse uppträder helt orädd och lugn. I en del fall är det kanske inte så lämpligt att skaffa en elev/valp till en lärare/hund om denne har alltför onormala beteenden att lära ut. Är den äldre hunden t.ex. aggressiv mot andra hundar, eller vek och rädd i vardagliga situationer, är det bäst att avstå från att skaffa en hund till.

Genom att ofta sära på hundarna undviker du att den nya

hunden lär sig alltför mycket av den äldre. Nykomlingen behöver få vara ensamhund tillsammans med dig, leka och tränas socialt – ofta och mycket. Då kommer den att präglas på dig och du blir den som valpen helst vill vara med. Det är lätt att bli bekväm när man har två hundar som gärna leker med varandra. Får de alltid vara ihop finns risk för att valpen kommer att ty sig mer till den andra hunden än till dig och du får kontaktproblem.

Den äldre hundens behov av aktivitet och kontakt med dig kommer förmodligen att öka när den lille gjort entré. "Gammelhunden" har fått konkurrens, vilket kan vara nog så jobbigt för honom, så se verkligen till att han fortfarande får den uppmärksamhet och stimulans han behöver och är van vid. Även han behöver få göra saker ensam med husse/matte och slippa konkurrensen med valpen.

Avel – stort ansvar

I samband med funderingarna på att köpa en hund till kommer ofta tanken på en valp efter den egna hunden. Din hund är säkert bäst och vackrast i dina ögon. Men för att passa som avelshund ska den vara mycket bra mentalt och exteriört även när den granskas av erfarna och raskunniga domares kritiska ögon. Det finns mycket annat än mentalitet och exteriör att ta hänsyn till och ha kunskaper om för att välja bra avelshundar, bl.a. defekter, sjukdomar, linjer, föräldrar, syskon och deras avkommor, rastyp, ålder och kondition. Har du inte dessa kunskaper så får du ta hjälp utifrån.

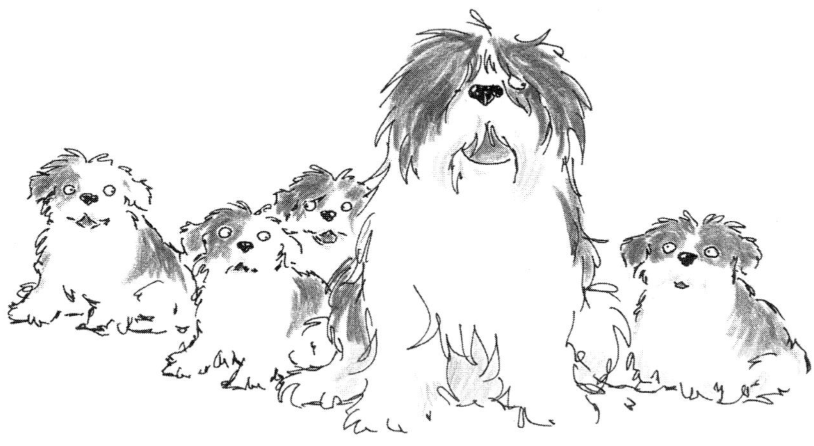

Avla själv

Att vara hunduppfödare är spännande och roligt, men svårare, jobbigare samt mer kostsamt och ansvarsfullt än vad de flesta tror. Och långt ifrån alla hundar duger till avel. Självklart tycker du att din hund är jättebra på alla sätt. Emellertid är det lätt att bli ”hemmablind” och därför ska en avelshund ha officiellt dokumenterade meriter, som visar att den motsvarar rasens exteriöra och mentala standard. Och allra viktigast är att den inte har, eller är anlagsbärare av, sjukdomar eller defekter.

Vare sig du har en hanhund eller en tik bör du förvissa dig om att din hund är rastypisk både till utseende och sätt genom att delta på flera utställningar, arbetsprov och anlagstester. Be dessutom någon raskunnig seriös person om hjälp att påvisa din hunds fördelar och nackdelar. Kontakta rasens avelsråd, som kan hjälpa dig att bedöma din hunds lämplighet i avel. De kan också ge råd om passande hanhund.

Nästan bara väl meriterade hanhundar efterfrågas av tikägare. Självklart finns ingen anledning för tikägaren att "chansa" vid val av hanhund – dokumenterade meriter och friska linjer är oftast ett grundkrav för att någon ska vilja para med en hane. Låna bara ut din hane till mycket bra tikar och kolla upp tiken och kombinationen med erfarna rasspecialister eller avelsråd.

Avstå för tikens och rasens skull

Endast friska hundar utan kända sjukdomar eller defekter bör få föra sina anlag vidare till kanske sex–sju nya valpar, som i sin tur får valpar som för anlagen vidare osv. En del raser ingår i SKKs bekämpningsprogram mot ärftligt betingade sjukdomar. Det kan innebära att avkomma inte får registreras efter hundar med vissa defekter eller efter hundar som inte har "defektstatus" registrerad.

Det har kanske tagit mer än hundra års arbete för generationer av intresserade uppfödare att skapa en ras med ett speciellt utseende och för ett speciellt användningsområde. Var därför rädd om rasen och undvik att medvetet bli medskyldig till att förstöra den. Ställ dig frågan "Kan min hund tillföra rasen något bra?". Om du inte kommer fram till att den kan det, så avstå från att låna ut din hanhund eller para din tik. Låt din älskade tik slippa besväret och riskerna med dräktighet, valpning och valpar och i stället få förbli din bästa och vackraste hund.

Skulle det visa sig att din hund håller måttet som avelshund finns flera aspekter för tikägaren att ta hänsyn till. Du måste ha gott om ledig tid för att ta hand om tik, valpar och valpköpare. Tiken ska få vistas i valpmiljön – du vet ju inte exakt när hon ska valpa – under uppsikt hela tiden den sista veckan före beräknad valpning. Därtill måste du vara hemma och sköta tik och valpar nästan dygnet runt, kanske ända upp till fyra månader efter valpning. Även om valparna är leveransklara vid 8–9 veckors ålder betyder det inte att alla valpar fått ett bra hem vid den åldern. Nej, som uppfödare måste du räkna med risken att ha osålda valpar kvar hemma under flera månader. Att passa på att ta en valpkull under semestern är följaktligen helt orealistiskt.

Skyldigheter och ekonomi

Du måste också ha tid att ta emot och hjälpa dina valpköpare både under valptiden och i framtiden. Du kan råka ut för att få tillbaka en valp du levererat och innan du hittat ett nytt bra hem till den kan ännu ett par månader ha gått. Uppfödarens moraliska skyldighet gentemot såväl valpar som valpköpare upphör ju inte i och med att valparna flyttat till sina nya hem. Var beredd på att stötta dina valpköpare under de närmaste åren.

Att föda upp en valpkull kostar pengar och är oturen framme vid valpningen kan det bli väldigt dyrt. Ett kejsarsnitt med efterföljande veterinärvård är kostsamt och dessutom en mardröm för den som inte har en duktig amma till hands. Har du tur och allt går bra får du ändå ligga ute med en massa pengar, i väntan på eventuella valpinkomster, för t.ex. parningsavgift, veterinärvård, registreringsavgifter, veterinärbesiktning av valparna, vaccinationer, ID-märkning, utrustning och foder under flera månader.

Ska du ha en valpkull måste du ha utrymmen som lämpar sig för valpar. Och även ha grannar som står ut med valpars olåt alla tider på dygnet. Du som bor i lägenhet bör nog avstå från en valpkull med tanke på den sanitära olägenhet som kan uppstå av lukter från kiss och bajs samt för grannsämjans skull.

Beslutar du dig för att para din tik gör du klokt i att vända dig till någon erfaren uppfödare för att få råd och stöd innan och under valptiden. Du kan även ta kontakt med kennelkonsulenten i ditt område. Namn och telefonnummer får du genom SKKs kansli.

Självklart behöver du skaffa en del utrustning för tik och valpar samt lära dig så mycket som möjligt om bl.a. valpning och uppfödning. Genom SKK kan du köpa boken Hunduppfödaren, som vänder sig till såväl den som ska ta sin första kull som till de mer erfarna uppfödarna.

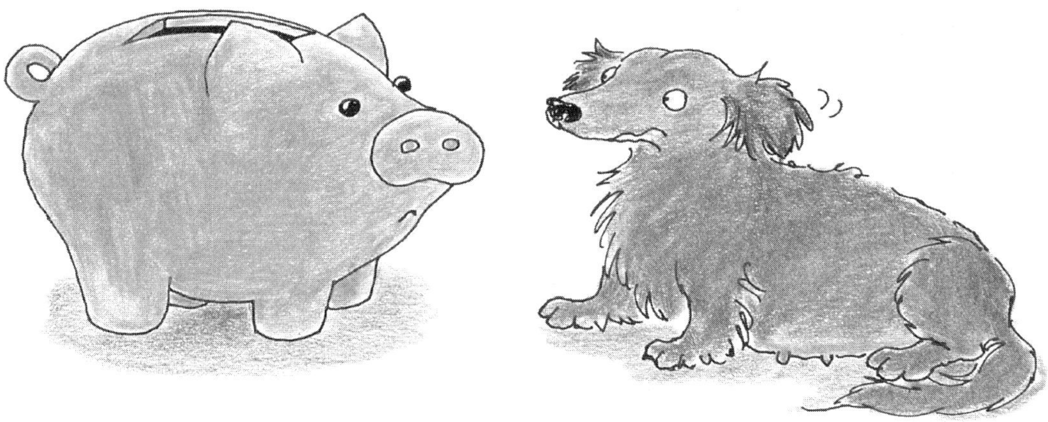

Hunden och lagen

Som nybliven hundägare måste du ha klart för dig att långt ifrån alla människor delar din entusiasm över hundar. En del människor gillar helt enkelt inte hundar! Det är bara för oss hundägare att acceptera det. Och faktiskt se till att de inte får sina aversioner förstärkta genom att vi inte visar dem hänsyn.

Det finns också en väldigt stor grupp människor som kanske vill men inte kan umgås med hundar – allergikerna. Här måste alla hundägare ta sitt ansvar och inte handla så att andra får besvär eller blir sjuka på grund av våra hundar. Det är framför allt med tanke på allergiker som det finns förbud mot hundar på många ställen. Är du osäker på om du får ta med en hund in i någon lokal, låt då bli med tanke på allergikerna.

Ju mer hänsyn vi hundägare visar, desto mer hundvänligt samhälle borde vi få. Hundhållningen i Sverige är, jämfört med många andra länders, utomordentligt god och merparten av hundägarna är förhållandevis kunniga och ansvarstagande. Men tyvärr inte alla. Därför finns lagar som reglerar rätten att ha hund.

Skada och olägenhet

Första paragrafen i Lagen om tillsyn över hundar och katter lyder "Hundar och katter skall hållas under sådan tillsyn som med hänsyn till deras natur och övriga omständigheter behövs för att förebygga att de orsakar skador eller avsevärda olägenheter."

Lagen gäller visserligen för alla hundar, men konsekvensen av den beror t.ex. på hur hunden är och hur man bor. Risken för att en hund som befinner sig långt ifrån en trafikerad väg ska orsaka en trafikolycka är förstås liten. Medan exempelvis en aggressiv hund som är lös invid en lekplats självfallet innebär en risk för omgivningen.

En hund som lämnas ensam hemma större delen av dagen mår psykiskt dåligt och kanske ylar och skäller sig igenom dagarna. I ett hyres- eller radhus kan den hunden mycket väl "orsaka avsevärd olägenhet" genom att störa grannar. Om en hund däremot sköts väl och inte stör kan ingen hyresvärd förbjuda någon att ha hund i sin lägenhet.

Bitsk hund

I andra paragrafen står "Hund som visar benägenhet att bita människor eller husdjur må icke vara lös utomhus, så framt den ej hålles inom område, som är betryggande inhägnat och till vilken utomstående ej äga tillträde."

Det här innebär alltså att en hund som inte är att "lita på" alltid måste rastas i koppel, eller hållas i en rastgård, som den absolut inte kan ta sig ur. Och utomstående ska heller inte kunna ta sig in till hunden. Det räcker följaktligen inte med en "varning-för-hunden-skylt" – små barn kan ju inte läsa – eller ett vanligt villastaket, som nästan vilken hund som helst kan ta sig över eller under.

Tack och lov är de allra flesta hundar inte folkilskna, men vanlig hänsyn kräver att man inte låter sin hund rusa fram och skälla och hoppa på främmande människor. Det finns många människor som är hundrädda. För dem spelar det ingen roll om hunden kommer rusande med ett glatt skall och en snällt viftande svans. De blir lika vettskrämda i alla fall och sällan lugnade av en husse som står femtio meter bort och skriker att "den vill bara hälsa och är sååå snäll". Nej, lär din hund att inte hälsa på främmande utan tillåtelse eller håll den kopplad där du riskerar att möta folk.

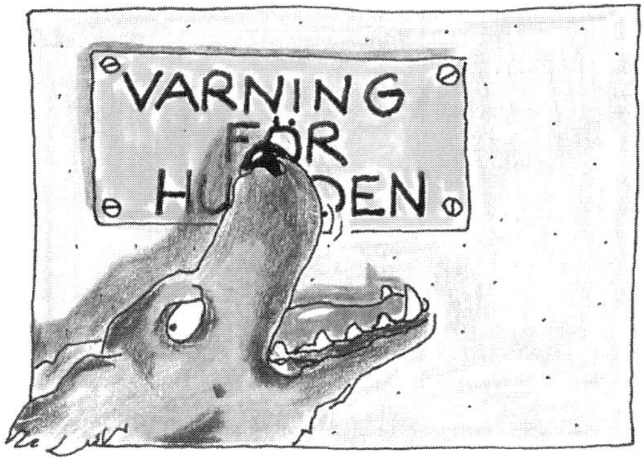

Strikt ansvar

Du har ansvar för allt som din hund ställer till med. Man brukar tala om hundägarens strikta ansvar. Lagen stadgar "Skada som orsakas av hund skall ersättas av dess ägare, ändå att han ej är vållande till skadan."

Det betyder att om hunden orsakat en skada, trots att ägaren gjort allt vad som krävs i form av vård eller tillsyn, så är ägaren ändå ersättningsskyldig. Hur oskyldig matte eller husse än är, betraktar lagen alltid ägaren som ansvarig till hundens vållande av skada. Anta att din hund sliter sig och rusar ut på en väg, föraren väjer och kör in i ett träd. Då får du stå dels för eventuella personskador, dels för skadorna på bilen. Skulle olyckan vara framme vill det till att du har en ansvarsförsäkring som täcker skadan. Hör med ditt försäkringsbolag om hemförsäkringen täcker dina eventuella utlägg för något som hunden orsakar.

Hundvaktens ansvar

Om du reser bort och lämnar hunden i någon annans vård under semestern, eller ber kompisen rasta din hund, hur blir det då med ditt strikta ansvar? Har du fullt ansvar för vad din hund ställer till med fast du inte själv är på plats?

Här är lagtexten lite diffus. I andra stycket står "Vad nu stadgat som ägare till hund gäller ock den som mottagit hunden till underhåll eller nyttjande."

Det måste stå helt klart vem som har ansvaret för hunden i just det ögonblick hunden orsakar en skada. Och det kanske inte alltid är så lätt att bena ut. Anta att du vet att din hund biter av ett koppel på nolltid. Grannen tar med hunden på promenad, stannar till vid affären, binder upp hunden och går in och handlar. När grannen kommer ut igen är hunden borta. Den har bitit av kopplet, rusat ut framför en cyklist så denne ramlat omkull och skadat sig och cykeln. Du hade inte berättat för grannen att jycken är duktig på att kapa koppel. Det borde du gjort för att gå helt fri från ansvar.

Ibland är gränsdragningen för ansvaret klarare. Har du exempelvis lämnat in din hund på pensionat under semestern övergår ansvaret för din hund till ägaren av hundpensionatet. Tag alltid för vana att upplysa den som tar hand om din hund, om hundens eventuella egenheter och olater för att undvika problem i onödan.

Den som dömts att betala skadestånd har i sin tur rätt att kräva ersättning av den som vållat eller medverkat till att skadan skett. Vid personskador är det emellertid ovanligt att en domstol dömer så att hundägaren får rätt till ersättning av den som egentligen varit vållande till skadan, hur klantigt denne än har betett sig.

Koppeltvång

Under hela året måste du ha kontroll över din hund i alla situationer, överallt. Detta gäller speciellt under den s.k.

"hundförbudstiden", 1 mars–20 augusti. Då är det barnkammare i naturen eftersom de allra flesta djur föder sina ungar under den här perioden. Dräktiga däggdjur och ruvande fåglar är mycket känsliga för störningar. För att djur- och fågelungar ska ha en chans att överleva får de absolut inte störas av lösspringande hundar.

I Jaktstadgan står bl a följande "Under tiden 1 mars–20 augusti skall hundar hållas under sådan tillsyn att de hindras löpa lösa i marker där det finns vilt. Under den övriga tiden på året skall hundar hållas under sådan tillsyn att de hindras från att driva eller förfölja vilt, när de inte används för jakt."

Gäller alla hundar

Tro inte att lagen endast gäller jakthundar. Nej, givetvis kan alla hundar, oavsett ras och ålder, jaga vilt. Därför gäller lagen alla hundar överallt där det finns vilt. Och fåglar och andra djur finns i minsta parkdunge.

Jo visst, men min hund saknar jaktinstinkt, säger en del okunniga hundägare. Det kan vara hur det vill med den saken, men det spelar ingen roll eftersom alla hundar kan **störa** djuren. Även den minsta valp är nyfiken och kan därmed t.ex. skrämma upp en ruvande fågel eller ett rådjurskid.

För att följa lagen ska din hund föras i normallångt koppel under "hundförbudsperioden". Endast synnerligen lydiga hundar får då vistas i skog och mark utan koppel. Och då i omedelbar närhet av föraren som ska kunna kalla in hunden ögonblickligen, oavsett vad den fått syn eller vittring på. De flesta hundar och hundägare uppfyller inte dessa krav!

Den som underlåter att följa lagen riskerar att straffas med böter och kan vid grov oaktsamhet till och med dömas till fängelse.

Hälsoskyddslagen

Det finns ytterligare en generell lag du måste känna till som vanlig hundägare; Hälsoskyddslagen. I den stadgas bl.a. att "husdjur och andra djur som hålls i fångenskap skall förvaras och skötas så att sanitär olägenhet ej uppstår".

Vad innebär då sanitär olägenhet? Jo, det är exempelvis då grannar störs av ihållande hundskall (även dagtid), då hund förorenar på lekplatser, gångbanor eller planterade gräsmattor samt då hund orsakar elakartad lukt.

Lokal ordningsstadga

Utöver ovanstående lagar har varje kommun sin Lokala ordningsstadga. Ring kommunkontoret i din kommun och ta reda på vilka regler som gäller. Vanliga regler är bl.a. att hundar inte får vistas på begravningsplatser, ej heller där torgförsäljning pågår eller på allmänna badplatser.

Det finns faktiskt flera andra lagar som reglerar hundhållningen än de som tagits upp här.

Eftertankar

”Snälla” hundägare?

Alltför ofta hör och ser jag hundägare som, i såväl tanke som handling, förmänskligar sina egna och andras hundar. Jag tror att den absoluta merparten av dessa hundägare verkligen tycker om sina hundar och vill dem väl. Men utan kunskap om hundar är det svårt att vara ”snäll” på hundars vis. För hur ska man kunna hantera och utveckla något på rätt sätt om man inte vet hur det fungerar?

Jag tänker på den rara farbrorn i grannskapet, vars mycket feta hund överöses med kärlek i form av mat. Men också på en bekants glada hund som aldrig får vara lös och därmed heller aldrig kan leka och umgås med andra hundar. Matte har inte brytt sig om att lära den att komma på inkallning.

Många tycker det är mysigt att låta hunden ligga i soffan och gosa när den vill. Men ibland hoppar hunden upp när den råkar vara smutsig... ”och då blir de tvåbenta plötsligt jättearga”. Nåde den hund som inte förstår att soffor är svårtvättade!

Det är OK att slita och dra runt med matte i kopplet ända till den dagen då matte dras ned i ett dike och gör illa sig. Då ”blir matte helt vansinnig, skriker och slåss”. Eller ena dagen är det tillåtet att hoppa upp mot främmande och hälsa medan det nästa dag plötsligt är förbjudet och följs av skrik, slag, ryck och slit för hunden. Skulle hunden själv kunnat räkna ut att en tvååring skulle ramla omkull av dess tyngd ...eller?

Ja, ovanstående är bara ett fåtal exempel – listan kan lätt göras väldigt lång – på hur okunniga, bekväma och inkonsekventa en del hundägare är, samtidigt som de själva tycker att de är så snälla och verkligen älskar sina hundar.

Andra hundägare håller på fasta regler och ser till att de efterlevs, ger mycket kel, kärlek, lek, fysiskt umgänge och positiva uppmuntringar istället för klander. De tränar, tränar och tränar för att öka hundens möjligheter till ett friare och tryggare liv. De skaffar sig kunskaper om hundens fysiska såväl som psykiska och sociala behov och reaktioner. Och de har en positiv attityd och en målsättning med sitt val att "leva livet med hund".

Vem är egentligen snäll mot sin hund? Jo, den som försöker förstå att hunden inte är en "liten människa", utan ett domesticerat/tämjt rovdjur som följer sina urfäders instinkter fast den lever hos oss människor. Vi måste förstå att hunddjur inte har samma behov och språk som vi och, som det flock- och rovdjur de är faktiskt är, mår bra av en rättvis, konsekvent och tydlig flockledare, som ger trygghet.

Bitte Lind

BOKTIPS

L. Fält – *Hundens språk och flockliv*
M. Stavenborn – *Hundens vanligaste sjukdomar*
B. Wikströms – *Hundens sjukdomar*
K. Lorenz – *Sådan är din hund*
SKK – *Hundägaren*
SKK – *Hunduppfödaren*
M. Mohlin – *Se vad jag säger – om hundars språk, Aktivitetsboken, Inkallning är så mycket mera, Lydnadsboken, Innan det smäller – om förebyggande skottränina, Agilityboken*
Rasböcker
Speciallitteratur